Women of the Year

Women of the Year

Jacqueline Duke, editor

Chapters by
Edward L. Bowen
Tom Hall
Craig Harzmann
Steve Haskin
Avalyn Hunter
Judy L. Marchman
John McEvoy
Eliza McGraw
Ray Paulick
David Schmitz

ECLIPSE PRESS

Lexington, Kentucky

Library of Congress Control Number: 2004104473

ISBN 1-58150-116-1

Printed in The United States
First Edition: October 2004

ECLIPSE PRESS

Contents

Preface

The assumption that female Thoroughbreds face a competitive disadvantage against males involves an ill-defined admixture of prejudice, observation, experience, Biblical and social custom, a masculine sense of entitlement, and probably a bit of physiological justice.

Just how the sport of racing would deal with this assumption has been an ongoing process. England's *Racing Calendar* in the middle eighteenth century published a "Schedule of Weights and Distances for Royal Plates" (races). Distinctions were struck as to distance and individual racecourse, not as to gender, while the weight scheme for other races was based on the height of the horse.

Then, Admiral Henry John Rous, who prevailed for years as president of England's Jockey Club, published a weight-for-age scale in 1850. The recommended scale assigned weights by distance, age, and time of year. At any distance or age, mares were to be allowed five pounds early in the year, then three pounds, and finally only two pounds. (Geldings were allowed three pounds, reflecting a presumption about them that apparently was then in vogue.)

While this scale was not universally imposed, racing on both sides of the Atlantic has adhered to a generally similar standard while being willing to adjust. In the United States today the gender concession is between three and five pounds, depending on age. For example, the two modern fillies who won the Kentucky Derby, Genuine Risk (1980) and Winning Colors (1988) each carried 121 pounds to their male rivals' 126.

Weight concessions and the infrequency of fillies' challenges of males on the modern racetrack are the two ways in which the presumptions about females are most commonly expressed. The corollary of this mindset of the Turf is that fillies and mares who do defeat males are highly special. In American racing the heroines have come along with enough frequency that a female's outrunning a male is not seen as a freakish occurrence, but it is not so commonplace as to deny each such Amazon her recognition as deserving unusual status. This has been true for more than two centuries.

In Colonial America in 1752, the fabled Maryland mare Selima defeated the Virginia male Tryal in a battle for intercolony pride and a great deal of money for the day, $10,000. On June 7, 1774, not long before things got really dicey in the Colonies, the mare Slamerkin sealed her brief unbeaten record by defeating the imported English horse Slim at Philadelphia. Then, the early decades of the next century saw the likes of Lady Lightfoot's successes against Tuckahoe and other males, and in a storied afternoon of heat races the distaffer Fashion's defeat of the great horse Boston.

The American Turf has continued to produce its angels and Amazons. The present volume is a tribute to those who attained what is regarded as Horse of the Year status.

Certification of that status has not always been a consistent matter. In 1970 *The Blood-Horse* published a book entitled *The Great Ones*, an exposition of the careers of seventy-six runners. For an appendix the principal author of that volume, Kent Hollingsworth, who was then editor of *The Blood-Horse*, waded his way through sundry historical accounts to determine a legitimate, although unofficial, list of champions dating back a century to 1870.

Officially recognized voting for champions, in divisions and as Horse of the Year, did not begin until 1936. Between then and 1971, *Daily Racing Form* and then the Thoroughbred Racing Associations conducted the polls given the status of national recognition. Thereafter, the combined Eclipse Award scheme has been in place.

Hollingsworth approached the effort of determining which horses qualified as "champions" in earlier years as a respectful horseman and historian. The commentaries of such other historians as Walter Vosburgh, John Hervey, Joseph A. Estes, and Joe Palmer were instrumental in determining who would receive Hollingsworth's imprimatur as champion. For those years when the opinions of the past were not considered clear, those divisions were simply left off the chart.

In subsequent years the distinction between a "voted" champion and a horse on a list has been obscured. There are Turf writers today who will look at *The Blood-Horse*'s annual update of champions and refer imprecisely to, for example, Beldame, as having been "voted" Horse of the Year for 1904.

Whatever the source of her distinction, any female who is regarded in either a contemporary or retrospective sense as the best racehorse of a particular year is a very special lady. The fillies and mares who have been assigned or voted the status as Horse of the Year are revisited in these pages. There are only ten of them, again an indication that such feats are rare.

Most of these Women of the Year met males on the racetrack, and all of them brought to the racetrack a compelling combination of speed, strength, class, and sass. Selima, Slamerkin, and Fashion would welcome any of them into a unique and lasting sisterhood.

by Edward L. Bowen

Miss Woodford

(1883-84)

Racing in the 1880s, Miss Woodford became the first horse of either gender to earn more than $100,000 in America.

When it comes to racehorses, however, money is not universally held to be the truest yardstick. A racehorse might happen upon a sea change in purse distribution and thus eclipse in bankroll those that came before and achieved higher prestige. Alternatively, a horse might hang up a record in earnings not so much with brilliance but by longevity and fortitude. For better or worse, the greatness of racehorses is most often evaluated via that ardent, if imperfect, phenomenon called human opinion.

In either context Miss Woodford

Miss Woodford.

found her status undiminished, for she gathered her record bankroll during five sterling campaigns in which she won thirty-seven of forty-eight races. In *The Great Ones*, published by *The Blood-Horse* in 1970, principal author Kent Hollingsworth summarized the recorded opinions of a veritable blue-ribbon panel of old: "Of trainers who spent more than a half-century racing or racing against good fillies, James Rowe Sr., John W. Rogers, R. Wyndham Walden, Green B. Morris, A. Jack Joyner, Tom Healey, and Sunny Jim Fitzsimmons each declared Miss Woodford the best filly of them all."

The object of such respect from a coterie of America's most renowned horsemen needed an extraordinary ability and constitution merely to deal with her owners, for she was early on recruited into the stable of the Dwyer Brothers. Mike and Phil Dwyer were rambunctious surveyors and purveyors of the American dream, but they might well have run afoul of animal treatment sensitivities had they been around today.

In business the Dwyers were a sort of two-man Ray Kroc of their day. Originally proprietors of a small butcher shop in Brooklyn, they combined business savvy and the economic sweep of their times to establish a wholesale meat business that helped launch such endeavors as heading several New York area racetracks as well as establishing a dominant racing stable. Indeed, it has been suggested that the segue of American racing from a sport — a pastime — among gentlemen to a hard-charging business enterprise was, if not instigated, at least pushed along by the Dwyer brothers' philosophy.

The more obstreperous of the brothers, Mike, was as enamored of betting as he was of winning the race. He seemed to hold the ambition of bringing to their collective knees the bookmakers who flourished legally at the time, but some reports suggest

Women of the 1880s

Clara Barton establishes the American branch of the Red Cross and becomes its first president...Sophia Packard and Harriet Giles open a school for black women in an Atlanta, Georgia, church basement. Their school will become known as Spelman College...The first "Harvey Girls" go west to work as waitresses in Fred Harvey's restaurants on the Santa Fe Railroad.

that he was not particularly astute with his major plunges. He and a like-minded pal, Boss Richard Croker of Tammany Hall, took a major hit one year when they tried to make a big score in England with their American horses. By the time Mike Dwyer died in 1906, reporters guessed that he had dropped an aggregate of $1.5 million by backing heavy favorites.

As racing men, they were known for heavy use of their horses as much as for heavy gambling. Hanover, their champion colt who came onto the scene at the end of Miss Woodford's career, was raced twenty-seven times at three in 1887, winning twenty. More dramatic than sheer numbers of races was the bunching up of his starts: In July of that year, his seventeen-race winning streak ended with his sixth race within a month. Later, when lameness finally forced even the Dwyers to give Hanover a rest, they had the offending forefoot "nerved" so that he could come back sooner by being unencumbered by pain.

Their techniques succeeded, though, for they raced a glorious series of champions, including Hindoo, Kingston, Luke Blackburn, and George Kinney, as well as Miss Woodford and

James Rowe.

Hanover. Eventually, Mike Dwyer's high-rolling nature got too deeply under his brother's skin for the partnership to continue. While Mike was known for betting $50,000 on a race, it was said that one would have to delete three zeroes from that figure to describe the largest bet Phil would ever make.

When they split, Phil retained their well-known red-and-blue silks. Mike, free now to express his personality with his own private colors, looked to the fancy uniforms of the New York militia unit known as the Zouaves, with their Algerian fezzes and tassels. In the sweep of American racing, few things could accurately be described as singular. One of them may well be a jockey's lament that the tassel on his cap hung down so low that it interfered with his vision. Mike adjusted the tassel length and, undeterred, campaigned the champion Ben Brush in his fine new silks of white with gold trim.

While loving the action of racing, the Dwyers cared nothing for the tedious processes of breeding, raising, and breaking their own. This attitude on occasion proved a boon to other breeders, who thus could both sell their top racing prospects to the Dwyers and take on the brothers' retiring racers as prime young breeding stock. Over the years the breeders of Miss Woodford found themselves on both sides of this equation.

Tradition has it that two brothers-in-law with the delightful names of Colonel Ezekiel F. Clay and Colonel Catesby Woodford bred Miss Woodford. However, the official record in Sanders D. Bruce's fledgling *American Stud Book* assigned George W. Bowen the honor. This discrepancy is bridged by the folksy legend that Bowen traded the mare Fancy Jane to Clay and Woodford for a barrel of whiskey but was tardy in alerting Bruce to this bit of enterprise. So, when Fancy Jane foaled her filly by Billet in 1880, Bowen was still listed as her owner and thus as breeder of her spring foal.

Phil Dwyer (second from left), one of the owners of Miss Woodford.

The Billet—Fancy Jane, by Neil Robinson, filly was named for Woodford's sister, Maria. Woodford and Clay were partners in Runnymede Farm outside Paris, Kentucky, which today is still a flourishing Thoroughbred farm owned by a kinsman whose name melodically bespeaks his heritage — Catesby Woodford Clay. Today's master of Runnymede is a grandson of Ezekiel Clay.

Ezekiel Clay, a nephew of abolitionist Cassius Clay and a cousin of the persistent presidential candidate Henry Clay, purchased the farm after he returned to Kentucky following the Civil War. He named the property Runnymede, for the English site where the Magna Carta was signed. A grandson of Kentucky's second governor, James Garrard, built the original portions of the Greek Revival home on the farm in 1832.

Clay and Woodford sent Miss Woodford to the races under trainer J. Hannigan, and she earned her way into the consciousness of the Dwyer Brothers. Actually, she raced in the name of George Bowen & Co., which would create doubt about the whiskey-for-horse legend but for the fact that when she was traded to the Dwyers, it was Clay and Woodford who got the other horses involved in the swap.

Miss Woodford debuted at two in 1882 at the Chicago Driving Park, where she won the Ladies Stakes. She then finished second to Ascender in the Nursery Stakes and was shipped to Saratoga. As befits the quality associated with the Spa, she ran into the best colt of the moment in the Dwyer Brothers' George Kinney and finished third behind him in the Flash Stakes. (Standing up for the family, Miss Woodford's full sister, Belle of Runnymede, won the Alabama Stakes later on the same card.)

Miss Woodford then strung together consecutive triumphs in four stakes, the Spinaway and Misses stakes at Saratoga and the unimaginatively named Filly Stakes and Colt and Filly Stakes back in Kentucky (Lexington). She then finished third in a race called the Blue Grass Stakes at Churchill Downs in Louisville. She had won five of eight races at two and earned $6,600.

Then the Dwyers came calling. They had on hand a great racehorse, Hindoo, who had won thirty of thirty-five races, including eighteen in a row, but, at four, had developed enough lameness that trainer James Rowe Sr. was loath even to gallop him. They threw in a couple of fillies,

Mike Dwyer (seated) co-owned Miss Woodford.

Red-and-Blue and Francesca, valuing the three at $15,000. In the deal Clay and Woodford got Hindoo and the fillies and turned over Miss Woodford and nine thousand dollars, meaning the budding star was valued at six thousand dollars. This was a win-win deal. The Dwyers got a filly emerging into greatness, and Clay and Woodford got what proved a highly successful stallion along with a prospective mate for him. They bred a Hindoo—Red-and-Blue filly, who was named Sallie McClelland and became co-champion two-year-old filly of 1890 for Byron McClelland. In Hindoo's first crop, Clay and Woodford bred the colt Hanover, whom they sold to the Dwyers for $1,350 and who eventually surpassed Miss Woodford's earnings record.

With future Hall of Famer Rowe training Miss Woodford for the Dwyers, the filly came out at three on June 5 and won the Ladies Handicap, an enduring event that then carried the considerable purse of $3,040. The Ladies was run at a mile and a half at that time and represented a stern first-time out for the season. Miss Woodford continued to win, taking the Mermaid Stakes by six lengths and the Monmouth Oaks by eight. She then followed in the footsteps of her sister, Belle of Runnymede, by winning Saratoga's Alabama Stakes by four lengths.

None of these four races found her facing particularly formidable opposition, despite several of the events' importance. She then ran into Empress, who raced for a Maryland governor, Oden Bowie, and had finished ahead of Miss Woodford in the Flash Stakes the previous summer. Giving Empress eight pounds, Miss Woodford finished second to her in the Pocahontas Stakes, but she bounced back to defeat Carnation, a frequent foil, in the West End Hotel Stakes by six lengths.

The original Monmouth Park in New Jersey put up a purse of $6,750 for the Monmouth Stakes to attract a unique field. This was more than twice the amount the Dwyers' splendid colt George Kinney earned by winning the Belmont Stakes. The Dwyers entered Miss Woodford with George Kinney, and they were facing Pierre Lorillard's Iroquois, a five-year-old who two years earlier had become the first American-bred to win England's grandest race, the Epsom Derby. Iroquois also had won another English classic, the St. Leger, and he beat Miss Woodford to the $100,000 earnings mark, he being the first American-bred to attain that figure although his earnings came primarily abroad.

That the only American-bred Epsom Derby winner in history was facing the best American-raced three-year-old of the year along with such other good runners as Eole, Monitor, and Miss Woodford would seem to make this a truly great event. "Race of the Century" no doubt crossed the minds and lips of the organizers. However, Iroquois apparently was but a shell of his former self. He had become a bleeder while in England and missed his entire four-year-old season. He returned to racing at five, but he generally trained for shorter races in recognition of his condition. He won the six-furlong Stockbridge Cup on June 21 and six days later embarked on the ocean voyage from England, arriving in New York on July 11. The Monmouth Stakes was run on August 25. In the meantime, Matt Byrnes, who trained Lorillard's American stable, feared training Iroquois very hard because of the classic winner's tendency to break blood vessels. Under light training, Iroquois, a big eater, had a tendency to gain weight.

A year later the great English jockey Fred Archer, who had ridden Iroquois in the Derby and St.

Leger, visited New York. According to Walter Vosburgh, writing in The Jockey Club's *Racing in America* series, Archer said of the horse that "they shouldn't have raced him here. He was in no condition when he left England to race over a mile."

For the Dwyer stable the approach of the Monmouth Stakes brought not so much a question over condition of the horses but over jockey assignment. Jimmy McLaughlin rode both George Kinney and Miss Woodford for the Dwyers, and both were entered. McLaughlin was a sort of Jerry Bailey of his day, winning major races in multiples — six Belmonts, four Travers, eight Tidal Stakes, three Alabamas, etc. Years later, McLaughlin said in an interview that "the Dwyers wanted me to ride the mare [in the Monmouth Stakes]. I thought George Kinney was the better of the two." Such was the jockey's standing that he had his way. Years after his retirement McLaughlin still regarded George Kinney as the second-best colt he ever rode, putting him behind only another Dwyer champion, Luke Blackburn, who won twenty-two of twenty-four races at three in 1880.

On the basis of what Miss Woodford had done at that time, it seems questionable that the owners would have regarded her as superior to George Kinney coming up to the 1883 Monmouth Stakes. Moreover, as the race was run, one interpretation could be that Miss Woodford was used as a pacemaker. Ridden by jockey Hughes, who rode for the Dwyers in McLaughlin's shadow, Miss Woodford led early and put away Monitor, but then faded to finish last. McLaughlin happily brought George Kinney along and, as he said years later, "had the satisfaction of winning the race by four lengths" over Eole. (*Krik's Guide to the Turf* reported the winning margin as one and a half lengths.) Iroquois, for all his travails, finished third.

The ignominy of finishing last was soon swept away by Miss Woodford's launch of a sixteen-race winning streak — one short of the streak of her future stablemate, Hanover, and the equal of twentieth century skeins by Citation, Cigar, and Hallowed Dreams. Miss Woodford's winning streak touched three seasons.

First in the sequence came the $4,950 Great Eastern Handicap, which found her facing Empress again, as well as the distinguished male Drake Carter and seven others. Miss Woodford won by eight lengths. An exceptionally rich event for the day, the $9,537 Lorillard Champion Stallion Stakes prompted a trip back to Kentucky, where she won the Churchill Downs extravaganza by half a furlong. The arrogant margins continued: six lengths in the Hunter Stakes back in New York (Jerome Park) and twelve lengths in the District of Columbia Stakes.

On October 26 Miss Woodford made her final start of the year in a race of unusual magnitude and conditions. This was the mile and five-eighths Pimlico Stakes, which had a twist that presaged some of the more aggressive promotional efforts of racetracks one hundred years or so later. In recent years Monmouth Park has been among tracks with the initiative to dangle a purse increase for an established race on the condition that the event could attract specific horses, i.e., winners of Triple Crown races in a given year. Conversely, in the 1883 Pimlico Stakes, the Maryland Jockey Club was flirting with a big-time purse to attract runners who had already distinguished Monmouth's August spectacle, the Monmouth Stakes. Conditions for the Pimlico Stakes required owners put up five hundred dollars per starter, the total of which would comprise the purse unless three or more horses (representing different owners) that had started in the Monmouth Stakes came back to reassemble, in which case, the association would put up five thousand dollars. As matters transpired, this purse promise was not enough to elicit the requisite field, but Iroquois was entered, and such was his lingering public appeal that the Maryland Jockey Club went ahead and provided the five thousand dollars for a four-horse field representing only two owners, the Dwyer stable and Lorillard.

Iroquois had followed his loss in the Monmouth Stakes with another defeat days later and had not run again. It was widely recognized that he was not at his best, but word was about that he had had two fast trials coming up to the Pimlico race, and the public still responded to his unique distinction as a homebred Epsom Derby winner and source of great national pride. On the day of the race, the Dwyer entry was favored, but sentiment went for the pioneer.

Only a week earlier, McLaughlin had been aboard George Kinney when Lorillard's Drake Carter snapped the colt's four-race winning streak with a six-length win in the Potomac Stakes, at the same mile and five-eighths distance. In the Pimlico Stakes, whether in response to George Kinney's defeat or to stable fiat, McLaughlin was aboard Miss Woodford while Hughes rode George Kinney. Race conditions called for the three-year-old filly to carry 107 pounds, but McLaughlin came in at 109. Drake Carter carried 107, George Kinney 110, and the older Iroquois 125.

McLaughlin put Miss Woodford on the lead, but not as a pace-maker's set-up ploy. Drake Carter came along to challenge and then take the lead, but Miss Woodford spurted out to lead by three lengths turning for home. Iroquois prompted a vocal public response when he made what appeared a menacing move, but he could not mount a prolonged challenge. Miss Woodford won, and George Kinney came on to be second to complete a one-two Dwyer Brothers finish.

Contemporary publications put different spins on Miss Woodford's victory. The *Turf Field and Farm* noted that Miss Woodford was "taken in hand" and won comfortably, whereas The *Spirit of the Times* observed that George Kinney "came up so fast that McLaughlin, on Miss Woodford, had to call out to Hughes to hold his colt, which the latter did." They agreed that the winning margin was three lengths.

Regardless of the nuances, with her defeat of George Kinney, Iroquois, and Drake Carter, Miss Woodford had won ten of twelve races at three and earned $51,121. Historians tend to rank her as what would today be called Horse of the Year, although one surmises her jockey might not have agreed. In the modern era of voting for championships, the only instances of three-year-old fillies being elected Horse of the Year came in a unique back-to-back sequence in 1944 and 1945 when Twilight Tear and Busher were accorded the honor.

At four Miss Woodford ran in nine races — a light menu for a Dwyer runner — and won every one. Whereas she had begun her three-year-old season in a major stakes, this time Rowe raced her twice in purse races before she took the Coney Island Stakes. Next came the Ocean Stakes, in which she met George Kinney once more, McLaughlin again on the mare. No longer quite the force he had been at three, George Kinney went down to defeat again.

Miss Woodford continued with victories in the Eatontown Stakes and $3,535 Champion Stakes, the latter finding her superior to

Drake Carter, Monitor, and Eole at a mile and a half. Next, in a purse race, the filly who had beaten the best going a mile and five-eighths showed enough raw speed to zip seven furlongs in 1:28 3/4, missing the American record by a quarter-second. Two weeks later she demonstrated her versatility in an extreme manner, defeating Lorillard's high-class Drake Carter by ten lengths at two and a half miles in a match race. Lorillard and the Dwyers put up five thousand dollars a side for the match, and the Coney Island racetrack added two thousand dollars.

Only two days after that distance test, Miss Woodford came out again, for the $3,650 Great Long Island Stakes. Incredibly, this was not just a two-mile race, but two of them. While heat races more or less had given way to single events by that time, a touch of the old days prevailed when Miss Woodford was pitted against Drake Carter again, as well as Modesty. Ed Corrigan's filly Modesty was a western version of Miss Woodford who had won the Kentucky Oaks and defeated colts in the first American Derby. (In those days, before California came to the fore, Kentucky and Chicago were regarded as "the West" insofar as horse racing was concerned.) Miss Woodford won the first heat by three lengths in 3:33 and the second heat by four lengths in 3:31 1/4. The combined times established an American record. The two races comprised the Great Long Island Stakes and, like other heat races, are traditionally counted as one victory. Parsing the issue in the modern context of single (dash) races, one might feel justified in adding another victory to Miss Woodford's record and thus regard her winning streak to be seventeen races.

For the 1884 season Miss Woodford had won nine of nine to earn $21,070 and again was recorded years later as the consensus pick as the best, "Horse of the Year." In the modern context of voting, it is instructional that no female has won more than one Horse of the Year title, incidentally a fact that gives added gloss to Azeri for even being seen through much of 2003 as a candidate to duplicate her 2002 Horse of the Year title.

When Miss Woodford began her campaign at five in 1885, she had not known defeat since that loss to George Kinney in the Monmouth Stakes two summers before. She launched her 1885 season with her fifteenth triumph, which came in a five-hundred-dollar purse race at Jerome Park in New York. As recorded in the race description in *Goodwin's Guide*, the Equibase chart precursor of the day, she won "very easily under a strong pull by a short neck." One wonders whether this evidenced a nonchalant attitude about winning streaks, an extraordinary confidence on McLaughlin's part, or a set-up by the Dwyers to get a better price on her next race.

Whatever the agenda, in her next race Miss Woodford faced a tough task when entered in the mile and one-eighth Coney Island Stakes. She was asked to give nineteen pounds in actual weight to Lorillard's three-year-

James Rowe in a discussion with Frank McCabe, who also trained Miss Woodford.

old filly Wanda, who had won eight of thirteen as champion of her division the year before. Moreover, two other champions were in the field: Louisette, who raced for Lorillard's brother George and had been champion three-year-old filly of 1884, and Sam Bryant's Gen. Harding, a four-year-old who had been champion at two.

Gen. Harding and Louisette were in front early and then Wanda moved up to challenge, but Miss Woodford emerged as best of a field of four champions, beating the three-year-old filly by a length, with Louisette third.

The Coney Island marked the sixteenth consecutive victory for Miss Woodford. Her next race, the Farewell Stakes, interrupted her winning streak. She lost to yet another in the powerful stable of the Lorillard brothers, Thackeray, to whom she gave nine pounds. The hiatus from the winner's echelon was brief. Miss Woodford bounced back to win the Ocean Stakes, Monmouth Cup, and Freehold Stakes. Thus, she had won nineteen of her past twenty races over three seasons.

Victories were not so consistently forthcoming thereafter. On August 6 she finished fourth in the Eatontown Stakes to the year's Suburban Handicap winner, Pontiac. This ranked with her last-place finish in the 1883 Monmouth Stakes among only two times she was out of the first three. Four days later she faced for the first time Ed Corrigan's Freeland, a six-year-old gelding destined to be a consistent rival for the next few events. In the $4,425 Champion Stakes at Monmouth Park, Freeland beat Miss Woodford a length at a mile and a half. Eight days later they hooked up again, at a mile and a quarter, in the $4,000 Special Stakes. Pontiac was also in the field, and after Miss Woodford put him away, she had Freeland to face. Freeland passed her in the stretch, but Miss Woodford came back bravely, failing by only a short head.

The Dwyers did not take to losing kindly and immediately challenged Corrigan to a match race, $2,500 a side. The sporting folk who ran Monmouth came with another $2,500 and, only two days after the Special, Miss Woodford and Freeland came out for the match at a mile and a quarter. Miss Woodford took the lead at the start and prevailed by a head in another grim and testing battle.

After such strenuous activity trainer Rowe declared Miss Woodford needed to stop for the season. The Dwyers could not imagine such a thing right in the midst of an exciting season merely because a horse might be wearing down. Apprised of their insistence as to this matter, Rowe resigned. The owners were not much for the "Oh, don't be hasty. Come on back. If you feel that strongly, you can rest her if you really want to." Instead, they promoted barn foreman Frank McCabe to head trainer, and the season proceeded.

Three weeks after the match, Miss Woodford appeared for yet another meeting with Freeland, in a $5,000 Sweepstakes at New York's Brighton Beach. That time Freeland won easily, by four lengths, going a mile and a quarter. Five days later the mare whose former trainer had said she needed a rest was tested at two-mile heats for the Great Long Island Stakes. Gamely, Miss Woodford won the first heat by a neck and the second by a length and a half. She was surely a true and faithful servant of whoever was chosen as master of her training.

Miss Woodford won the equivalent of seven Eclipse Awards.

That was her final start of the year. She had won seven of twelve and earned $19,370. While Freeland wrested from her the historians' recognition as Horse of the Year, Miss Woodford retained her hold on the older distaff division.

At six Miss Woodford was fresh and ready for more when she came out in the $1,000 Harlem Stakes at Jerome Park on May 31, 1886. A victory there set her up for one of the most remarkable moments in her career. A $10,000-plus race called the Eclipse Stakes was on tap out in St. Louis, and she was sent thither for the mile and a half race whose organizers hoped would also attract her nemesis, Freeland. The old gelding was not sound enough at the moment, so Corrigan sent his vaunted distaffer Modesty. California horseman Lucky Baldwin's Volante, whose thirty-five victories included the American Derby and Saratoga Cup, was also entered, as was Porter Ashe's Alta.

Alta led after a mile, by which point Miss Woodford put her head in front. Volante tested her, but the mare prevailed. Afterward, the *Spirit of the Times* opined that she had "clearly established herself as the Queen of the Turf," but that she had been "pushed to the very utmost by her California rival, Volante." Miss Woodford thus won the richest race she ever ran for, and it was that victory that pushed her over the $100,000 mark.

(A tragic aspect of the otherwise glorious occasion was that the press stand attached to the main grandstand was pushed beyond its limits, with forty or so people crowded into it, "some of them having no business there," according to the *Spirit*. Soon after the start of the race, the press stand collapsed. In *The Great Ones*, author Hollingsworth could not resist the quip that Miss Woodford "brought down the house." Local reporter Romayn A. Dyer was killed in the melee, but amazingly none of some two dozen other injuries were regarded as serious.)

Back in New York, Miss Woodford faced an old campaigner named Barnum in the mile and three-quarters Coney Island Cup. There was no clowning in this Barnum production. The pair ran together for all but the first quarter-mile, and so close was the finish that the judges were unable to separate them, and so it went into the record as a dead heat victory for each runner.

Captain Sam Brown won the

important Suburban Handicap with Troubadour, and a match race between that one and Miss Woodford was quickly arranged. Troubadour won by nearly a length in the $3,000 special event. It was Miss Woodford's only defeat at six. She reeled off three more victories: the Ocean Stakes, Monmouth Cup, and, on July 24, Saratoga's First Sweepstakes.

The First would be last. Miss Woodford was lame afterward, and her glorious racing career suddenly was over. She had won six of seven that year to earn $20,000, and again was rated as the champion older distaffer.

True to their methods the Dwyers put Miss Woodford on the market once she was finished as a racer. James Ben Ali Haggin, who had vast land and Thoroughbred holdings in California as well as at Elmendorf Farm in Kentucky, bought the champion as a broodmare prospect. Miss Woodford had nine foals, of which five won. None were outstanding, but two were stakes winners: George

MISS WOODFORD				
Billet, 1865	Voltigeur, 1847	Voltaire, 1826	Blacklock, 1814	Whitelock Coriander Mare
			Phantom Mare, 1816	Phantom Overton Mare
		Martha Lynn, 1837	Mulatto, 1823	Catton Desdemona
			Leda, 1824	**Filho Da Puta** Treasure
	Calcutta, 1853	Flatcatcher, 1845	Touchstone, 1831	Camel Banter
			Decoy, 1830	**Filho Da Puta** Finesse
		Miss Martin, 1844	St. Martin, 1835	Actaeon Galena
			Wagtail, 1829	Whisker Sorcerer Mare
Fancy Jane, 1869	Neil Robinson, 1857	Wagner, 1834	Sir Charles, 1816	Sir Archy Citizen Mare
			Maria West, 1827	Marion Ella Crump
		Belle Lewis, 1848	**Glencoe**, 1831	Sultan Trampoline
			Tranby Anna, 1838	Tranby Lady Thompkins
	Knight of St. George Mare, n.d.	Knight of St. George, 1851	Birdcatcher, 1833	Sir Hercules Guiccioli
			Maltese, 1845	Hetman Platoff Waterwitch
		Glencoe Mare, 1850	**Glencoe**, 1831	Sultan Trampoline
			Varico, 1831	Sumpter Northumberland Mare

Kessler, by Salvator, won the Great American and Hudson stakes at two in 1896, and Sombre, by Midlothian, won the Androus and Olympic stakes at two in 1898.

Her five campaigns, as noted initially, found Miss Woodford winning thirty-seven of forty-eight races to earn $118,270. She was second seven times and third twice.

Oddly though, despite the encomia that have flowed to Miss Woodford from both contemporaries and historians, her standing in the eyes of her own jockey was more reserved. McLaughlin did not regard her as the best filly or mare he ever rode, stating many years later that "Miss Woodford was a sturdy mare of the masculine type, but Firenze, in my opinion, was a greater performer. Firenze could run all day." Although he was not Firenze's regular rider, McLaughlin did partner her on ten occasions and rode against her twenty-two times as she won forty-seven of eighty-two races from 1886 to 1891. Firenze, who followed Miss Woodford as the second female to earn $100,000, was a noted distance mare who defeated such highflying males as Hanover, Tenny, and Kingston. She was rated a champion in three years.

Nevertheless, Miss Woodford had Firenze's number in terms of years as perceived champion. In today's context Miss Woodford presumably would have been recipient of seven Eclipse Awards — one division title for each of the five years she raced and two Horse of the Year honors. A mare to match that has yet to be seen.

by Edward L. Bowen

Imp

(1899)

Her fans called her "the Coal Black Lady," and the press called her the queen of the Turf. Whichever nickname you liked, there was no doubt that Imp was one of the most successful and experienced race mares of all time. She was born in 1894 and ran 171 races from 1896 to 1901. She won sixty-two (sixteen of them stakes), took second place in thirty-five, and third place in twenty-nine. Imp was Horse of the Year in 1899 and sixty-six years later was inducted into the Racing Hall of Fame.

Imp raced at an exciting time for America during the decade known as the Gay Nineties. New inventions and discoveries abounded: X-ray, the wireless

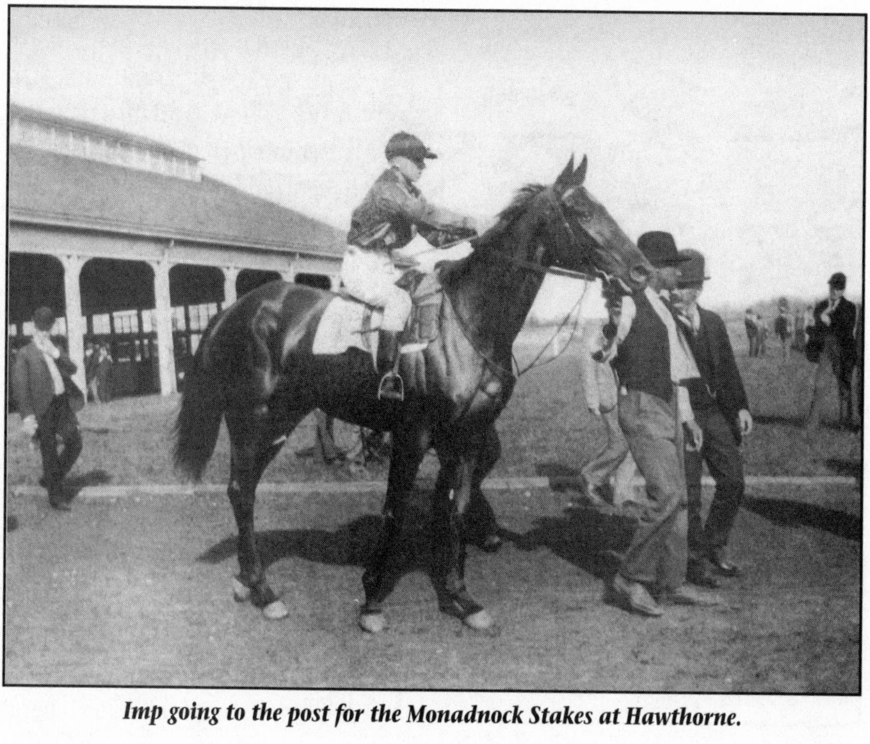

Imp going to the post for the Monadnock Stakes at Hawthorne.

telegraph, the snapping mousetrap, radium, and the zeppelin. Henry Ford built his first car, and Spain sank the U.S. battleship *Maine* in Havana, Cuba, prompting the Spanish-American War. It was a time of adventure, too. Admiral Robert Peary claimed he had reached the North Pole, and the Klondike gold rush drew fortune-seekers and reporters. The cakewalk took over dance floors, and bicycles filled the streets. Americans quested for the liveliest entertainment and found it in Thoroughbred racing, particularly at Saratoga, which reached its pinnacle as a place to enjoy the races.

Women's rights came to the forefront at the turn of the century as well. Susan B. Anthony and Carrie Chapman Catt stood at the helm of the solidly established suffrage movement. In private parlors and in public lecture halls, debates raged whether female Americans should have the right to vote, a crucial step on the road to gender equality. In the meantime, a female horse was tearing up the country's tracks, proving herself the equal — and often the better — of her male competitors.

Imp was a leggy black mare with a white diamond. Her color, large frame, and broad head resembled that of her sire, the imported stallion Wagner. She was rather homely, but as a reporter for the *Cincinnati Enquirer* wrote: "Imp is not a pretty mare to look at in the paddock, but when running she is perfection itself." Her dam was Fondling, by Fonso. Ironically for the parents of such a heavily raced filly, Wagner and Fondling had each raced only once. Imp was owned by Daniel "Uncle Dan" Harness, an Ohioan who had shared ownership in postbellum champions like General

Women of the late 1890s

The women's suffrage movement advances in some states...Charlotte Perkins Gilman writes *Women and Economics*, in which she argues that the lost talent of women hampers the entire economy...Florence Kelley and the National Consumers League begin a campaign against child labor and sweatshops and in favor of minimum wage legislation, shorter hours, improved working conditions, and safety laws...In Kansas, Carry Nation begins her campaign to close saloons; she attacks bars and smashes bottles containing alcohol with her hatchet.

"The Coal Black Lady" in front of Pioneer Bowling Alleys.

Duke (a Belmont winner), Vauxhall, and Bayonet. Harness was very fond of Imp, who had been born on his High Bank Farm. He had named her Imp because of the mischievous way she gamboled around the paddock as a foal.

Charles E. Brossman trained Imp for most of her career. Brossman, who later became a Turf writer, had trained many horses around small-time Ohio fairs. He and Harness split all winnings, with Brossman paying training costs. Brossman's first success was a filly named Bessie Bisland, and the year after she won the Harlem Cup he began training Imp as a yearling. Imp started her career as one of many platers on the Ohio and Kentucky tracks and did not have a particularly auspicious two-year-old season. Although she won her first race, she won only two others out of her eleven starts as a two-year-old in 1896.

During her three-year-old season, though, Imp continued running often and improving. She raced in Kentucky during the spring and won some overnight and claiming races there. She usually ran at the front and often led wire to wire. She raced in Chicago from August through the fall and won eight races there at Harlem and Lakeside. She won her last race of the season by fifteen lengths, bringing her record as a three-year-old to fourteen victories out of fifty races. A loyal following had begun to develop in her hometown of Chillicothe, Ohio. The *Chillicothe Gazette* reported her homecoming at the season's end with pride: "Imp, the fleet and beautiful 3-year-old daughter of Wagner and Fonso, and the best piece of horse flesh in the possession of 'Uncle Dan' Harness, in fact with few superiors in her class in the state, was shipped from Chicago to this city yesterday evening."

In 1898 Brossman took Imp to New York for the Suburban Handicap during her four-year-old season, which had so far consisted of winning ten of eleven starts. The Suburban, which was run at the Sheepshead Bay track on Coney Island, had started in 1884, when the track's mile and one-eighth circumference was the largest in America. She finished sixth in the popular race, which brought spectators out of Manhattan in droves.

Although she did not seem to stand a chance against New York horses, she won a race at Gravesend on June 13. She lost again after that and soon went back to Chicago to run. She languished on the track that summer, but by September she picked up steam, and her four-year-old record stretched to twenty-one wins out of thirty-five starts. Her four-year-old season also initiated her success at the stakes level, as she won the Hawthorne Monadnock Stakes, the Harlem Speed Stakes, and the Hawthorne Dash Stakes among others.

Imp made her biggest impression in 1899 as a five-year-old, when she earned Horse of the Year honors. It also was an important year for the rest of the country as well. William McKinley, the last Civil War veteran to serve as president, was in the White House. E.B. White, Duke Ellington, and Humphrey Bogart were born. It was a year of conclusions — the Spanish-American War ended, and the French government pardoned military officer Alfred Dreyfus after accusing him of providing information to the German government, spawning "the Dreyfus affair," which heightened anti-Semitism in Europe. It was also a year of firsts. Oysters Rockefeller was first served in New Orleans. The paper clip and spring mousetrap were invented. Carnation

Imp with groom Tom Tandy.

prepared its first can of evaporated milk. The first automotive fatality occurred when an electric taxi hit a man in New York City. The first Hague peace conference took place, and the first American juvenile court opened.

And Imp became the first mare to win the $10,000 Suburban. The race would make her famous. With her victory she paved the way for other female Suburban winners like Beldame (1905), Bateau (1929), Harmonica (1948), and Busanda (1951). The Suburban victory proved that despite her humble beginnings, unimpressive appearance, and heavy schedule, Imp should be heeded as a contender.

That year the Suburban fell on the first day of the Sheepshead Bay meeting. It was a huge occasion for male New Yorkers of all castes, but only lower-class women were at the track for the big race in a time when genteel women sometimes eschewed sporting events like horse races. "Society with a capital S was not very largely in evidence, as to the feminine portion of it at least," reported the *New York Times*. "Every gambler of note was there, though but a modicum of them found places in the boxes and reserved seats of the second tier of the grand stand where, with their ladies, they were able to touch elbows with such of the social elect as were there to see the fun." With such a heterogeneous crowd in attendance, the scene was set for an exciting day of racing as well as for a lively social occasion.

Women who were unfettered by societal convention may have been there to join in the fun of a day at the track, but even they could not place bets themselves. "Men, willing or no, were pressed into service as messengers for the women who had dollars to bet on some horse that they had dreamed would win," reported the *Times*. And it was apparently a big day for betting. "Bedlam was a quiet spot compared with the betting ring in the half hour before the race was run."

Since Imp raced in the days before the starting gate, a starter dropped a flag to send the horses off. Much of the field misbehaved, and the favorite, Banastar, seemed particularly rambunctious as the starter attempted to line up the horses. It took forty-five minutes and twelve false starts before the thirteen-horse field was ready to go. Between the aborted starts

Dan Harness.

Imp's jockey, Nash Turner, placed his foot on the rail for a while to give the mare, who was carrying 114 pounds, a rest. As the horses charged across the starting line, Banastar's jockey pulled him up after about four lengths. The stewards later fined him two hundred dollars for abusing Banastar at the post and suspended him for ten days for meddling with the start of the big race.

Turner kept Imp behind the early trailblazers, waiting for his opportunity. At the first turn Briar Sweet led the pack, with George Keene just behind. Imp and Fillgrane matched strides directly behind him. At mid-backstretch Fillgrane ran out of juice. The other horses were starting to press forward when Turner dug in his heels and took Imp to the front of the field. At one point Bannockburn made a bid for the lead, but Imp "seemed to have the wings of the wind to help her busy feet along," according to the *Times'* reporter. She led from the five-eighths pole, and Turner (unnecessarily, according to one reporter) only went to the whip once. The *Cincinnati Enquirer* reported that, "Still moving in her long, low, frictionless manner, the Western wonder maintained her marvelous pace."

Police had tried in vain all day to keep the infield crowds from pressing the rail. But as the horses thundered down the stretch, all the people excitedly pushed up against the fence to get a better view, forcing it to collapse. Turner had to veer to keep Imp from getting stuck in the mess as the rails fell. People screamed as the horses ran by because it seemed that surely someone would get crushed under flying hooves. All the spectators survived, though, and Imp churned on to win. Her closest rival, Bannockburn, never got closer than two lengths. The *Chillicothe Gazette* wrote that "Straight as an arrow that black whirlwind ran down the stretch...Not only is Imp the fleetest thoroughbred that Ross County ever produced, but Ohio as well, and the best of her sex and species of which the county can boast."

After the race the band played "Hail To The Chief" for Turner, and he gave credit to his mount. In his interview with the *Enquirer*, Turner said that Imp had been willing and kind. "As we reached the betting ring I felt that I would win," he said, "but Imp began to falter and I had to shake the whip at her a couple of times. I did not touch her with the whip and won driving all out by about a length."

As soon as the win was official, a messenger on horseback carried the news out to a thrilled Harness, who was home in Ohio. The *Thoroughbred Record*'s Ohio correspondent quoted him as saying, "I don't give a damn about the money, just wanted to show them Kentucky boys that we can grow a race horse in Ohio now and then." He rejected the deluge of offers to buy the mare after her Suburban win. "I am an old man and there is no pocket in a shroud," he said. "Imp is all I want."

After the Suburban, Imp's fame grew and grew. The turn-of-the century press was not noted for its reticence, and the *New York Press* extolled Imp: "Than Imp, no greater mare ever was saddled on this continent...Imp is the queen of the equine queens — a

perfect racing machine; one of the best thoroughbreds ever has been the good fortune of American Turfmen to look upon. She is something more than the best mare in training. She has earned a higher honor — that of being the best thoroughbred, horse or mare, now racing in America." Horse of the Year honors seemed fitting for such a significant and record-setting racehorse.

Imp's Suburban win stamped her as a "queen among equine queens," but also as a pioneer. With her success she demonstrated that the race belonged to the fastest horse, not just the fastest colt. Other "firsts" were happen-

Imp's return to Chillicothe after winning the Suburban Handicap in 1899. In the carriage are Dan Harness (right) and Charles Brossman.

ing for female human athletes as well at the turn of the century. Although it wasn't until 1906 that Lula Olive Gill became the first woman jockey to win a horse race in California, other gender milestones were being set in sports. Jane Yatman rode seven hundred miles in eighty-one hours, five minutes on Long Island to set a new women's cycling endurance record. And two women ice hockey teams played a game on the artificial ice at the Ice Palace in Philadelphia.

As these women broke new ground, though, others campaigned for things to stay the same. The suffrage movement was probably the most pressing women's issue — and a crucial issue for all Americans — of the day, and even as activists fought for women's right to vote, some women fought to keep voting a male privilege. In 1899 the *New York Times* reported on an anti-suffrage organization that listed several reasons why women should not have the vote. "The physiological aspect is the kernel of this question," the anti-suffragists argued. "No possible future conditions can ever alter the physiological differences between the sexes. Once the incontrovertible and unalterable fact of physical limitation is faced and acknowledged all the plausible arguments which have grown up about this question of the suffrage, obscuring its inmost meaning, fall away." While obviously not involved in the suffrage question, Imp's success nevertheless struck a blow for gender equality. Unlike the anti-suffragists, Imp was obviously unaware of the differences between herself and the colts she beat. She simply kept racing, and winning.

Whenever she was led to the winner's circle, the racetrack band would strike up a popular tune of the day called "My Coal Black Lady." The song, written by W.T. Jefferson in 1896, included the lyrics, "She says she is my honey, and she has no use for money, and to her I'll be true. There ain't no other fellow that can hope to cut a figure with this lady friend of mine. When we start a-walkin', we just set 'em all to talkin'. We are winners every time." The song ended, "Don't trifle with my coal black lady," a warning her fans considered appropriate for other horses planning to race her.

Imp also drew attention for her "sleeping stunt." She ran with her head held low and looked deceptively sluggish as she streaked along. The *Cincinnati Enquirer* once reported that "still moving in her long, low, frictionless manner, the Western wonder maintained her marvelous pace." Her groom, Tom Tandy, would shout at jockeys from the rail, "Let her sleep. Don't wake her up!"

Imp lost four races after her Suburban triumph, but nevertheless the racing secretary still assigned the "Coal Black Lady" the top weight of 115 pounds in the Brighton Handicap on July 6. Because of threatening weather, attendance was down, but just as in the Suburban, the field held the promise of a big day. Ethelbert, a champion three-year-old, had just won the Lawrence Realization and was favored to win the Brighton as well.

Martimas, a Futurity winner, also had plenty of support. The race stood a chance to make history, since it was "not often a race crowd has the chance to see a Futurity winner, a Realization winner, and a Suburban winner arrayed against one another in a single contest," as the *New York Telegram* said.

The betting crowd backed Ethelbert, forgetting, as the *New York Times* reported, that "the very sturdy and honest Western mare was in the field." Ethelbert had an inside position and started out at the lead. But as the horses passed the stands for the first time, Imp took the lead. By the first turn she was ahead by a length. More concerned with Bangle and May Hempstead, Ethelbert's jockey kept his horse back perhaps more than advisable, because Imp wound up two lengths ahead by the time the horses reached the backstretch. Basically, after the first quarter mile, Imp had a commanding lead.

"Those who best knew the mare and her method of running," the *Times* reporter wrote, "made the declaration with much certainty when she got her lead in the run from the judges' stand to the turn that there was nothing in the race that would be able to catch her unless it should be Martimas," which never happened. Imp won in 2:05 2/5 and also won $8,420, her largest purse yet.

All during 1899 Imp was unstoppable. At the August 30 Ocean Handicap at Sheepshead Bay, the *Thoroughbred Record* reported that as the pressure grew, "Still [jockey Pete] Clay sat motionless, allowing the mare to 'sleep,' and only in the last few strides did he bend low over her neck and appear to ask her to 'sleep harder.' "

He took her to the front of the pack right away, but the favorite, Voter, caught up with her, and they ran together until the stretch, when Voter dropped back. Clay looked behind him, and nearly lost the race when a horse named Charentus came up for a final bid. But Imp rallied and won by half a length with another victory chalked up to her now-notorious "sleeping stunt."

She kept going. On September 1, Imp won the Turf Handicap at Sheepshead Bay. "It is doubtful if there is another horse in training on the American turf to-day that can repeat Imp's performance in the Turf Handicap, galloping one mile and a quarter on grass in 2:07 1/8 with 128 pounds on her back," said the *Cincinnati Enquirer*. After the first furlong people started shouting "Nothing in it but Imp," and "She'll come home alone." She finished lengths ahead of the others on the bit, and in the end she matched a time record that had stood since 1844.

September remained a lucky month for Imp, and she was in the winner's circle again after the mile and a quarter First Special on September 12. Although the race day at Gravesend was sparsely attended (the Long Island Rail Road and Brooklyn Special Transit Company were feuding, so the LIRR deposited its passengers in a potato field two miles from the track), Imp did not seem to notice the absence of her usual cheering section. "Ohio Mare Ran Good Race In Mud," trumpeted one headline. During the mile, Imp and May Hempstead swapped the lead back and forth, but eventually "the black mare went on alone, finished as she pleased," reported the *Enquirer*. She won by two lengths.

Even with a packed schedule, Imp kept on winning, taking the mile and a half Second Special on September 23. Again the press extolled her victory. "Imp, the 'sleepy' black mare from Chillicothe, ran one of the best races that was ever run by a mare on an Eastern racecourse," said the *New York Telegraph*. Although Ethelbert was not entered, the race vindicated him after his defeat in the Brighton. Many racing fans had been disgusted with the champion colt for being beaten by a filly, but Imp's victory in the Second Special over Ben Holladay, known as a distance runner, showed that there was no shame in losing to her. By the bend of the stretch, Ben Holladay had only two lengths between him and Imp, but he never got closer. It was a case of "Imp first and the rest nowhere," wrote one reporter, harkening back to the saying about the undefeated Eclipse, from whose sire line Imp descended.

Imp's success delighted her hometown fans. At the end of the racing season, Chillicothe residents threw her a victory parade, during which she acted very much the queen. Her most regular jockey, Pete Clay, wearing Harness' silks, rode her down the street past the thrilled crowd. She wore a wreath of flowers and was accompanied by police, a brass band, and the mayor. The *Chillicothe Gazette* wrote that under all the attention she was "playful as a school girl [and] agile as a kitten...She shared the generous applause that hundreds of admiring spectators were only too glad to give. Imp seemed to realize that she was on dress parade and acted accordingly by dancing over the street, her easy, graceful motion arousing the enthusiasm of her observers."

Imp's next year — her six-year-old season — proved far more checkered than her golden year of 1899 had been. Charley Brossman wanted her to win the Suburban again, but she finished fourth, unable to repeat her famous performance. She finished ten and a half lengths behind Kinley Mac at the finish. (She beat Kinley Mac again at the Second Special at Gravesend later in the season, though.)

She did lose the mile and one-eighth Brookdale Handicap by a nose to Jean Beraud. She also lost her usual jockey, because days before Brossman had fired Clay,

Imp's final trainer, Peter Wimmer (right).

who had long worn Harness' black and gold silks. Although Clay had perfected the art of letting Imp "sleep," he kept urging her forward instead. As he dismounted on May 15, Brossman fired him. (Clay had apparently figured out he was becoming Brossman's second choice for Imp.) The *New York Telegraph's* reporter quipped that "P. Clay will not ride the thundercloud mare Imp again in all his life, unless he gets her out of the stable in the night and scurries off with her across the landscape."

Her first stakes victory in 1900 was in the Parkway Handicap on May 30. In this race she impressed her fans by not spooking at a barrier that was giving the other five horses trouble. The *New York Telegraph* said that, "While the other five contestants began their twistings, backing and breaking as soon as they faced the barrier, the black wonder from Chillicothe just stood and looked at the proceedings with an intelligence almost human. The great mare seemed to watch that machine as much as to say to the starter, 'Don't mind me. I will be there or thereabouts as soon as you let that barrier go.' " More than four-fifths of the racing crowd liked that calm attitude and bet on her, and she gratified them with her win.

In the Advance Stakes a month later she was in the lead after the first half mile and never looked back. It was a mile and three-quarters race, and when Imp finished thirty lengths ahead of the pack in 2:59 1/5, not only had she beaten the Sheepshead Bay record, but she had also beaten Ben Holladay's American record for that distance.

On October 25, 1900, she won the mile and one-sixteenth Mahopac Handicap at the Empire City racetrack, leading the whole race. She continued to be a crowd favorite, as the *New York Times* reported, "Though the result was exactly what nine out of every ten spectators had anticipated confidently, the cheering and applause that greeted the old black mare from Ohio were as spontaneous and genuine as if she had really achieved a great success."

Harness apparently considered Imp purely a racehorse, and even as she passed her prime, did not give much thought to letting her retire or become a broodmare. In 1901 Imp was still winning some races as a seven-year-old, including three overnight races at Saratoga and Morris Park. She was third in the Saratoga Cup. At a race at Morris Park on October 22, the *Thoroughbred Record* reported that Imp looked like a likely winner, as she was handicapped at 109 pounds, or fourteen pounds less than weight for age, and faced a field of unimposing challengers. Imp won by a head, and her fans continued to applaud her at every turn. The reporter wrote, "The roof of the grandstand resounded with shouts of the public, winners and losers alike appearing to view with the greatest possible enthusiasm the victory of the veteran mare. When she returned to the scales, a couple of thousand people who had gathered around the stewards stand clapped their hands and showed their appreciation for several minutes, while the band played 'My Coal Black Lady.' "

Charley Brossman was no longer training Imp. He and Harness had differences over the trainer's handling of the mare, and she had been turned over to Peter Wimmer (who had been training Ben Holladay when the horse lost to Imp at Gravesend in 1899). It was Wimmer's job to help Imp make a graceful exit,

IMP	Wagner, 1882	Prince Charlie, 1869	Blair Athol, 1861	**Stockwell**, 1849	**The Baron** **Pocahontas**
				Blink Bonny, 1854	Melbourne Queen Mary
			Eastern Princess, 1858	Surplice, 1845	Touchstone Crucifix
				Tomyris, 1851	Sesostris Glaucus Mare
		Duchess of Malfi, 1873	Elland, 1862	Rataplan, 1850	**The Baron** **Pocahontas**
				Ellermire, 1852	Chanticleer Ellerdale
			Duchess, 1864	St. Albans, 1857	**Stockwell** Bribery
				Bay Celia, 1851	Orlando Hersey
	Fondling, 1886	Fonso, 1877	King Alfonso, 1872	Phaeton, 1865	King Tom Merry Sunshine
				Capitola, 1858	Vandal Margrave Mare
			Weatherwitch, 1858	Weatherbit, 1842	Sheet Anchor Miss Letty
				Birdcatcher Mare, 1853	Birdcatcher Colocynth
		Kitty Herron, 1875	Chilicothe, 1867	**Lexington**, 1850	Boston Alice Carneal
				Lilla, 1856	Yorkshire Victoire
			Mollie Foster, 1869	Asteroid, 1861	**Lexington** Nebula
				Little Miss, 1860	Sovereign Little Mistress

but she began losing more and more as time went on. "Take a good look at her, boys," Wimmer reportedly told one crowd. "You'll never see the old mare on a track again." The *Chicago Record-Herald* reported that she finished a far last at a Sheepshead Bay race, "galloping home a miserable wreck of her former self." She was as game as ever and started out in the front of the pack, but simply could not keep up any longer. Her last race was at Aqueduct on November 9, 1901. Reports of her exact winnings vary, but they were more than $70,000. When Daniel Harness died in 1902, his executors sold Imp to Ed A. Tipton, the head of the auction firm, for $4,100. Imp was up for auction at Fasig-Tipton's Sheepshead Bay Fall Sales in 1902. She was sold to John E. Madden for six thousand dollars and had six foals at Madden's Hamburg Place, the most notable of which was a stakes winner named Faust.

Imp died in 1909, shortly after giving birth to her sixth foal, which was never named and apparently died as well. She is buried in a private horse cemetery on Hamburg Place, east of Lexington, Kentucky.

With her talent and perseverance, Imp kept the hearts of fans she had won along with the 1899 Suburban. Her handlers saw to it that she was constantly tried and retried by the intense schedule they set her whole racing life. Instead of shrinking from such a challenge, Imp met it head-on, as her fans well knew. People could not help but respond with adoration as throughout her life, Imp kept showing the trademark grace that well suited a queen of the Turf.

by Eliza McGraw

Many thanks to the National Museum of Racing and the Ross County Historical Society in Chillicothe, Ohio, for their help in researching Imp.

Beldame

(1904)

It didn't take long for Beldame, the 1904 Horse of the Year, to be honored in the grandest of ways. After her retirement in late summer of the following year, Aqueduct instituted the Beldame Handicap for two-year-old fillies, run that November. The name of the winner, Flip Flap, who ran the five furlongs in a minute flat and collected the biggest part of the $1,570 purse, long has faded from memory. But the memory of Beldame remains as strong as ever and comes alive each fall with the running of the grade I Beldame Stakes at Belmont Park.

Beldame was the best filly ever bred by her owner, August Belmont II, who also bred Man o'

Beldame at Morris Park.

War but sold that great champion colt as a yearling. A leading Wall Street financier and the most prominent man in racing for years, Belmont served as president of Belmont Park, named in honor of his father, and was chairman of the New York State Racing Commission, as well as the longest-serving chairman of The Jockey Club, from 1895 to 1924.

Ironically, Belmont did not race Beldame that championship season because of pressing business matters that included building a subway system in New York City and instead leased her to friend and business associate Newton Bennington. Considering that Horses of the Year are hard to come by, a good case could be made for Bennington being the luckiest man in the history of racing. Beldame's Horse of the Year and three-year-old filly championships are credited to him.

Beldame's achievements her three-year-old season were such that she earned a place among the all-time greats. Kent Hollingsworth, a former editor of *The Blood-Horse,* succinctly summed up her three-year-old season in *The Great Ones*. "At three Beldame was magnificent. She sprinted; she stayed. She humiliated her feminine rivals, then beat good colts, gave them weight and beat them again, and then whipped the best handicappers over a distance of ground. She won twelve of her fourteen races."

Prominent Turf writer Neil Newman also thought her extraordinary. Commenting in the late 1940s, he found Beldame to be one of four "super-colossal" fillies that he had seen since 1900. The other three were Artful, born a year after Beldame; 1915 Kentucky Derby winner and Horse of the Year Regret; and 1945 Horse of the Year Busher. The great ones Newman felt didn't measure up included such stars as Top Flight from the 1930s

Women of the 1900s

Wild West star Calamity Jane appears at the Pan-American Exposition in Buffalo, New York...The Women's Trade Union League is founded to help working women organize...Helen Keller is the first deaf and blind woman to graduate from Radcliffe College. She graduates cum laude...Lillian D. Wald, Florence Kelley, and other reformers establish the National Child Labor Committee to work for legislation to eliminate child labor...Psychologist G. Stanley Hall describes the specialty of professional work as alien to the female mind.

and Gallorette and Twilight Tear from the '40s.

"Her action was faultless; she always galloped with her head held low," Newman wrote. "She had a mind of her own, and was inclined to be a bit headstrong, but got along perfectly with the boy who galloped her...She was a very masculine type, was never in season while in training."

Beldame's headstrong manner showed itself in a peculiar way. A finicky eater, she failed to show much of a liking for oats but loved corn, consuming seven or eight ears down to the cob. When it came to oats, she never ate more than three quarts a day.

Racing during the first part of the twentieth century was a whole different ball game from what it is today. (And speaking of ball games, the first World Series took place when Beldame was a two-year-old in 1903 and was won by the Boston Red Sox over the Pittsburgh Pirates.) Race meetings were much shorter than they are today, and a card usually consisted of five or six races. Instead of just Aqueduct and Belmont Park, the New York metropolitan area also boasted tracks such as Brighton Beach, Gravesend, Morris Park, and Sheepshead Bay, all of which closed years ago. Saratoga, founded in the 1860s, was upstate and several hours by train.

In addition to short race meets, betting was done with bookmakers instead of through the present-day pari-mutuel system.

Belmont's rival owners did not differ much in the way of substance from many of today's top owners. Men of social and financial means, they included the likes of William Collins Whitney and his son, Harry Payne Whitney, plus James R. Keene, Mike Dwyer, and Kentucky horseman John E. Madden.

Although Beldame received high marks in several races during her two-year-old season in 1903, she showed more promise than overall prominence. Making her first start for Belmont and trainer John Hyland in the June 10 Clover Stakes at Gravesend, Beldame finished second as the 5-2 favorite, beaten one and a half lengths for the five furlongs. She was nearly left at the start but "closed a tremendous gap and was going faster even than the winner at the end; was much the best and is evidently a high-class filly."

Beldame proved that *Daily Racing Form* chart caller correct by winning the July 1 Vernal Stakes at Sheepshead Bay in a front-running effort.

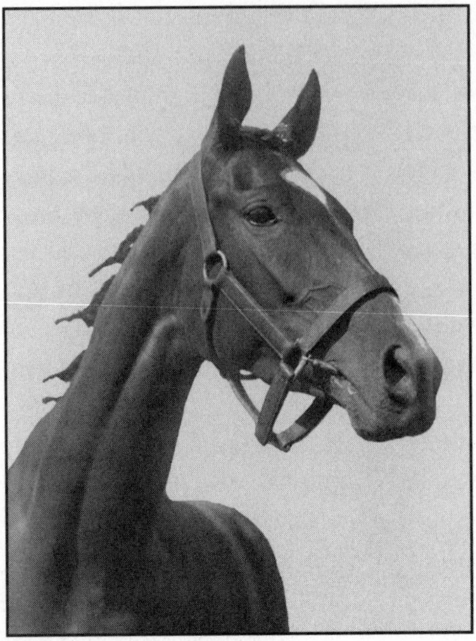

Beldame.

She made the trip north to Saratoga and came down with what appeared to be a skin infection. Belmont and Hyland disagreed on what caused the infection, with the owner feeling it was hives or shingles and the conditioner, mosquito bites. To make matters worse, Beldame lost an allowance race on August 22 to the year's best two-year-old filly, Hamburg Belle, and the two men found something else about which to argue. Belmont then declared Beldame from the rich Futurity Stakes (won by Hamburg Belle), and it wasn't long before an irate Hyland told Belmont he was quitting, effective the end of October.

Prior to Hyland's departure, Beldame made three more starts. She overtook Ocean Tide to win the September 2 Great Filly Stakes at Sheepshead Bay by a head, with Mineola a nose farther back. As good as Beldame's effort was, Mineola's was considered better, as she "finished running faster than the leaders and probably was the best," according to the chart.

In her last two starts for Hyland, both at Morris Park, Beldame ran third in the September 28 Matron Stakes and fourth in the October 3 Nursery Handicap against males.

By the time of Beldame's next race, against males November 5 at Aqueduct, the filly had a new trainer, Fred Burlew, and a new listed owner in Bennington. Beldame won that overnight handicap by four lengths, showing characteristics of "a superlative mudlark, (Beldame) won all the way and, cantering at the end, was much the best in the going."

For the year Beldame had won three races — two stakes — and placed in two stakes from seven starts. She had earned $21,185. Since there was nothing like today's Experimental Free Handicap, it was hard to determine where Beldame ranked compared to champion Hamburg Belle and the other juvenile fillies.

The disagreement between Belmont and Hyland had come after years of success together. Hyland, a robust man who ran a tight ship, had won two Belmont Stakes for Belmont, with Hastings in 1896 and homebred Masterman in 1902. Hastings and Masterman were never champions, but Hastings' name lives on as the grandsire of Man o' War. Hyland also trained Belmont's two-time Horse of the Year, Henry of Navarre.

In addition to training Hastings, Hyland played a big role in the Man o' War legend from another angle. One of his young employees was Louis Feustel, later Man o' War's trainer. Feustel, who started working with the Belmont horses at age ten, galloped Hastings until the day the colt ran off with him for two miles.

Hyland also did his part to help promote racing away from the track. The following appeared in a Racing Hall of Fame article in 1956, the year Hyland was elected.

"During the early 1900s, the clergy of New York were calling for the abolishment of racing. Riding the subway one day, Hyland found a lost wallet and returned it to its owner, who happened to be a clergyman. The clergyman wrote a letter to the *New York Times* saying all horsemen were not bad and that he supported the continuation of horse racing."

Both Belmont and his father would have appreciated Hyland's civic act. The first August Belmont was born in Germany in 1816 and arrived in New York as a representative of the French-based Rothschild banking firm. With the Rothschild connection and refined European manners, he quickly was welcomed into New York society.

Belmont was a man about town. He enjoyed art and politics, and "no one in this country, or perhaps in Europe, had a more complete and better selected wine cellar," wrote one newspaper. As national chairman of the Democratic Party for a dozen years, he made a strong speech for unity at the 1860 convention. The regular Democrats nominated Stephen Douglas, but the southern Democrats picked John Breckinridge in a separate convention. Both candidates went down in defeat to Abraham

Lincoln's Republican Party, and a civil war resulted.

Six years later Belmont made his way into racing when fellow financier Leonard Jerome sought his help in organizing the American Jockey Club and Jerome Park. By the close of the first season, the authoritative Belmont was the leader of the American Jockey Club, with Jerome seemingly powerless, "a ghost of Don Quixote," as one newspaper reported. In the second season, Jerome Park instituted the Belmont Stakes. In the third season, Belmont won it with homebred Fenian.

Belmont based his breeding operation at his Nursery Stud near Babylon on Long Island, New York, but he relocated it to leased land near Lexington, Kentucky, in the mid-1880s after becoming convinced of the Bluegrass region's better soil, weather, and stallion selection. After suffering a decline for several years, starting in the late 1870s, Belmont's stable rebounded in the second part of the next decade. Belmont topped the owners' list in 1889 and 1890, setting a record in the latter year, but didn't live long enough to see the full effects of the stable's renaissance. He died in November 1890. Some of the stock that was so much a part of his success would now contribute to his son's good fortune.

August Belmont II, born in New York City in 1853, joined his father's banking firm and eventually became a full partner in Belmont & Co. An excellent rider, he was one of the founders of the Meadow Brook Club, a riding club. At the time of his father's death, Belmont was no more than a spectator in racing but later became interested in purchasing some of the breeding stock and continuing the Nursery Stud tradition.

That tradition was nurtured through a quarter-century of careful bloodstock selection. Dan Bowmar III, in his *Giants of the Turf*, wrote "the elder Belmont had assembled the best group of race mares and producers in America. After Woodburn Farm began to wane about 1880, Nursery became supreme among American studs."

The elder Belmont's racing stock was sold in December 1890 and the remaining horses in the fall of 1891. Through an agent, August Belmont II bought seven broodmares, including Bella Donna, paying $8,800 for her. She would become the dam of Beldame in 1901.

Belmont also bought a yearling

filly at the dispersal and got a quick return on his $11,000 investment. Named Lady Violet, she became both a multiple stakes winner and multiple stakes producer.

Overall, both sessions of the sale combined for a record $639,500 from the sale of 131 horses. Beldame's sire, Octagon, was a proven performer on the racetrack as a Belmont homebred. In the span of three days, he won the Toboggan Handicap and Withers in May 1897. He later ran third in the Belmont Stakes and beat older horses in winning the Brooklyn Derby. As a stallion, it's safe to say Beldame was his best runner.

August Belmont II (right) bred and raced Beldame.

Beldame, a dark chestnut foaled at Nursery Stud near Lexington, raced as a three-year-old in several stakes that still command the utmost respect: the Alabama, Carter, Ladies, and Metropolitan. Other stakes such as the Dolphin, First Special, Second Special, and September are long gone.

Beldame's three-year-old season was marked by a number of wire-to-wire scores, and it didn't matter if the races were short or long, on fast or off tracks, or against males or females. She started the season in the Carter Handicap in April 1904 at Aqueduct and led all the way to beat sixteen rivals, most of them older males, under a feathery 103 pounds. She then was assigned only ninety-eight pounds in the Metropolitan Handicap but broke poorly and was beaten four lengths by the highly accomplished four-year-old male Irish Lad. She finished third at 20-1.

After that, Beldame was favored in all but one of her remaining starts that year. In the Ladies, first

Beldame winning the Ladies Handicap in 1904.

run in 1868 and won by such greats as Miss Woodford and Firenze in the 1880s, she ran off with her rider before the race and galloped around until finding her away back to her barn. Returned to the track, she led throughout the mile race and won by three-quarters of a length.

Up to that time Beldame had been ridden by six different jockeys and won under three of them. After the Ladies and for the remainder of her career, Frank O'Neill was her rider.

Both O'Neill, who had ridden Beldame in her last two-year-old start and the Carter, and Beldame's trainer, Fred Burlew, had grown up in St. Louis. Burlew took notice of O'Neill during the 1902–03 winter meeting in New Orleans. Burlew signed the teenager to a contract and took him to New York.

Burlew was a rarity, showing similar concern for his stable help as he did for his horses. His men slept on cots with sheets instead of on straw. Burlew ensured they ate well, and he paid their medical bills.

Burlew, who later trained 1922 Kentucky Derby winner Morvich, and O'Neill are members of the

Racing Hall of Fame. O'Neill, who rode the great Roseben numerous times in 1905, was on him when he won the six-furlong Manhattan Handicap under 147 pounds at Belmont Park. O'Neill later developed into a leading rider in France.

After the Ladies, Beldame won four consecutive races before finishing second in the Test Stakes at Brighton Beach. Her ten-length victory in the Gazelle Stakes at Gravesend under high weight of 124 pounds was special, the *Daily Racing Form* reported: "Beldame, almost pulling O'Neill from the saddle, won all the way and far outclassed her field and is one of the greatest fillies seen in this country." In the Mermaid Stakes at Sheepshead Bay, Beldame won by seven lengths under top weight.

In the Test Handicap at Brighton Beach in July, Beldame met her match in Hermis. Horse of the Year the previous two years, Hermis carried 133 pounds as the slight favorite compared to Beldame's 115 and beat her by a length while equaling the mile track record. It was Beldame's last loss of the year.

Beldame next won the Alabama Stakes by six lengths as the 1-20 favorite in what was "an exercise gallop," before facing arguably her sternest test. In the one and three-quarters-mile Saratoga Cup, first run in 1865 and won by stars such as Kentucky and Preakness, Beldame faced Africander, who had set a record in winning the previous year's running, plus other accomplished stars in The Picket and Major Daingerfield.

The weights were in Beldame's favor as she won over the sloppy track under 108 pounds. "Beldame made the running throughout never fully extended...and she was pulling up at the finish. Nothing ever got near her and she simply played with the others," the *Form* reported

Beldame won four stakes to close out the season, taking the Dolphin and September stakes at Sheepshead Bay, then the First Special and Second Special at Gravesend.

Newman thought Beldame's victory in the weight-for-age First Special under 114 pounds her greatest race. "Burlew now averred Beldame could beat any horse in the United States, scale weight at any distance," Newman wrote in *The Blood-Horse*. "He proved this to the satisfaction of everyone in her next start and greatest triumph."

The even-money favorite in the one and a quarter-mile First Special, Beldame defeated Caughnawaga, Stalwart, Pulsus, and Ort Wells. "This was an exceptionally high-class field, but Beldame vanquished them in effortless fashion," Newman wrote.

Beldame's victory in the Second Special came over Broomstick, who later developed into an outstanding sire.

That was it for the year for Beldame. She was an easy choice for Horse of the Year and top three-year-old filly. Ort Wells was champion three-year-old colt; Hermis, top older male; and Gunfire, best older female. Some thought Beldame was the best three-year-old filly in the world, better than England's remarkable Pretty Polly, who had won the two filly classics, the One Thousand Guineas and Oaks, plus the St. Leger Stakes over colts.

"It has been stated that Pretty Polly was lucky to have been foaled in 1901, as there were no good three-year-olds to oppose her this year," wrote the *Thoroughbred Record*. "While this may be true, it cannot be said of Beldame, as there were several real good three-year-olds as well as our best handicap horses that

Beldame at Saratoga in 1904, prior to her victory in the Alabama Stakes.

met defeat at her heels...Her victory in the Saratoga Cup we think emphatically demonstrated to the turf that she was by all odds the best horse of any age running in this country and it is the opinion of a great many that she is the superior of Pretty Polly..."

The *Thoroughbred Record* kept Beldame's name alive during the winter months by announcing a contest to find a mate for the filly. At the time there was no intention of retiring Beldame, who was resting up for her four-year-old campaign in 1905.

Open to readers worldwide, contestants had to submit an essay supporting their candidate for the best mate in the world for Beldame. A committee, consisting of judges from a number of countries, would decide the winner. Judges from the United States included Belmont and Captain Thomas B. Merry, whose book, *The American Thoroughbred and Breeders' Hand Book* was one of the three prizes. The others prizes were Bruce Lowe's *Breeding Racehorses by the Figure System*, and William Allison's *The British Thoroughbred Horse*. The winner would be given his choice of the three.

Allan Winn of Chicago won on the strength of his reason for choosing Meddler, who seemed like a logical and easy choice, as he was the leading sire by progeny earnings in 1904.

"I select Meddler as the best mate for Beldame for the reason that she coming from a great sire family (No. 10) should be mated to a representative of a great running family to produce the best results, and as Meddler is a great champion of a family of champions, he, in my opinion, is more suited to a sire filly like Beldame, than even the greatest Herod horse in the world."

Seven committee judges also elected Meddler. Six stallions, including Broomstick and England's St. Simon, received two votes each, and several stallions one vote apiece.

Beldame's transformation from racemare to broodmare would not be realized until the following year. Her first start at four would be at the new Belmont Park, which took the place of Morris Park.

The construction of Belmont Park signaled the belief that racing's future in New York was tied to the expansive land of Long Island rather than the mainland. Built at an enormous cost of two million dollars, Belmont Park offered a mile and a half main track. A beautiful enclosed walking ring helped make it popular among owners and fans.

Beldame was one of the stars that May 4, 1905, afternoon, the track's grand opening. The day also was special in another way.

August Belmont II had completed the building of Belmont Park and the merging of a subway system to his satisfaction and was ready for some additional challenges and enjoyment. He was back as Beldame's owner.

Burlew continued as Beldame's trainer. Belmont had offered the job to his new conditioner, Andrew Jack Joyner, but the latter figured it would be difficult to improve on near perfection and declined.

Belmont started opening day in a big way when his Hastings colt Blandy won the first race at the new track. Bennington, who previously had raced Beldame as a lessee from Belmont, also shared in some of the day's glory. His two-year-old First Water won the third race.

The big race of the day was the Metropolitan Handicap, and it featured not only Beldame but the previous year's champion two-year-old male Sysonby. The Metropolitan has lived on in memory, but not because of what Beldame accomplished. Sysonby, owned by James R. Keene, and five-year-old Race King provided the dramatics by dead heating for first. For Sysonby it marked the start of a superlative unbeaten season.

Beldame who ran ninth in the Metropolitan, could not replicate her three-year-old season at four, enduring a sub-par year. But there were highlights. She won the Suburban Handicap under 123 pounds, top weight by scale, to become only the second female to win that great race. Imp had won the 1899 running.

The enormity of Beldame's Suburban remained fresh in writer John Hervey's mind for years. "The performance was so brilliant that it caused her to be proclaimed the greatest racer of her sex that had ever graced the American turf, for it came as a climax after a wondrous previous career," he wrote in 1928.

Beldame also captured the 1905 Standard Stakes and her stakes placings included a runner-up effort in the Saratoga Cup in August.

Beldame was retired after the Saratoga Cup with a record of seventeen wins from thirty-one races and earnings of $102,135. She was only the third filly, after Miss Woodford and Firenze, to earn $100,000.

Her four-year-old season in which she won two of ten races

August Belmont II (left) and trainer Jack Joyner.

failed to detract from her overall greatness. "No terms were too strong to use in describing Beldame's greatness and popularity," wrote the *Morning Telegraph* after her retirement. "She was a public idol. She is retired to stud with a grand record and is one of the biggest money winning mares of the American turf."

Hervey, writing as Salvator in the *Thoroughbred Record*, was one of many sorry to see her go. "It speaks volumes for the mare's physical superiority that she was not sent to the hospital long ago. Apparently, her underpinning is marvelous. But she was bound to crack somewhere — and it was her temper and speed that suffered. She lost the last phenomenal burst of the latter that she had possessed, and when it came to the pinch, in the stretch, she stopped trying — the same old, old story."

Belmont selected Meddler as Beldame's first mate. Whether it was because of his belief in Meddler's prowess or Winn and the committee's belief in the stallion, only Belmont knew. By the time the foal arrived in early 1907, Belmont had every right to feel extra confident in his selection because Meddler had been the leading sire in 1906. That first foal was a filly, which Belmont named Consensa, but he later changed the name to Ballot Bred after she arrived in England. Sent to France, Ballot Bred produced several foals, one of whom, Bistouri, was returned to the United States and became a successful sire, getting 12 percent stakes winners from his 131 foals. Ballot Bred later was returned to Nursery Stud and produced three foals.

As good as she was as a race mare, Beldame was the complete opposite as a broodmare. Belmont sent her to such top stallions as Fair Play, Hastings, and Rock Sand, and the best she could do was come up with three winners from seven foals. One of her fillies, Belvale, became the ancestress of 1941 Santa Anita Handicap winner Bay View and successful sire Revoked.

Beldame's dismal broodmare performance prompted Hervey to write in the *Thoroughbred Record* in 1928 that Beldame might have raced with objectionable stimulants that hindered her racing and broodmare career. Bennington took exception to the charge, replying, "there was never a greater injustice than this statement carries," and that Burlew "was violently opposed to stimulants of any kind.

"Beldame was a very nervous, high-strung mare; as quiet and

docile around the stable as any mare that ever raced; she seemed to instinctively know when she was being prepared for a race and as the hour approached the more nervous she became," Bennington continued.

Beldame and Belmont died in 1924. Belmont, who attained the rank of major while serving in World War I, died December 10 of that year. Beldame, who passed away at Nursery Place, was a member of the second crop of inductees in the Racing Hall of Fame, being honored in 1956.

Beldame's memory remained alive after her death. The Beldame Handicap for two-year-olds fillies gave way to the present-day Beldame for distaffers aged three and up starting in 1939. It quickly took on the appearance of a championship-bearing event. Fairy Chant, the winner in 1940 and '41, was a champion both years. The following year, Vagrancy won a division of the Beldame and was voted both champion three-year-old filly and handicap female.

Subsequent winners of the Beldame (a grade I event since races were first graded in 1973) include such stars as Gallorette, Conniver, Next Move, Parlo, Tempted, Berlo, Cicada, What a Treat, Gamely, Shuvee, Desert

Beldame — 1904 Horse of the Year.

Vixen, Susan's Girl, Waya, Love Sign, Life's Magic, Lady's Secret, Personal Ensign, Go for Wand, Serena's Song, and Sharp Cat. The Breeders' Cup Distaff has replaced the Beldame as the most important filly and mare race in the United States, but a Beldame win still packs plenty of punch on a mare's résumé.

The Beldame Stakes remains special in another big way. The New York Racing Association has renamed stakes that once honored great race mares of the distant past. Stakes for Firenze and Maskette immediately come to mind. But the one honoring Beldame remains unaltered.

by David Schmitz

BELDAME	Octagon, 1894	Rayon D'Or, 1876	Flageolet, 1870	Plutus, 1863	Trumpeter Britannia
				La Favorite, 1863	Monarque Constance
			Araucaria, 1862	Ambrose, 1849	Touchstone Annette
				Pocahontas, 1837	Glencoe Marpessa
		Ortegal, 1889	Bend Or, 1877	Doncaster, 1870	Stockwell Marigold
				Rouge Rose, 1865	Thormanby Ellen Horne
			Lizzie Agnes, 1878	Macaroni, 1860	Sweetmeat Jocose
				Polly Agnes, 1865	The Cure Miss Agnes
	Bella Donna, 1885	Hermit, 1864	Newminster, 1848	Touchstone, 1831	Camel Banter
				Beeswing, 1833	Dr. Syntax Ardrossan Mare
			Seclusion, 1857	Tadmore, 1846	Ion Palmyra
				Miss Sellon, 1851	Cowl Belle Dame
		Bonnie Doon, 1870	Rapid Rhone, 1860	Young Melbourne, 1855	Melbourne Clarissa
				Lanercost Mare, 1848	Lanercost Physalis
			Queen Mary, 1843	Gladiator, 1833	Partisan Pauline
				Plenipotentiary Mare, 1840	Plenipotentiary Myrrha

Regret

(1915)

If ever a horse could be said to have been born with a silver bit in its mouth, Regret would certainly qualify. Foaled at Brookdale Farm near Red Bank, New Jersey, she was to become one of 192 stakes winners bred by Harry Payne Whitney. Six times the leading American owner by stable earnings in the period 1905–1930 and also the leading American breeder from 1926 to 1932, inclusive, H.P. Whitney was a member of a racing dynasty that had been founded by his father, William Collins Whitney, and would be continued by his son, Cornelius Vanderbilt "Sonny" Whitney. Behind much of the success of the Whitney horses was trainer James G. Rowe, Sr., a three-time

Regret at Saratoga.

Women of the 1910s

Activist Margaret Sanger is indicted under the Comstock Act for distributing a birth-control pamphlet entitled "Family Limitation."...The U.S. Navy hires 12,000 women as clerks in the same job classifications and for the same pay as men so that it can send men overseas...When the United States enters World War I, the Army Nurse Corps has 8,000 trained nurses ready to serve...British oceanliner *Lusitania* is sunk by German submarine; 1,195 perish...Lucy Diggs Slowe wins the singles title at the first American Tennis Association (ATA) national tournament, becoming the first female African-American national champion in any sport.

champion jockey who switched to training in 1876 and had previously trained for the Dwyer brothers, August Belmont, and James R. Keene. Rowe, who trained no less than thirty-four acknowledged champions during his legendary career, including undefeated Colin, was inducted into the National Museum of Racing's Hall of Fame in 1955.

Regret's pedigree was as patrician as her connections. Her sire was Broomstick, a winner of the historic Travers Stakes and three times America's leading sire, while her paternal grandsire was the Kentucky Derby winner Ben Brush, the leading sire of 1909.

Regret winning the 1914 Sanford Memorial.

American Derby. Jersey Lightning produced only five foals, but they included Regret's full brother Thunderer, winner of the 1915 Futurity Stakes; the All Gold colt Vivid, winner of the 1916 Champagne Stakes; and stakes winner Barnegat.

James Rowe had trained fine horses for nearly forty years by the time Regret came along, and he quickly realized that the pretty blaze-faced chestnut was something very special after she began her education as a racehorse. Much the best of the Whitney yearlings when tried against her peers during training, she was brought along slowly as a juvenile and did not make her first start until the Saratoga meeting of 1914.

Saratoga has historically been the stage for unveiling many a fine two-year-old, but Regret's first assignment was ambitious even for a Saratoga debut. She was supplemented to the Saratoga Special, where her opponents would include the season's leading colt,

Her dam, Jersey Lightning, won only one race and never won or placed in a stakes, but she had at one point shown enough ability for Rowe to train her with a tilt against males in the Withers Stakes in mind. Jersey Lightning was a daughter of the great racehorse and sire Hamburg out of Daisy F., a winner of twenty-three races including the 1889 Spinaway Stakes. One of the fine mares purchased by H.P. Whitney from the dispersal of his father's racing stock in 1904, Daisy F. was by the 1890 Kentucky Derby winner Riley out of Modesty, winner of the 1884 Kentucky Oaks and of the first

Pebbles. Already the winner of the Whirl and Eastview stakes, Pebbles looked a formidable opponent on paper and conceded only a three-pound sex allowance to Regret, but the Whitney filly was nonetheless installed as co-favorite based on her works and the reputation of her connections. Her backers' faith proved well justified as jockey Joe Notter (the leading American jockey of 1908 and Regret's regular partner through her first two seasons) sent Regret straight to the front. She led all the way and coasted home by a length over Pebbles with Paris third.

The racing secretaries of Regret's day were not noted for being overly chivalrous, and they loaded 127 pounds on the chestnut filly's back for her next race, the Sanford Memorial. Neither the weight nor a sloppy track made any difference to Regret. Her seven rivals were for the most part indifferent, and under a

Regret victorious in the 1914 Hopeful.

tight hold she cruised home a length and a half to the good over Solly.

The rich Hopeful Stakes a week later nearly produced a very different outcome. The track came up deep and muddy, and Regret, again under 127 pounds, was shuffled back early in the field of eleven; worse, she got boxed in on the rail where the going was very deep and tiring. Notter finally managed to work the filly over to the firmer going in the middle of the track, and she began picking up horses immediately, but she had to call on every ounce of courage to get up in time to win by a half-length. She had conceded thirteen pounds of actual weight to runner-up Andrew M. while Pebbles, again conceding only the three-pound sex allowance to the filly, finished third. Future Futurity Stakes winner Trojan finished among the also-rans.

Regret's victory in the Hopeful

completed her conquest of Saratoga and also completed her juvenile campaign. In just fourteen days she had gone from being another unraced youngster to the undisputed queen of the juvenile division. She had faced colts three times, beaten them three times, and taken the measure of the season's champion juvenile colt, Pebbles, twice. That was enough for Whitney and Rowe, who took their star filly home for a long rest. The spring would bring many rich races, and they wanted her fresh and fit for the new year.

Perhaps to the surprise of Whitney's circle of blue-blooded friends, Regret made her 1915 debut in the Kentucky Derby. Such a course might be considered suicidal today because of the lack of prep races, but that was not what disturbed Whitney's friends; most of today's preparatory races for the Triple Crown races simply did not exist in 1915, and it was not uncommon for a top three-year-old to make its seasonal bow in a major stakes. (In fact, Regret wound up starting as the Derby favorite off works alone.) It was the choice of race itself that would have disturbed the New York racing aristocracy to which Whitney belonged. Although 1913 cham-

Regret with trainer James Rowe (left) and owner Harry Payne Whitney (right).

pion two-year-old male Old Rosebud had galloped off with the roses in 1914, he had been the first top-class horse to win the race since Regret's grandsire Ben Brush had won the 1896 Derby eighteen years earlier. In between, the Derby had been won by a succession of horses who were at best second-raters by the standards of the New York elite. Only Plaudit, the 1898 winner, and Worth, the 1912 winner, could be said to approach the top rank, but Plaudit did not win any of the major New York races at three to solidify his reputation. Worth is generally considered the champion two-year-old male of 1911, but he earned his title during the depths of the New York racing blackout when American racing was at a nadir and is little remembered today.

Colonel Matt Winn, general manager of Churchill Downs and the impresario behind the Derby's resurgence, knew very well that New York horsemen thought of his beloved racetrack as a provincial backwater. But he also knew that New Yorkers liked the jingle of cold cash as well as anyone else, and in 1915, the Kentucky Derby offered a winner's purse of $11,450 plus a gold cup, which by far trumped the winner's purses of $1,275 for the Preakness Stakes and $1,825 for the Belmont. In fact, the Derby was the richest race of the season open to three-year-olds and one of the richest races on the entire U.S. racing calendar that year. Winn also knew that Whitney was among the leaders of the New York racing scene and that where he led, others would follow. So he unleashed all of his considerable Irish charm and persuasiveness in Whitney's direction and was rewarded by seeing Regret's name in the Derby entries. Pebbles, owned by James Butler, also entered the race, so Winn was able to bask in the publicity generated by the rematch of the top two juveniles of the previous season.

Regret doubtless neither knew nor cared about the human machinations surrounding her Derby appearance. Nor did she know or care that fourteen fillies had previously tried to capture the roses without success (though Lady Navarre had run second in 1906 and Flamma, Gowell, and Bronzewing had run third in the 1912, 1913, and 1914 editions, respectively). Regret was there to run, and run she did. Breaking sharply with Joe Notter in the saddle, she led the field into the first turn by a half length, with Pebbles second and Sharpshooter third. A mile later the order was exactly the same, except that Joe Notter had eased his hold a notch to meet a brief challenge by Pebbles. Regret repulsed the threat easily and drew off to win easing up by two lengths in 2:05 2/5, leaving fifteen rivals in her wake. Excepting the connections of the losing horses, everyone was happy. Whitney had gotten a lucrative victory; Colonel Winn had gotten an invaluable dollop of publicity for the Derby and the promise of future entries from the elite of the American racing scene; and Regret got her victory oats. Later, Winn credited Regret's victory with making the Derby "an American institution."

Regret's victory apparently delighted Whitney, who, in accepting the Derby trophy, exultantly said, "She [Regret] has won the greatest race in America, and I am satisfied." But trainer Rowe was not quite so sanguine. Regret had not shipped well from Brookdale to Louisville and had gone off her feed for several days before the Derby, apparently with a respiratory ailment of some sort. Her pre-Derby works had not been impressive, and for several days there was some doubt as to whether she would start at all. While she recovered well enough to race and win, she was left with a slight defect in her breathing — not enough to make her a full-blown "roarer" but nonetheless there — and no less an authority than the great handicapper Walter Vosburgh came to believe that the daughter of Broomstick never quite recovered after her Derby victory.

Tragedy as well as illness intervened before Regret's next start. On May 7, 1915 — the day before the Kentucky Derby — a German warship sank the *Lusitania*. Among the casualties was Alfred Gwynne Vanderbilt, brother-in-law of H.P. Whitney, who had given up his life jacket to a woman he did not know before going down with the ship. The news did not reach Whitney until just before the Derby. He honored his commitment to run Regret in the Derby since her name had already appeared among the entries and betting had commenced, but in respect for his brother-in-law's memory Whitney raced no more that year. Those of his horses that continued in training were leased to L.S. Thompson (a family friend who bought Brookdale Farm from Whitney in 1915) for the remainder of the year. Thus, when Regret resurfaced among the entries for the Saranac Handicap at Saratoga, she raced under Thompson's colors

Regret (outside) is narrowly defeated by Borrow in the Brooklyn Handicap.

rather than Whitney's familiar brown cap and Eton blue jacket.

Once again Regret was coming into a stern test off a long layoff. She had not raced in more than three months, and among her rivals for the Saranac was The Finn, winner of the Belmont and Withers stakes against his own division and the Manhattan Handicap against his elders. Further, she was asked to concede weight to all her rivals except The Finn, who was co-highweight with her on the scale and conceded the filly only her three-pound sex allowance (Regret carried 123 pounds to 126 on The Finn). But once again Regret proved equal to the task. Keeping her undefeated record intact, she cruised wire to wire to win by one and a half lengths over Trial By Jury (114 pounds), winner of that year's Jerome Handicap. The Travers Stakes winner, Lady Rotha (106 pounds), was another three lengths back in third, and The Finn — later acknowledged the season's champion three-year-old male off nine good victories — finished among the also-rans. Whether because of her breathing problem or some other trouble, Regret raced no more that year; yet so authoritative were her two victories that she was commonly acknowledged as the best horse in training in 1915, regardless of age or sex. This was quite a compliment considering that the horse generally acknowledged second best, champion handicap male Roamer, had won eight of thirteen starts while conceding substantial weight to stalwarts such as Short Grass, Stromboli, and Borrow.

Regret did not reappear under colors for a year, and the reasons are not readily apparent from surviving records: perhaps she suffered a flare-up of her respiratory ailment, or perhaps minor injuries suffered while in training prevented an earlier return. In any event she finally returned to the races in the Saratoga Handicap of 1916, and her performance in that race suggested that she either had not fully recovered from whatever physical problems she suffered or was not completely fit. Although she broke sharply and set a blistering pace despite being under a pull, she weakened suddenly after a half mile and ended up running dead last behind the veteran gelding Stromboli. It was an ignominious tumble from the unbeaten ranks, and the feelings of Regret's connections were only partially assuaged by a win three weeks later over Fair Play's much inferior full brother Flittergold in a mile overnight race. That was it for Regret's 1916 campaign, and she retired to the farm to lick her wounds. It was her only season of racing in which she would not be acknowledged as a champion.

Many owners would have gone ahead and retired Regret for good at this point; the breeding dogma of the time was that heavily raced mares often did not make good broodmares, and Regret at four was clearly not the same racehorse she had been at three. Whitney, however, did not shy away from testing his fillies in the heat of competition, and he stocked enough fine broodmares that there was no particular need to rush Regret to the paddocks. Perhaps, too, he and Rowe were determined to find out and correct the causes of the filly's problems as a four-year-old before giving up on her as a racer. And so Regret returned to the racing wars as a five-year-old. For the first time in her life, Regret took part in a race restricted to her own sex: This was a five and a half furlong overnight affair at Belmont Park, and she handled the assignment easily, defeating the good fillies Yankee Witch and Admiration while conceding them ten and twenty-two pounds, respectively. Three weeks later she made her next start in the fabled Brooklyn Handicap of 1917, which marked the first-ever meeting of Kentucky Derby winners on the racecourse. Three winners of the Run for the Roses — Old Rosebud, Regret, and 1917 winner Omar Khayyam — faced off that day, along with the excellent handicappers Roamer and Stromboli. Nonetheless, another Whitney runner, Borrow, stole the show. No slouch himself, Borrow had won the prestigious Middle Park Plate in England as a juvenile and had been the co-leading handicap male of 1914 with Great Britain, but in 1917 he was nine years old and considered well past his best days. For the Brooklyn he carried 117 pounds against 122 on Regret, and the entry of Regret and Borrow started as second choice behind A.K. Macomber's good handicapper Boots.

The story of the race is simply told. Showing all her old speed, Regret broke forwardly under jockey Frank Robinson and led the field through the first mile and one-sixteenth while repelling one challenger after another, but Borrow loomed up in the last hundred yards and just beat her home by a nose, setting a new American record of 1:49 2/5 for the mile and one-eighth. Intimates of the Whitney stable later claimed that Willie Knapp on Borrow had ignored Whitney's orders to let Regret win if possible, and other witnesses reported tears in Whitney's eyes as he led Borrow into the winners' enclosure. However, still other witnesses' accounts recall Old Rosebud (who finished a length away in third) as having made a strong bid at the same time that Borrow launched his drive, and Knapp may have driven hard in the fear that Regret would give way to the older champion. The exact truth, whatever it was, cannot now be known as the parties to it have long since passed on.

Regret appeared next in the Gazelle Handicap. It was her only appearance in a sex-restricted stakes race, and she could not have had an easier time of it. Although she was given 129 pounds by the handicapper, she had no trouble in disposing of second-place Bayberry Candle (123 pounds) and third-place Wistful (105 pounds); the last-named filly had won the inaugural Coaching Club American Oaks earlier in the season. Regret won by three lengths and was officially described as "eased up" at the end.

The Whitney mare made her last appearance under silks in an overnight race at Aqueduct on September 25, 1917. Facing only one overmatched challenger (Ima Frank, who carried only 109 pounds to Regret's 127) and under a tight hold all the way, Regret cruised home three lengths to the good in track-record time of 1:24 1/5 for the seven furlongs. Despite racing only four times during the year (the busiest season of her career), she was widely acknowledged as the leading older female of 1917, making her a champion for the third time in four seasons on the track.

Regret ended her racing career with nine wins and one second from eleven starts for earnings of $35,093. She had never finished behind a member of her own sex, and she had become a part of racing legend as the first filly to win the Kentucky Derby, the race she helped establish as a national event. It would be sixty-five years before another blaze-faced chestnut filly, Genuine Risk, would rob Regret of her title as the only filly ever to wear the roses. It would also be twelve years before another Whitney runner captured the Kentucky Derby, and thereby hangs a tale.

Encouraged by his success with Regret, H.P. Whitney had entered his finest colts and fillies in the Derby annually thereafter to no avail — horses like Thunderer, Upset, Wildair, Tryster, Prudery, and Transmute — though he had come agonizingly close, finishing second by a head with Upset in 1920. But in 1927, Whiskery (whose dam Prudery had run third in the 1921 Derby) withstood a stern drive against Osmand to win the great race. That night Sonny Whitney became bored with the post-race celebration of the rich and famous in his father's house and wandered outside. There, in a field not too far from the stable, he found the stable hands gathered about a bonfire, holding a party of their own and singing spirituals. And the guest of honor? Regret, who had been brought over from her quiet broodmare paddock so that she might share in the festivities. It was a defining moment for young Whitney, who would later recall the sound of spontaneous joy and the sight of Regret silhouetted against the flames as one of his most cherished racing memories.

By that time Regret had been a broodmare for nine years, and it had become apparent that her reputation as a producer was not ever likely to equal her success as a racer. She began well: her first foal, the Pennant filly Penitent, was a stakes-placed runner and produced the Coronation Stakes winner Easter Hatter. Regret next produced the Chicle gelding Revenge, winner of the Yonkers

Handicap. It was all downhill afterward with the racing records of Regret's foals, although some of her daughters turned out to be good producers — not least her 1921 foal, Nemesis, whose sire Johren had been the consensus champion three-year-old male of 1918 but who was to prove a very bad stallion. Nemesis was unable to win in fourteen starts, but she redeemed herself as a broodmare by producing the Hartsdale Stakes winner Red Rag, the Gazelle Stakes winner Avenger, and the stakes-winning steeplechaser Rhadamanthus. Avenger, in turn, produced the stakes winner Spiteful and unplaced My Hattie, whose son Repetoire won the 1950 Remsen Stakes and the 1951 Wood Memorial.

Barren in 1922, Regret produced a full sister to Nemesis in 1923; this was Stigma, who was no improvement on her sister as a race mare but did produce the fine steeplechaser Blot. The year 1924 was another barren one, and the following year Regret produced Repenter, one of the few foals sired by the nearly sterile champion Grey Lag. No credit to either of his illustrious parents, Repenter could not win in five starts and was gelded.

Regret took another year off from production in 1926. Her mate that spring was the high-class St. Germans, a sire of much greater stature than either Johren or Grey Lag, and in 1927 this breeding produced Rueful, Regret's first winner since Revenge. Rueful won only three of twenty-two starts and never won or placed in a stakes race, but she produced the high-class handicapper First Fiddle, winner of twenty-three of ninety-five starts and just under $400,000. Rueful also produced the stakes-placed mare Despondent, whose stakes-winning daughter Miss Dundee continued the line into the 1960s by producing four minor stakes winners.

The Derby winner revisited St. Germans in 1927 and the following spring produced unraced Mea Culpa, whose grandson Divine Comedy won three good handicaps in 1959–60. Regret was again barren in 1929, then produced Redress in 1930. A full brother to Rueful and Mea Culpa, the gelded Redress may not have been the classiest of Regret's foals, but he was certainly the toughest. He started 174 times, won twenty-two races, and placed in another thirty-six efforts to earn $19,020.

Regret's next two foals were both by Mad Hatter, an excellent racehorse but a disappointing sire given the fine opportunities he received. He certainly did not make much of his matings with Regret: March Heiress (1931) never raced, Brabble (1932) won only once in fifteen tries, and none of the fifteen foals the sisters produced between them were of any distinction. The Derby winner's final foal was Tale of Woe (1934), a three-parts sister to First Fiddle as both were by Royal Minstrel. Not nearly of the class of her famous kinsman, Tale of Woe won once in five starts and produced no living foals.

The broodmare career of Regret can be summed up as fair but disappointing. She produced one stakes winner, one stakes-placed runner, and four winners from eleven foals. Six of her daughters produced foals that were able to place or win in stakes races, but only two of Regret's "grandchildren," Avenger and First Fiddle, could be considered above the ordinary as flat racers, and neither made any lasting mark as breeding stock although Avenger did produce one stakes winner in the St. Germans filly Spiteful. In an odd

REGRET

Broomstick, 1901	Ben Brush, 1893	Bramble, 1875	**Bonnie Scotland**, 1853	Iago Queen Mary
			Ivy Leaf, 1867	**Australian** Bay Flower
		Roseville, 1888	Reform, 1871	**Leamington** Stolen Kisses
			Albia, 1881	Alarm Elastic
	Elf, 1893	Galliard, 1880	Galopin, 1872	Vedette Flying Duchess
			Mavis, 1874	Macaroni Merlette
		Sylva Belle, 1887	Bend Or, 1877	Doncaster Rouge Rose
			Saint Editha, 1873	Kingley Vale Lady Alice
Jersey Lightning, 1905	Hamburg, 1895	Hanover, 1884	Hindoo, 1878	Virgil Florence
			Bourbon Belle, 1869	**Bonnie Scotland** Ella D
		Lady Reel, 1886	Fellowcraft, 1870	**Australian** Aerolite
			Mannie Gray, 1874	Enquirer Lizzie G
	Daisy F., 1895	Riley, 1887	Longfellow, 1867	**Leamington** Nantura
			Geneva, 1880	**War Dance** La Gitana
		Modesty, 1881	**War Dance**, 1859	Lexington Reel
			Ballet, 1871	Planet Balloon

coincidence, Regret's career as a broodmare foreshadowed those of her sister Derby winners: Genuine Risk, the 1980 victress, produced only two living foals, neither of which ever raced, while Winning Colors (1988 Derby) has produced only the minor Japanese stakes winner Golden Colors from eight foals of racing age despite being bred to a selection of high-class stallions.

Regret barely lived long enough to see her final foal into the world, dying on April 14, 1934. She was buried in the Whitney equine cemetery at Whitney Farm near Lexington, Kentucky, which succeeded Brookdale Farm in 1915 as the base of H.P. Whitney's breeding operations. The property in which the cemetery lies was later sold to Gainesway Farm by Sonny Whitney in the 1980s, but the cemetery has been preserved, and Regret's simple marble headstone can still be seen there in company with that of her sire Broomstick and other notable Whitney runners.

Another memorial to Regret exists at the National Racing Hall of Fame in Saratoga Springs, New York, where Regret has been enshrined since 1957. And while Regret's broodmare record has long since sunk into obscurity and her championships have all but been forgotten, she is still remembered as the first filly to win the Kentucky Derby, a memory that will endure for as long as roses are still run for on the first Saturday in May.

by Avalyn Hunter

Twilight Tear

(1944)

Only the lights from the foaling barn pierced the darkness. Inside the white barn with red trim, Lady Lark grunted in the throes of labor, her sweat-soaked bay body a glistening contrast to the deeply bedded straw on which she lay. The impending birth had perhaps evoked more interest than usual since the foal was one of the first from the "house" stallion, Bull Lea. Those attending the mare moved with an assuredness born of countless nights of midwife duties, and soon a bay filly awkwardly struggled to coordinate the instinct to nurse with those long, spindly legs that would one day carry her, under the

Twilight Tear and Conn McCreary at Belmont Park.

name Twilight Tear, into the annals of racing history. It was April 2, 1941.

Beyond that arc of light in the dark silence of a spring night, the rumble of war hung like distant thunder. For more than two years Hitler's armies had goose-stepped their way through Europe and Northern Africa; countries had fallen like dominoes to the Axis powers: Czechoslovakia, Poland, France, Belgium, Norway, Denmark. The German Luftwaffe had attacked England, and Britain, France, New Zealand, Australia, and Canada had declared war against Germany.

In a little more than eight months, December 7, American neutrality would be shattered when Japan's attack on the U.S. fleet at Pearl Harbor realized Japanese Admiral Isoroku Yamamoto's fear and awakened the "sleeping giant and filled him with a terrible resolve." On December 8 the United States responded with a declaration of war. World War II changed things forever.

When American men put down their plows and pliers and picked up rifles, American women dropped their aprons and donned coveralls. A new face joined the pantheon of American war icons Uncle Sam and G.I. Joe.

Uncle Sam had been a popular recruiting tool for the doughboys of World War I. Posters showed a tall man with a goatee dressed in a blue suit, white shirt, and red bow tie, a shock of gray hair protruding beneath the brim of a top hat decorated with a blue band and white stars. A grim sense of purpose etched on an avuncular face and a directly pointed finger expressed the slogan, "I Want You for the U. S. Army."

World War II posters recycled Uncle Sam, but this generation's war was not just their father's war. New placards showed a pretty girl wearing a no-nonsense look of determination and blue coveralls, her hair hidden by a red-and-white polka dot ban-

Women of the 1940s

More than 310,000 women have jobs in the U.S. aircraft industry. Wartime propaganda urges women to join the labor force for the duration of the war...Physicist Elda Anderson is recruited to work on the development of the atomic bomb at Los Alamos, New Mexico...The All-American Girls Professional Baseball League is founded by Chicago Cubs owner Philip Wrigley...The Democratic Party endorses the Equal Rights Amendment.

dana, flexing her right arm with a clinched fist and gripping her muscle with her left hand. Her battle cry, "We can do it!" And do it they did. The number of working women increased by 50 percent during the war years, and the perception of all the things that women could achieve increased two-fold. Redd Evans and John Jacob Loeb put a name to the face of working women when they wrote the song "Rosie the Riveter" in 1942, with its lines "That little girl will do more than a male will do" and "There's something true about, red, white, and blue about Rosie the Riveter."

To that little filly growing up in the paddocks of Warren Wright's Calumet Farm, these words would have a special significance, for she, in many ways, would become Rosie the Riveter's equine equivalent.

Warren Wright had been in the racing and breeding business for ten years when Twilight Tear was born. Having inherited the Calumet Baking Powder Company fortune, he had already transformed his father's Standardbred operation at Calumet into a Thoroughbred showplace and his success in the racing world had been on the rise. A meticulous man in his appearance and in his business practices, he operated by one rule: "Get the best; only the best will do." Wright began the foundation for his success by acquiring the best bloodstock, yearling by yearling and broodmare by broodmare. One of the first horses he bought was the good race mare Ladana, a stakes-winning filly who was lucky to still be alive. In an attempt at a betting coup, one of the stable lads working for her owner, Rancocas Stable, administered the poison chloral to the filly prior to a start in the Burnt Hills Handicap at Saratoga. The filly frothed at the mouth and had blisters where the poison had touched her, but she recovered after a month and won her next race. Wright purchased her in 1932. She raced for him that year but failed to win any of her three starts.

Not only was it her racing ability that attracted Wright but also her pedigree. Speed is key to any good racehorse, and Ladana carried the blood of the prime source of speed in American breeding, Domino, "the fleetest runner" the American Turf had ever seen. But the daughter of Lucullite out of Adana, by Adam, didn't descend from his sire line; rather, she was a product of his powerhouse female family. Stakes-placed Adana was a veritable font of stakes winners, producing three in France before being imported to America, where she produced three more including the influential stallion Ariel. Ladana's second dam was Mannie Himyar, a full sister to Domino and to the great race mare Correction, all descending from the foundation mare Gallopade.

Wright bred Ladana to E.R. Bradley's outstanding runner and sire Blue Larkspur. The resulting foal was Lady Lark, a high-strung filly who was not much on the racetrack, winning once in five starts. But with that pedigree she would certainly be a welcome addition to the Calumet broodmare band, at least for a while.

Often fate intervenes in the affairs of not only men but also horses. In building his racing stable, Wright had purchased at the 1936 Saratoga yearling sale a brown colt by Bull Dog, whom he named Bull Lea. The colt improved on his $14,000 purchase price, winning such important stakes as the Blue Grass Stakes and Widener Handicap. An injury early in 1939 sent him to stud. The Blue Larkspur mare Lady Lark was among the first group of mares bred to Bull Lea. It was to be a fortuitous cross. At the end of Bull Lea's career, twelve of his fifty-seven stakes winners had been produced from Blue Larkspur mares. Ironically, by the time the first crop of Bull Lea reached the races, Lady Lark had changed hands. After Twilight Tear was weaned, Wright consigned Lady Lark to the 1942 Lexington Fall Sale conducted by Fasig-Tipton where Walter Salmon bought her for his Mereworth Farm for $1,700.

Although the world may have been in chaos, life on the farm was routine, especially for young horses learning their lessons. So it was for Twilight Tear who as a yearling in 1942 underwent breaking and training at Calumet Farm.

Overseeing the process and a key figure in the Calumet team was Ben A. Jones, who was no newcomer to racing, bringing his son Jimmy as an assistant. Jones had already won the 1938 Kentucky Derby with Lawrin when he came to Calumet in 1939. Known as Plain Ben, he was the embodiment of his name. A Missouri native, Jones had grown up a hard-nosed son of an even harder-nosed Welsh father who founded the town of Parnell, Missouri. As a youngster Jones had ridden cow ponies and had cut his training teeth on the bullring tracks of the West and Mexico. A man who eked out his day-to-day living from racing horses in that harsh environment had to learn a thing or two about training them. When Jones moved his tack east, those lessons came with him, and he applied them in more upscale stables with higher-class horses. His success with Calumet was instantaneous. He saddled his first horse for Calumet on September 20 and not until October 11 did he have a horse finish out of the money. From sixteen starts he saddled the winners of nine races, with four seconds, one third, and one fourth.

Jones' mantra was speed. At Calumet he quickly found it. Wright's breeding program was beginning to coalesce and produce the kind of stock that Jones would revel in, and stakes winner after stakes winner bore the devil red-and-blue silks to the winner's circle. Jones had won his second Kentucky Derby with Calumet's Whirlaway when the crop of 1941 came to him as two-year-olds. Included in this clutch of inexperienced youth were two of particular note, Twilight Tear and a chestnut son of Hyperion named Pensive.

By this time the war had influenced every aspect of American life, including racing. Sacrifices were the norm. Such items as gasoline, sugar, butter, coffee, and meat were in short supply. A nationwide food rationing was instituted in spring of 1942, and ration books became part of every citizen's home-front war effort. Victory gardens sprouted in lawns and fields across America. And like the millions of Americans making personal sacrifices, Calumet responded in patriotic fashion with its own version of the victory garden. To aid the war effort, 150 acres of bluegrass pasture were converted to growing hemp for rope, a necessary commodity for the armed forces. To make room for the hemp, Wright sold a dozen mares privately.

Racing was curtailed due to the ban on transportation, and race meets were consolidated at tracks in cities that were the hubs of transportation. Just as with all of society in an America at war, racing constantly evolved, redefining itself in its service to the sport, to society, and to the war effort. Racing raised huge sums of money for war relief and the Red Cross. Entire cards were devoted to that purpose, and at the end of the year more than five million dollars had been raised at the various tracks still conducting racing. When that sum was added to the 1942 amount, more than eight million dollars filled the war relief coffers. And Americans went to the races in droves.

Against this backdrop Twilight Tear made her debut on June 25, 1943, at the Arlington at Washington Park meeting. How different the sights and sounds must have been for her, the comparative quiet and solitude of morning workouts replaced with the clamor and crowds of an afternoon at the races. Twilight Tear was slow to break from the gate and lagged behind early in the five and a half-furlong race. After settling in stride, she closed the gap to the frontrunner Letmenow and won by three parts of a length. Finishing third that day was Brownell and Leslie B. Combs' filly Durazna, who, like Twilight Tear, was from the first crop of Bull Lea and out of a Blue Larkspur mare. Although the two only met on the racetrack twice, their separate paths intertwined, for each carved out championship seasons and helped put Bull Lea on the rising-

Twilight Tear with trainer Jimmy Jones heads for her next race.

star list of new sires.

Eight days later Twilight Tear moved from maiden winner into stakes competition in the Arlington Lassie Stakes, a race that would establish itself among the "queen makers" of two-year-old fillies. A large field of fifteen assembled for the six-furlong event. For this outing she was coupled with her stablemate Miss Keeneland, and the entry was the even-money favorite. Twilight Tear had obviously learned a great deal from her first race. This time she pressed the pace set by Iron Maiden (who, ironically, would become a broodmare for Calumet and produce 1957 Kentucky Derby winner Iron Liege), before taking a three-length lead heading into the stretch and holding off her stablemate, winning by two and a half lengths. Also in the beaten field was a kindred sister so to speak, Harriet Sue. Yet another daughter of Bull Lea, Harriet Sue was produced from a daughter of Black Servant, Blue Larkspur's sire.

As fall approached, racing for the Calumet runners shifted from the Midwest to the East. At Pimlico, Twilight Tear encountered a nemesis that would plague her throughout her entire career, a wet track. Entered in the six-furlong Junior Miss Purse, Twilight Tear floundered home third by nearly three lengths, the victim of a speed duel and the sloppy conditions. Miss Keeneland finished fourth. Four days later Twilight Tear redeemed herself on a fast track in a prep for the Selima Stakes. Once again Miss Keeneland was her immediate victim.

The Selima Stakes held a great deal of prestige in determining two-year-old filly champion. Calumet's Nellie Flag had set a precedent for the farm by winning the Selima and the championship in 1934, and Twilight Tear was expected to mirror her. Of course, it rained, and the muddy track once again proved too much of an obstacle. Twilight Tear took the lead after the first quarter and maintained a length advantage throughout most of the mile and one-sixteenth race. Her stablemate Miss Keeneland, who was receiving eight pounds, collared her in deep stretch and pulled away to a length win.

It couldn't be called sibling rivalry since Miss Keeneland and Twilight Tear were in no way related; however, it certainly was a matter of stablemate rivalry and bragging rights. As if to affirm the Selima result was a fluke and perhaps a result of Miss Keeneland's weight advantage, Jones entered both, this time equally weighted, in the Carvel Hall Purse at a little more than a mile. It might not have looked promising when the rain poured down and the track turned up sloppy, but he elected not to scratch either. This time Twilight Tear used her speed to get to the front and control the pace, skimming over the Pimlico surface and leaving Miss Keeneland in her wake.

Calumet's freshmen fillies came to hand faster than the colts. While the girls were seasoned performers by September, Pensive, the main colt in the stable, was nearing his first start, a six-furlong maiden race, which he duly won. A five-length victory five days later set him up to meet the leading colts of his crop in the Futurity Stakes, in which he closed from tenth to finish fourth behind John Marsch's Occupy, the leading two-year-old colt. It was a promising performance.

Championship honors ended in a tie between Twilight Tear and Durazna, who had come into her own in the second half of the racing year, winning in the Midwest. Her crowning achievement was a victory over Occupy in the Breeders' Futurity at Churchill Downs. Weights on the Experimental Free Handicap found Durazna and Miss Keeneland with 121 and Twilight Tear with 119; the promising Pensive, 116.

After November, racing in the East closed for the season, and the big stables moved to warmer climes. The Calumet string wintered in Florida, where the newly turned three-year-olds began preparation for the ultimate prize, the Kentucky Derby. Jones was patient with his sophomores and planned to ship to Churchill Downs early in March, so he was in no hurry to tighten the screws on his young runners.

Twilight Tear and Pensive were the leading contenders for the classics and were on similar courses for return to the races. The filly was up first, and Jones was ambitious and wily for her first start of the year. He chose Hialeah and the Leap Year Handicap against older males for her debut. It was a stern test, but he would find out what the strapping, sixteen-hand filly was made of.

Twilight Tear proved to be as docile and sweet a race filly as her dam had been irascible. Racing commentator Tom O'Reilly perhaps described her temperament best when he referred to her as "Sleepy Time Gal." And her temperament was to stand her in good stead through a long and

Champion Twilight Tear wintered at Hialeah.

arduous three-year-old campaign. On February 29, she faced seven older males, her first start in more than three months, and finished third, beaten only two lengths. The next day Pensive, too, finished third in his debut, after dropping to last place and then closing strongly in the stretch.

On March 10, Twilight Tear won convincingly against three-year-olds. Conn McCreary, contract rider for Calumet, rode her that day and became her regular jockey. By then Susie, as she was called around the barn, was being considered as a possible filly entry in the Derby and a likely candidate to become the first filly since Regret to win the coveted stakes. She added another win seven days later before shipping north to Pimlico.

When the Derby nominations came out, her name was among them, along with that of Pensive, who was forging his own path toward Kentucky. However, there was some uncertainty as to whether Calumet would even have a runner in the Derby. Jones, not yet impressed with Pensive, was enigmatic about whether he would start Twilight Tear in the Derby, saying that he preferred to see if a colt stepped up to the plate and fillies were a little harder to handle in the spring. Wright, wintering in Florida, like his horses, was not opposed to running the filly in the Derby, adding "were she to win, I would not care if she never ran again."

The decision would come in the crucible of the Chesapeake Stakes. Both Twilight Tear and Pensive had been nominated, and both were pointing nicely toward the race. The filly had suffered only one defeat so far that year, and Pensive had recently won the Rowe Memorial at Pimlico. But he had been inconsistent, and she had not started since March. So much depended then on the Boniface Purse on April 25, Twilight Tear's first start in more than a month. Jones indicated that should she acquit herself well she would run in the Chesapeake as an entry with Pensive. She won and was entered with Pensive. Only one would show up. Somewhere between the entry and the race that was contested on a heavy, wet track, she was out. Pensive finished a close second, beaten by Gramp's Image, whom Twilight Tear had defeated easily in the Boniface. However, her Derby fate had been sealed. Pensive would carry Calumet's banner into the fray.

Pensive did not let his connections down in the Kentucky Derby. He decisively dispatched a top-notch field of colts in a race that, according to the *Daily Racing Form*, was broadcast by short-wave radio to "every hut that is radio equipped on every fighting front, in every training base or headquarters and on every ship at sea or in port. Every fighting son of Uncle Sam will hear about the Derby."

Three days earlier Twilight Tear won her first stakes of the season, the Rennert Handicap over nine fellow three-year-olds. Many in the country began to feel that she was the best of the sophomore class, gender notwithstanding. But others remembered Durazna and her fine ending to the previous year and felt that those two would have to meet again to settle who was better. An easy romp in the Pimlico Oaks a week later gave Calumet its sixth stakes win of the meet and Twilight Tear her fifth straight victory.

The Acorn at Belmont on May 17 proved just as easy, and Jones talked of giving her a rest. But she neither looked nor responded like a tired filly. Instead of rest and relaxation, she faced a field of five other fillies on May 27, her fourth start in a month, in the mile and three-eighths Coaching Club American Oaks.

Pensive had added the Preakness to his Derby victory and stood on the verge of securing Calumet's second Triple Crown in three years. So, naturally, the question was put to Ben Jones as to who was the better. His response was a wry, sly grin.

While racing may have captured the headlines on the sports page, the progress of the war remained the top story. Signs of hope came from the European theatre. The Allied forces had begun finding the chinks in Hitler's armor. Some of the Allied forces had entered Rome while others stood on the cusp of the climactic event of the war in Europe, D-Day. Yet, ever present were reminders of the war. A sign in the Belmont infield next to the tote board instructed patrons the proper protocol in case of an air raid. "Keep Calm. Obey orders of wardens and police. Follow directional signals. Walk Do Not Run." Twilight Tear did not heed this advice. Leading from the start under regular jockey Conn McCreary, she increased her lead at every call, won by four lengths, and won easily. Finishing fourth that day, beaten nine lengths, was Belair Stud's Vienna whose path would intersect with the Calumet filly later in the summer in a memorable running of the Alabama Stakes. The CCA Oaks was Twilight Tear's seventh straight win, at distances from six to eleven furlongs.

The wear and tear of racing began to take its toll on her. For the first time she ran in bandages both front and rear. And this time there was a trace of iodine on her left hind sock. In a workout prior to the CCA Oaks, she had rapped herself, and filling in her legs necessitated treatment. Whether she would even make the race had been touch and go.

Despite being run in a relatively slow time, the CCA Oaks distance of eleven furlongs seemed to affect her as well, and she came back breathing heavily for the first time. Of course, this journey had been her longest.

The press hounded Jones increasingly as to whether Twilight Tear could whip Pensive. And he again rejoined in a noncommittal way, satisfied as long as Pensive kept beating the colts and Twilight Tear the fillies. But that was about to change. Pensive lost his Triple Crown bid by a half-length to Bounding Home.

Racing for Calumet moved back to the Midwest, and Twilight Tear was given a breather. No racing for her until the Princess Doreen, a month away. In this stakes at Washington Park, she would face a rival whom the press had conjured for her, and not without just cause, Durazna. When the entries were drawn for the race, not just two daughters of Bull Lea passed the entry box but three. Harriet Sue, who had won the Ashland Stakes and finished second in the Kentucky Oaks, was also entered. This race would certainly settle the matter for the filly championship in the minds of the press. Twilight Tear carried top weight of 121 pounds. McCreary was content to let her press the pace of Bell Song before taking command in midstretch and drawing off to win by one and a half lengths. Harriet Sue outfinished Durazna in the battle of the other Bull Leas, finishing third by a neck over Durazna. Twilight Tear had truly established herself as queen of the fillies. With few worlds left to conquer in the distaff division, Jones finally turned his attention to the colts to see if his equine Rosie could hold her own among the best males of her age, including her stablemate Pensive.

What would happen when one was measured against the other? Physically, Twilight Tear had the better of Pensive as the tale of the tape told. She was one-fourth of a hand taller and two inches greater in girth and width of chest. She was almost five inches longer from poll to tail and weighed twenty-five pounds more. But what about competitively? Who would prove the faster, stronger? Who would exhibit more heart?

This little drama would play itself out on the stage of the Skokie Handicap, when Jones entered both Twilight Tear and Pensive, but she would be without her regular jockey. McCreary had been in an automobile accident and was out for five weeks with a fractured right wrist and lacerations. Her partner in this most important race was Leon Haas, and he stood in well for the injured McCreary. Not only did Twilight Tear manhandle the field but she did so in track-record time, running the seven furlongs in 1:22 3/5 over the fast track. The expected duel never took place as Pensive turned in a dull performance and finished fifth. Once again Twilight Tear did her part for the war effort as profits for the day were for war relief and charity.

Act Two of the Twilight Tear-Pensive show took place in an allowance race, the Isolater Purse, again at Washington Park. This time the outcome was different. The winner was the same but Pensive finished closer. He let his stablemate set the pace and then cut her three-length lead in half at the wire. Surely, next time Pensive would redeem himself.

Act Three was the $50,000 Classic Stakes, an important fixture on the Midwest circuit. Again Pensive and Twilight Tear ran as an entry. Susie took the lead at the start of the ten furlongs and never looked back. She crossed the finish line two lengths ahead of Old Kentuck; Pensive trailed in third. For the third straight time she defeated the dual classic winner, settled decisively which of the Calumet runners deserved to wear the laurel, and won her eleventh straight start. Twilight Tear seemed as unbeatable as the Allied forces pushing closer and closer toward the liberation of Paris.

The Twilight Tear juggernaut had steamrolled through the spring and summer, and her connections targeted the historic Alabama Stakes on August 8 for her next campaign stop. Given his star's past performances, Ben Jones must have been supremely confident when he put her aboard the train in Chicago for

After the Arlington Classic with owner Warren Wright (right) and trainer Ben Jones.

the overnight trip to New York's Belmont Park and stayed behind himself. Her valkyrie-like reputation was such that she scared off most of the opposition. Only three rivals opposed her: Brookmeade Stable's Dare Me and Belair Stud's entry of Thread o' Gold and Vienna. Public confidence ran high as well, as the 23,860 fans backed the queen of the three-year-olds down to 1-20. Whether it was the long trip in the middle of the summer and her arrival at Belmont a few hours before post time or the tag-team approach by the Belair duo, Twilight Tear stunned the Belmont crowd. She lost. After following the pace of Thread o' Gold, Twilight Tear, under the strongest of restraints, seemed unwilling to take up the running when passed by Vienna, who made her move as her stablemate faltered on the front end. At the end of the mile and a quarter, Twilight Tear, under 126 pounds, finished three-quarters of a length behind Vienna to whom she gave twelve pounds. As quickly as Twilight Tear had arrived, she was gone, heading back to Chicago and a well-deserved rest before pointing for a fall campaign.

Pimlico Racetrack declared its fall flagship race, the Pimlico

Twilight Tear defeating top handicap horse Devil Diver in the Pimlico Special.

Special, the "most sporting of all races" and deservedly so, for its seven runnings included "the race of the generation" when Seabiscuit defeated War Admiral. Other victors included Horse of the Year War Admiral, Horse of the Year Challedon (twice), and Horse of the Year Whirlaway. An invitation-only race, Twilight Tear was on the list, and Calumet began the preparations to RSVP.

Returning to the scene of her second defeat of the year, Twilight Tear exhibited a renewed spirit for the racing wars. On October 2 in the Meadowview, an overnight handicap at five and a half furlongs, she had little trouble, winning by more than two lengths. Ten days later she had moved her tack to Laurel and won the Queen Isabella Handicap by three lengths under a new jockey, Doug Dodson. Her old nemesis, a muddy track, showed up for the Maryland Handicap. Twilight Tear, carrying a cumbersome 130 pounds, flailed in the heavy going and finished fourth, beaten fifteen lengths by Dare Me, who carried a featherweight 109. The Pimlico Special and Greentree Stable's Devil Diver, the leader among the older horses, were only eleven days away.

A bay son of St. Germans out of Dabchick, by Royal Minstrel,

A fighter plane named for Twilight Tear. Three swastikas painted near the cockpit mark the number of "kills."

five-year-old Devil Diver had compiled quite a record in the handicap ranks. Like Twilight Tear he had been a mark of consistency; he had won seven of his prior eleven starts. Starting with the Paumonok Handicap in his first 1944 start, he reeled off five straight wins including the Toboggan Handicap, Metropolitan Handicap, and Whitney Stakes, all bulwarks of the handicap division.

Once again the Pimlico Special with its $25,000 winner-take-all purse would be crucial in deciding year-end honors. According to the conditions of the race, Twilight Tear carried 117 pounds to Devil Diver's 126. One other entrant, Christiana Stable's Megogo, under 120 pounds, rounded out the field. The speed that Ben Jones so valued proved the difference. With catlike quickness, Twilight Tear broke from the gate, and Dodson took her immediately to the lead followed by Devil Diver under Eddie Arcaro. After a half the only female ever to have run in the Pimlico Special opened a three-length lead and her sweeping strides raked in yard after yard of the Pimlico surface. Four lengths ahead after a mile, she galloped home a six-length winner. The final time of 1:56 3/5 matched Seabiscuit's stakes record and came within one-fifth of the track record for the mile and three-sixteenths. Devil Diver finished second, ten lengths ahead of Megogo. Twilight Tear had nothing left to prove, so the nation's leading three-year-old and front-runner for Horse of the Year honors headed to Florida's Hialeah Park for a winter vacation.

The arrival of a queen is cause for celebration, and only the returning troops would have been given a more royal welcome than Twilight Tear when she arrived at Hialeah. Rather than arriving fashionably late, Susie arrived early, and the red-carpet treatment had to be moved to her stall. With a banner inscribed "Welcome Susie!" as a theme, Maurice Weiss and five of his band gathered at the Calumet barn and played the appropriate "Sweet Sue" and "If You Knew Susie." The band finished the serenade with "My Old Kentucky Home." Meanwhile, racing's "woman of the year" displayed her placid nature and unperturbedly munched on carrots. The coronation was not ill conceived, for at year's end Twilight Tear became the first female Horse of the Year since the honor's official inception in 1936. She also was named champion three-year-old filly.

So, in a stall at Hialeah, Twilight Tear waited for the upcoming season and her engagements in the Black Helen and Widener handicaps, races that would push her earnings past the all-time mark for fillies and mares set by C.V. Whitney's Top Flight. But the war effort intervened, and in December 1944, James F. Byrnes, the director of war mobilization, suspended all horse racing in the United States. This suspension would last until May 1945, when the nation celebrated the surrender of the German forces and victory in Europe.

When racing did resume, Twilight Tear was not ready to come back. In a workout at Churchill Downs in preparation for her debut, she bled and was rested until the Washington Park meeting. Two weeks after the Japanese had agreed to an unconditional surrender, she returned

Twilight Tear as a successful broodmare for Calumet.

to the races on August 28 in a six-furlong allowance race. It would be Twilight Tear's last start.

Chicago summers can be very hot and humid, conditions especially trying on horses that tend to bleed. She started well and pressed a rather rapid pace set by Fighting Don. At the head of the stretch, she hemorrhaged and was eased. She retired to Calumet Farm with a record of eighteen wins from twenty-four starts with two seconds, two thirds, and earnings of $202,165.

Although she may have been finished with the racing wars, Twilight Tear was not finished with her war effort. Twilight Tear would fly once more, not down the racetracks of America but in the skies over Europe. In 1944 in North American Aviation's factory in California, an airplane was assembled and shipped to the Eighth Air Force's 78th Fighter Group in England. There the Mustang P-51D-20 44-63864 was paired with a young American lieutenant, Hubert "Bill" Davis. Inspired by the fortitude of Calumet's formidable racing filly, he named the plane "Twilight Tear" and flew her in the bulk of

Twilight Tear with her Blenheim II filly A Gleam, who became an important stakes winner.

his thirty-five combat missions. Together they shot down three enemy planes and incapacitated another.

As a broodmare, Twilight Tear also etched her name in the ranks of outstanding producers. Upon her retirement she was bred to Calumet's Triple Crown-winning Horse of the Year Whirlaway, the first mating of two Horses of the Year. Her second mating to Whirlaway produced the stakes winner Coiner. She also produced the high-class handicap gelding Bardstown, a son of Alibhai who earned $628,752, and the outstanding racer and producer A Gleam. This daughter of Blenheim II linked Twilight Tear with Calumet Farm's last great champion in both name and bloodline. To the cover of Calumet's 1958 dual classic winner Tim Tam, A Gleam produced a filly named Moonbeam who when bred to Calumet's stakes-winning Raise a Cup produced

Before Dawn, the champion two-year-old filly of 1981.

In the same foaling barn in which she was born thirteen years earlier, Twilight Tear died giving birth. It was March 8, 1954.

Twilight Tear embodied the spirit of the changing face of America and American women, having proven herself equal to any male on the racetrack battlefield, in true "Rosie the Riveter" fashion.

by Tom Hall

Bull Lea, 1935	Bull Dog, 1927	Teddy, 1913	Ajax, 1901	**Flying Fox** **Amie**
			Rondeau, 1900	Bay Ronald Doremi
		Plucky Liege, 1912	Spearmint, 1903	Carbine Maid of the Mint
			Concertina, 1896	St. Simon Comic Song
	Rose Leaves, 1916	Ballot, 1904	Voter, 1894	Friar's Balsam Mavourneen
			Cerito, 1888	Lowland Chief Merry Dance
		Colonial, 1897	Trenton, 1881	Musket Frailty
TWILIGHT TEAR			Thankful Blossom, 1891	Paradox The Apple
Lady Lark, 1934	Blue Larkspur, 1926	Black Servant, 1918	Black Toney, 1911	Peter Pan Belgravia
			Padula, 1906	Laveno Padua
		Blossom Time, 1920	North Star III, 1914	Sunstar Angelic
			Vaila, 1911	Fariman Padilla
	Ladana, 1928	Lucullite, 1915	Trap Rock, 1908	Rock Sand Topiary
			Lucky Lass, 1909	Ormondale Lux Casta
		Adana, 1908	Adam, 1902	**Flying Fox** **Amie**
			Mannie Himyar, 1894	Himyar Mannie Gray

Busher

(1945)

Although the selection of the three-year-old filly Busher as 1945 Horse of the Year may have raised the hackles of some racing traditionalists, it wouldn't have elevated their eyebrows. Twilight Tear, also a three-year-old filly, had taken Horse of the Year honors the previous season, so there was precedent. And any objective review of 1945 racing should have emphatically concluded that Busher's campaign was the most impressive of any other horse in training, male or female.

No doubt there were some hidebound citizens in 1945 still troubled by the new presence in American society of female

Busher and Eddie Arcaro.

defense-plant workers, cab drivers, streetcar conductors, and pari-mutuel clerks who had come to the fore for the first time during World War II. But the majority had gotten used to this sociological development that saw some five million women in the nation's sixty-six million-person work force, the largest such total up until that time and a tremendous departure from the past.

In fact, Busher's deserved acclamation as the dominant runner of 1945 may have been seen as paralleling a female ascendancy in the nation as a whole. In this era of "Rosie the Riveter," why not a filly as Horse of the Year — especially the one subsequently acclaimed by eminent racing historian John Hervey (nom de plume Salvator) as the "Queen of Queens"?

When Busher was foaled on April 27, 1942, at Kentucky's Idle Hour Stock Farm, it could confidently be said she was "to the manor bred" — a product of some of America's truly regal bloodlines arriving at one of America's most successful breeding farms.

Colonel Edward Riley Bradley, one of the more colorful characters in the history of the American Turf, owned Idle Hour. This son of Irish immigrants was a Pennsylvania native, born in Johnstown in 1860. As a teenager he moved to the West to prospect for gold but found more lucrative work as a bookmaker at racetracks. Bradley later acquired gambling houses in at least four states, the most famous of which was the Beach Club Casino in Palm Beach, Florida. In famous 1934 testimony before a Senate investigating committee, Bradley, when asked what his business was, replied, "I am a speculator, racehorse breeder, and gambler." He was good at all three, accumulating a fortune measured in the millions. The popular Colonel (an honorary title) was also famous for his philanthropies.

Bradley entered horse racing

Women of the 1940s

During World War II more than six million American women enter the workforce; they are pushed back out of traditionally male jobs at war's end...Eleanor Roosevelt becomes a delegate to the newly created United Nations...The baby boom is in full swing; more marriages take place than at any other time.

before the turn of the century and soon adopted the use of "B" names for the horses he bred. Behave Yourself in 1921 became the first of Bradley's four Kentucky Derby winners. Others to carry the white silks with green hoops to Derby glory included Bubbling Over (1926), Burgoo King (1932), and Brokers Tip (1933). In all, Bradley started twenty-eight horses in the Derby. Four other Bradley contenders finished second and another ran third. His quartet ranks Bradley second only to Calumet Farm (eight) in Derby wins.

During his early years as a breeder, Bradley took a dislike to the fiery Fair Play line and thereafter avoided it, refusing even to breed to Man o' War. Later, however, Bradley became a great admirer of Man o' War's best son, War Admiral, whom he considered so attractive for both his talent and his looks that he unsuccessfully attempted to purchase him from owner Samuel Riddle. When the 1937 Triple Crown winner and Horse of the Year was retired, Bradley set aside his aversion to that equine family and sent some of his best mares to War Admiral's court. One of them was Baby League, a daughter of Bubbling Over out of the monumentally influential broodmare La Troienne. The result was Busher.

As a youngster Busher failed to make a great impression during the yearling trials conducted over the Idle Hour training track. Still, farm manager Olin Gentry ranked the smallish chestnut miss among the best of that Idle Hour crop. And she would eventually become more physically imposing, later prompting racing historian and illustrator C.W. Anderson to write that "Busher had one of the most beautiful and intelligent heads seen on any thoroughbred. Her eye held an expression of awareness that was characteristic of her grandsire, Man o' War."

Busher made her career debut on May 30, 1944, at Belmont Park. Taking on twelve other maiden fillies in a four and a half-furlong dash, she showed good early speed under jockey Ted Atkinson and scored by a half-length. She had been well prepared by trainer J.W. (Jimmy) Smith, who earlier during his riding career had been aboard Bradley's Blue Larkspur in the colt's last two starts in 1930.

Bradley viewed Busher's debut from a special glass and cypress-enclosed box that had been constructed for him atop the Belmont Park clubhouse. Nearing

Colonel E.R. Bradley.

eighty-five years of age, and in failing health, Bradley watched his horses run from this vantage point while avoiding the racetrack crowds. Bradley only attended Belmont during this period of his life, which led to Busher's relatively light (for those days) two-year-old campaign.

Following her maiden win, Busher was idle until August 2, when she returned in an allowance event at five and a half furlongs. This race represented an anomaly: Not only did Busher go off at the extraordinarily generous odds of 8-1, but it was the only time in her twenty-one-race career that she was not favored. She won easily by four and a half lengths. Most people assumed that the Colonel, betting man that he was, added considerably to his fortune that afternoon.

Busher's introduction to stakes competition came next, on August 16 in the six-furlong Spinaway, and it resulted in her first loss. After a poor start that saw her in eleventh place early, she came on late to finish fourth behind the victorious Price Level, beaten nearly four lengths. Two weeks later, with Eddie Arcaro replacing Ferril Zufelt in the saddle, Busher scored the first of her eleven stakes victories. This came in the Adirondack, in which she triumphed by two lengths over War Date.

Busher made the fifth start of her juvenile campaign in another allowance race, on September 19, as a prep for the Matron Stakes. Carrying 119 pounds, Busher unsuccessfully attempted to concede eleven pounds to Nomadic. Busher lost by a head as Nomadic sizzled six furlongs down Belmont's Widener Chute in 1:08 3/5. George "The Iceman" Woolf rode Busher that day.

Wheeled right back in the Matron Stakes, Busher turned the tables on both of her conquerors: Price Level, who finished third, and Nomadic, fourth. With Arcaro back aboard, Busher came from just off the pace to take the lead at the eighth-pole. However, Twosy gave her a tussle, briefly taking the lead before Busher rallied to prevail by a neck right at the wire. Busher thus became the fifth Idle Hour Farm filly to win the prestigious Matron. Her time of 1:09 2/5 was the second fastest in the history of the event. That was the last time Bradley saw her run. He died in 1946 at age eighty-seven.

Busher's final start as a two-year-old came at Laurel Park on October 14 in the Selima Stakes, last major race of the season for members of her division. In her first try beyond six furlongs, and first over a racing strip other than fast, Busher experienced some traffic trouble early. With racing room at a premium, Arcaro guided Busher over to the rail, keeping her safely away from the scramble for position going on ahead of them.

Ace Card led early in the mile and one-sixteenth race, followed closely by eventual star Gallorette. Going down the Laurel backstretch, Arcaro moved Busher closer to the leaders. Once the field turned for home, Busher shot from three lengths behind Ace Card to three lengths in front of her, Busher's final margin of victory, which she achieved without being fully extended. Gallorette wound up third, another two and a half lengths back.

Louis B. Mayer.

Busher's victory in the Selima marked her fifth in seven starts that season. It sewed up the two-year-old filly championship for her and also served notice that neither longer distances nor "off" tracks would trouble this impeccably bred performer. On the Experimental Free Handicap she drew the top filly assignment of 119 pounds. Busher's earnings of $60,300 led her division.

Bradley, who previously had owned and sold the Fair Grounds in New Orleans, in 1943 sold his interest in Hialeah Park to Joseph P. Kennedy, father of the future president. Some two years later, as his health continued to decline and he gradually dispersed his stable, Bradley parted with his final prized possession, Busher. Louis B. Mayer paid Bradley $50,000 for her in March 1945, a sizeable price at the time but one that proved to be a great bargain for the movie magnate.

Because of World War II the government curtailed racing in America for the first four months of 1945. The ban ended following Germany's surrender on May 7, some three weeks after the death of President Franklin Delano Roosevelt. Meanwhile, two other notable political careers were being launched: John F. Kennedy from Massachusetts filed to run for Congress, and Richard M. Nixon entered the campaign for a congressional seat in the California delegation. Both men won. Betty Friedan began contributing short fiction to women's magazines the same year, thus launching a writing career that eighteen years later would result in the groundbreaking book *The Feminine Mystique.* And 1945 was the year that Busher would follow in Twilight Tear's historic hoofprints.

That spring saw Santa Anita Park, which had been used as an internment center for Japanese Americans during the war, housing them in the horse stalls, finally restored to its original purpose. As at the other now reopened U.S. racetracks, fans came rushing back in great numbers.

Those at Santa Anita on May 26 were rewarded with the sight of Busher making her first start at age three. Just as Rosie the Riveter and her sisters had proved that females could succeed in male-dominated fields, Busher would make the same point on the nation's racetracks in 1945.

Busher's second owner was, like her first, a self-made millionaire who had moved west as a young man. The Russian-born Mayer, raised in St. John, New Brunswick, Canada, hit Los Angeles in 1918 with the first group of Hollywood movie pioneers. In 1924 he began a fabulously successful twenty-seven-year career as general manager and partner in Metro-Goldwyn-Mayer. Mayer created the hugely successful studio star system and for seven consecutive years earned more money than any other business executive in the nation.

Mayer got into racing in 1938 as an owner when his physicians urged him to find a hobby that would get him away from the movie business and out into the fresh air. He started by purchasing a pair of two-year-olds. Not long thereafter, Mayer entered the breeding side of the sport with characteristic energy. He bought a five hundred-acre farm, stocked it with well-bred mares, and imported the influential stal-

Busher and trainer George Odom (on right) after winning the Arlington Handicap.

lions Beau Pere from Australia and Alibhai from England. In only a few years Mayer was recognized as the most successful breeder-owner in California since the days of James Ben Ali Haggin and Ellis J. "Lucky" Baldwin early in the century. (In the 1945 running of the California Breeders Champion Stakes, Mayer homebreds Honeymoon, Moneybags, and Charivari, all sired by Beau Pere, ran one-two-three, a result that Hollywood Park fans greeted with a crescendo of boos.)

With the sale to Mayer, Busher acquired another famous ex-jockey as her trainer, George M. Odom, who knew the filly well. As Odom once told *Daily Racing Form* columnist Charles Hatton, he had seen Busher "the first time she ran, at Belmont. She was such a keen, sound filly." Odom began urging Mayer's associate Neil McCarthy to look into buying her from Bradley. They finally made the deal the next spring, much to the delight of Odom, who years later rated Busher the greatest filly he "or any other man" ever trained.

Recent racing has few examples of direct competition between top-class runners of the two sexes. Genuine Risk (1980) and Winning Colors (1988) were Kentucky Derby heroines, and Lady's Secret bested males in the 1986 Whitney Handicap, but to find other examples requires looking through the more distant past to such male bashers as Shuvee, Ta Wee, Silver Spoon, Bug Brush, the aforementioned Honeymoon, Beldame, Black Maria — and Busher.

Busher made thirteen starts under Odom's tutelage in 1945, a campaign in which she challenged male horses no fewer than six times — or almost half of her starts that year. As veteran racing official Thomas E. Trotter commented recently, "Such a thing is unheard of today, a three-year-old filly taking on colts and geldings that many times — and successfully. You'd have to have a special horse to pull that off."

The previous year Busher had sometimes been slow getting away from the gate in her races, a trait not normally associated with War Admiral's offspring. But at three, flashing Mayer's French blue and pink colors, she almost always quickly got into the mix,

beginning with her seasonal debut at Santa Anita. With the outstanding gate rider Johnny Longden in the saddle, Busher broke on top and stayed there, winning this six-furlong allowance test by five lengths at the lowest odds of her career thus far, 1-5. Mayer and Odom settled on Longden as Busher's regular pilot, and he rode her in all but one of her starts that season

One week later, in the seven-furlong Santa Susana, Busher carried Longden to an even easier triumph. Again breaking alertly, she took command early and rolled to a seven-length win in 1:23 3/5, carrying high weight of 121 for the second straight time.

She carried that same impost in her next start, the San Vicente Handicap on June 9, and it amounted to co-highweight with Sir Bim, but pure high weight on the scale, for here, Busher was going against colts for the first time.

The San Vicente probably would have been a relative stroll in the park for Busher had it not been for the unexpected antics of the good colt Quick Reward. Coming out of the gate, Quick

Busher winning the 1945 Cleopatra Handicap with ease.

Reward lost his rider, then played havoc with the field for much of the rest of the one-mile race. Bustling up the inner rail, Quick Reward forced Sea Sovereign into Busher, knocking her off stride. A lesser competitor might have spit out the bit at that point. Not Busher. She quickly recovered from the bumping and gained the lead nearing the furlong pole.

But then came Quick Reward again, charging up alongside Busher and nearly cutting her off. Longden held her together, however, and Busher displayed tremendous talent and determination in going on about her business to score by a disdainful length and a quarter. Her time of 1:36 3/5 was excellent under any conditions (it was the best mile time of that year at Santa Anita) and extraordinary under these. In so convincingly overcoming the traffic troubles she experienced in the San Vicente, Busher stamped herself as a filly of tremendous quality.

Busher's next race against males came in her next start, the nine-furlong Santa Anita Derby on June 23. For the second straight time she was odds-on

Busher winning the Arlington Handicap by daylight.

while going against colts (imagine that happening today!). Her former stablemate, the Idle Hour-bred Bymeabond, under George Woolf, drew 7-1 odds.

After she broke sharply, Longden settled Busher back just off the pace in the early going. Longden let out a notch down the backstretch, and Busher took command around the final turn, opening up a three-length advantage at the eighth-pole. It may have been that Longden was too confident, for had he stayed on the rail, the pursuing Bymeabond would have had to go around her on the outside. Longden permitted her to go wide, however, and Woolf was able to scoot up the rail with Bymeabond, who won by a half-length, with Busher giving him two pounds of actual weight (121 to 119) and seven pounds on the scale.

Busher's final outing of the Santa Anita meeting came on July 4. She faced her own sex again (but mostly older fillies and mares) in this one, the mile and one-sixteenth Santa Margarita Handicap. Her assignment of 126 pounds equaled that of the five-year-old Happy Issue. Busher won easily by a length and a half from older stablemate Whirlabout, being timed in 1:43. Then, it was off to Washington Park for one of the most impressive five-race campaigns ever conducted before Chicago fans.

Chicago summer racing in those days was the best in the country. The major tracks in California, Florida, and Kentucky did not operate during the summer, and Saratoga held an abbreviated meeting. As a result, most of the nation's top stables, jockeys, and horses shipped to Chicago's Arlington and Washington parks for the summer.

Busher made her Midwest debut in the July 25 Cleopatra Handicap. Lined up against her in this one-mile event for three-year-old fillies were old rivals War Date and Twosy, the former unbeaten that season, the latter the runner-up to Busher by a neck in the bitterly contested Matron Stakes the previous year.

Both Twosy and War Date received weight from Busher, but the respective spreads (ten pounds and four pounds) failed to faze the Mayer runner. Busher reached the line a widening four and a half lengths before Twosy, who had another two lengths on War Date. It appeared that no member of Busher's division could seriously threaten her.

Her connections then decided to provide Busher with another

career "first." In the Arlington Handicap on August 4, she would not only take on males — as she had in the Santa Anita Derby and San Vicente — but *older* males. Furthermore, with her 113-pound impost, Busher had to give all of them weight with the lone exception of Pot o' Luck, who was level with her on the scale.

This time, after she again broke well, Longden guided Busher directly to the lead. She bounced along in front all the way around the Washington Park oval, reporting four and a half lengths ahead of runner-up Take Wing. Pot o' Luck, considered Calumet Farm's best three-year-old colt, finished up the track. This was Busher's first attempt at a mile and a quarter, and she accomplished the distance in 2:03 4/5 while in front by daylight throughout.

At this point in her career, as author Kent Hollingsworth wrote, Busher was "considered invincible." Then, he added, "she promptly lost."

The upset occurred in the August 18 Beverly Handicap for fillies and mares at Washington Park. Busher received 128 for this mile and one-eighth event, and the brilliant Durazna, a mere 116. Durazna, a daughter of Bull Lea—Myrtlewood who had been champion two-year-old filly two seasons earlier, won by two and a half lengths over Letmenow (102 pounds) with Busher checking in third, another length and a quarter back.

There had been much talk that summer of a match race between Busher and Gallorette, who had been dominating the Eastern fillies. But Gallorette's connections declined, and Durazna's people accepted the challenge instead.

The one-mile match took place at Washington Park on August 29 — eleven days after Durazna had downed Busher in the Beverly. Both fillies carried 115 pounds, with the younger Busher the highweight on the scale.

This was a period when match races were still very much a part of the American racing scene, quite a few of them involving female runners. The Busher-Durazna clash was one of nineteen match races held in the 1940s. The previous decade featured eleven such events, including Seabiscuit's famous conquest of War Admiral in 1938. It has been nearly three decades since the last match race in this country pitting top-class horses against each other: the disastrous meeting of Foolish Pleasure and Ruffian in 1975 that resulted in Ruffian's fatal breakdown.

The Busher-Durazna battle was

memorable from the start. Busher grabbed the early lead Durazna snatched it from her. And, going head-to-head, these two combative dynamos alternated in front through fractions of :23 for the quarter, :45 3/5 for the half, and 1:10 4/5 for the six furlongs. In the final sixteenth Durazna gave way slightly, and Busher edged clear to win by three parts of a length, her mile in 1:37 4/5. This thrilling event had proven to be everything that fans seek in a match race.

In the current age of widely spaced races for horses that are often handled like Faberge eggs, it seems almost incomprehensible what next appeared on Busher's 1945 agenda. A mere five days after her ding-dong battle with the gritty Durazna, from which she emerged with a three-inch cut on her left hock, Busher took on not only a dozen handicap horses but Calumet Farm's mighty Armed, one of the nation's top handicap horses, in the Washington Park Handicap. Not only that, but Busher had to concede Armed four pounds on the scale of weights going a mile and a quarter.

Busher defeats champion Durazna in a match race at Washington Park.

It proved to be Busher's finest race. The seemingly ever-present Durazna led through the first half-mile before retreating, with Busher taking over at that point. Busher curved into the stretch three on top and going easily. But then Armed came to her, and Longden put Busher to a drive. As Hollingsworth phrased it, "Showing what class can do under pressure," Busher prevailed by a length and a half over Armed and broke a thirteen-year-old track record in the process. Her final time was 2:01 4/5.

Ironically, this was the only time Busher faced Armed, yet in 1999 the gelding was ranked number thirty-nine, one position ahead of her on *The Blood-Horse* roster of the top one hundred American Thoroughbreds.

A dozen days after beating Armed, and following another cross-country journey, Busher confronted colts again, this time in the Will Rogers Handicap at Hollywood Park. The recent physical demands made on Busher may have taken their toll — but not by much. Busher just failed to get up, losing by a head to Quick Reward, to whom she gave eleven pounds. However, the second money of six thousand dollars enabled Busher to replace Top Flight as the foremost money-winning filly or mare in history with her total of $276,120.

Busher defeats another Horse of the Year, Armed, in the Washington Park Handicap.

As she had in the past, Busher avenged herself on two previous conquerors when, in the September 29 Hollywood Derby, she downed both Quick Reward and Bymeabond while giving actual weight to each. She toted 123 pounds over the nine furlongs in 1:50 1/5 and won easily.

The final race of Busher's amazing three-year-old campaign came at Hollywood Park on October 6. In the mile and one-sixteenth Vanity Handicap for fillies and mares, Busher again gave weight to all. But she had little trouble scoring by two lengths over Canina, to whom she conceded twelve pounds. It was the thirteenth start of a season that resulted in ten wins, four against males, and total career earnings of $334,035.

Trainer Odom then began pointing Busher for the $75,000 Hollywood Gold Cup, but those plans were aborted when she fractured a cannon bone in a workout. That ended Busher's season.

The year-end polls paid justified tribute to Busher's 1945 exploits. She was the unanimous choice as best three-year-old filly, best three-year-old of either sex, best handicap filly or mare — and Horse of the Year.

After recuperating from her injury, Busher returned to light training in June 1946, under the care of trainer Graceton Philpot. Despite his cautious management, Philpot got Busher back to the races just one more time. On January 2, 1947, Busher showed up for a six-furlong allowance race at Santa Anita with Jackie Westrope as her rider. She dwelt at the start and ran fifth of sixth, beaten five lengths in so uncharacteristic a performance that Mayer then retired her. Busher's career dossier read twenty-one starts, fifteen wins, three seconds, and one third.

With his favorite horse gone from the racetrack, Mayer decided to disperse his vast Thoroughbred holdings. On the evening of February 27, 1947, some seven thousand people turned out at Santa Anita for the sale, which was broadcast on three radio networks. The sixty Mayer horses offered sold for a world record $1,549,800. Busher went through the auction ring on a bid of $135,000 made by Neil McCarthy. McCarthy later sold Busher back to Mayer, who the following year sold her for a world-record broodmare price of $150,000 to cosmetics queen Elizabeth N. Graham's Maine Chance Farm.

Busher produced five named foals. The best was Jet Action, a son of Jet Pilot, who won the

Withers Stakes and Roamer Handicap in 1954. On March 22, 1955, Busher died foaling a Jet Pilot filly at Spendthrift Farm near Lexington, where she was being boarded. She was thirteen.

In the column in which he dubbed her the "Queen of Queens," John Hervey placed great emphasis on Busher's feat of capturing the two great all-aged handicaps of the 1945 Washington Park meeting. To his mind "the impressive ease" with which Busher won the Arlington and Washington handicaps, "conceding weight to everything brought against her, is without parallel in turf history, American or foreign."

Those two performances by Busher, wrote Hervey in 1945, "cause genuine wonder." They still do today, nearly six decades later.

by John McEvoy

War Admiral, 1934	Man o' War, 1917	Fair Play, 1905	Hastings, 1893	Spendthrift Cinderella
			Fairy Gold, 1896	Bend Or Dame Masham
		Mahubah, 1910	Rock Sand, 1900	Sainfoin Roquebrune
			Merry Token, 1891	Merry Hampton Mizpah
	Brushup, 1929	**Sweep**, 1907	**Ben Brush**, 1893	Bramble Roseville
			Pink Domino, 1897	Domino Belle Rose
		Annette K., 1921	Harry of Hereford, 1910	John o' Gaunt Canterbury Pilgrim
			Bathing Girl, 1915	Spearmint Summer Girl
BUSHER				
Baby League, 1935	Bubbling Over, 1923	North Star III, 1914	Sunstar, 1908	Sundridge Doris
			Angelic, 1901	St. Angelo Fota
		Beaming Beauty, 1917	**Sweep**, 1907	**Ben Brush** **Pink Domino**
			Bellisario, 1911	Hippodrome Biturica
	La Troienne, 1926	Teddy, 1913	Ajax, 1901	Flying Fox Amie
			Rondeau, 1900	Bay Ronald Doremi
		Helene de Troie, 1916	Helicon, 1908	Cyllene Vain Duchess
			Lady of Pedigree, 1910	St. Denis Doxa

Moccasin

(1965)

Moccasin was a filly of contradictions. She was big and bold yet demure and biddable. She had blazing speed yet sometimes couldn't get out of her own way. But in 1965 Moccasin pulled all her disparate parts together to create one of the all-time greatest single seasons of racing.

She was a product of Claiborne Farm, A.B. "Bull" Hancock Jr.'s renowned showplace in the Bluegrass where blue-blooded Thoroughbreds roamed every field. Moccasin certainly had her share of that blue blood. She was a daughter of Nantallah, a Claiborne stallion by the great sire Nasrullah, whom Hancock

Moccasin at Keeneland.

had imported from England in 1951. Nasrullah had been a champion juvenile in England, while Nantallah was stakes-placed at two and won three of four at three before being retired.

Hancock had purchased Moccasin's dam, Rough Shod II, in 1951 as well, at the Tattersalls sales ring in Newmarket, England, for retired Republic Steel president Tom Girdler. Rough Shod II, a daughter of Gold Bridge—Dalmary, by Blandford, won once at three in 1947 before being retired in England. She produced one foal in her native country before being sent to the 1951 Tattersalls sale. She was imported in foal to My Babu, and the resultant foal was the filly Gambetta, who would go on to win the Debutante and Susan stakes at two. As a broodmare, Gambetta quickly followed in her dam's footsteps, producing stakes winner Staretta and three stakes-placed winners in her first four foals. Gambetta would go on to produce the brilliant filly Gamely, the 1967 champion three-year-old filly and 1968-69 champion older mare.

Rough Shod II's next important foal was Ridan, foaled in 1959. By Nantallah, Ridan showed precocity in winning the Arlington and Washington Park futurities among four stakes wins at two. He was named 1961 champion juvenile colt, but he didn't stop there. At three he won the Blue Grass Stakes, Florida Derby, Arlington Classic, and Hibiscus Stakes, and in one of the greatest racing duels of all time finished a scant nose behind Jaipur in the Travers Stakes after battling his rival the entire mile and a quarter.

When Girdler dispersed his Thoroughbred holdings in early 1961, Hancock quickly acquired the mare. That spring Rough Shod II foaled Lt. Stevens, a full brother to Ridan. Lt. Stevens was not quite at Ridan's level but was still a solid handicapper, winning the John B. Campbell, Palm

Women of the 1960s

The Civil Rights Act is passed. It prohibits discrimination in employment on the basis of race, creed, national origin, or sex...The U.S. Supreme Court rules, in Griswold v. State of Connecticut, that laws prohibiting the use of birth control are unconstitutional...The National Organization for Women (NOW) is founded by Betty Friedan and other delegates to the Third National Conference of the Commission on the Status of Women.

Beach, and Saranac handicaps. He later became a leading broodmare sire and is best known as the broodmare sire of 1987 Kentucky Derby winner and 1988 Horse of the Year Alysheba.

With Ridan's racetrack success still fresh, Hancock sent Rough Shod II back to Nantallah in 1962, and the mare was once again in foal to that stallion.

Moccasin was foaled at Claiborne Farm on April 16, 1963. She had a golden chestnut coat, a big blaze, and socks on three legs, but, flashiness aside, her breeding set her apart.

"You simply don't take a filly lightly who is a full sister to both Ridan and Lt. Stevens," her trainer, Harry Trotsek, told *Daily Racing Form* during Moccasin's two-year-old season. "So you always give her a little special attention and consideration."

Trotsek had received Moccasin on the luck of the draw. Hancock and longtime business partner William Haggin Perry each owned a half-interest in their racing stock and would divide the yearlings between their stables. They usually flipped to see who would pick first, and Perry won the toss for the crop of two-year-olds of 1965. He picked a Bold Ruler—Ritmar colt named Taipan. Hancock also picked a Bold Ruler, a chestnut filly named Isobella who was out of Monarchy, a full sister to Round Table. After Perry made his second pick, Hancock chose Moccasin. He had chosen Isobella first because at the time she had appeared much sounder than Moccasin, Hancock later told *The Blood-Horse*.

Moccasin, Isobella, and the rest of Hancock's picks received their early lessons at Claiborne Farm, then were shipped to Trotsek in Florida for the winter. There Moccasin received her first real test. Isobella seemed to show more ability early on, even outworking Moccasin, so Trotsek wasn't sure who was better. Isobella had a temper but worked with gusto. Moccasin, on the other hand, went about her lessons with little fanfare, just doing what needed to be done.

Trotsek brought some thirty years of training experience to his handling of Moccasin and her stablemates. A Cicero, Illinois, native, he had at age twenty sent out his first winner in 1931 at a Kansas City, Missouri, track. He saddled his first stakes winner in 1949 and since then had trained forty-five added-money winners, including 1954 Preakness winner Hasty Road, Oil Capitol, and so on. Trotsek had been leading trainer in 1953 with $1,028,873 in earnings. He was private trainer for Mr. and Mrs. Allie Reuben's Hasty House Stable from 1948 until 1964, when he took over training duties for Hancock.

Isobella made her first start on May 28, 1965, in a five-furlong maiden race at Aqueduct but finished eighth. She returned on June 24 for an easy wire-to-wire victory at the same distance but later had to be sent to Claiborne after injuring a knee. During the early winter Trotsek had had Moccasin's ankles pin-fired, more as a precaution and "tightener," and the filly recovered easily.

Even with the speed Moccasin had shown in her training, when she made her debut on August 6, 1965, at Saratoga, neither Trotsek nor Hancock could anticipate what she had in store — for them and for her opponents. The big chestnut filly disposed of eleven other maiden fillies with astounding ease, winning the five and a half-furlong event by eight lengths after leading the whole way. Ironically, shortly after Moccasin's debut win, the *Daily Racing Form* reported the death of Rough Shod II, who had died that April at age twenty-one after foaling a Sir Gaylord colt at Claiborne. The year before she

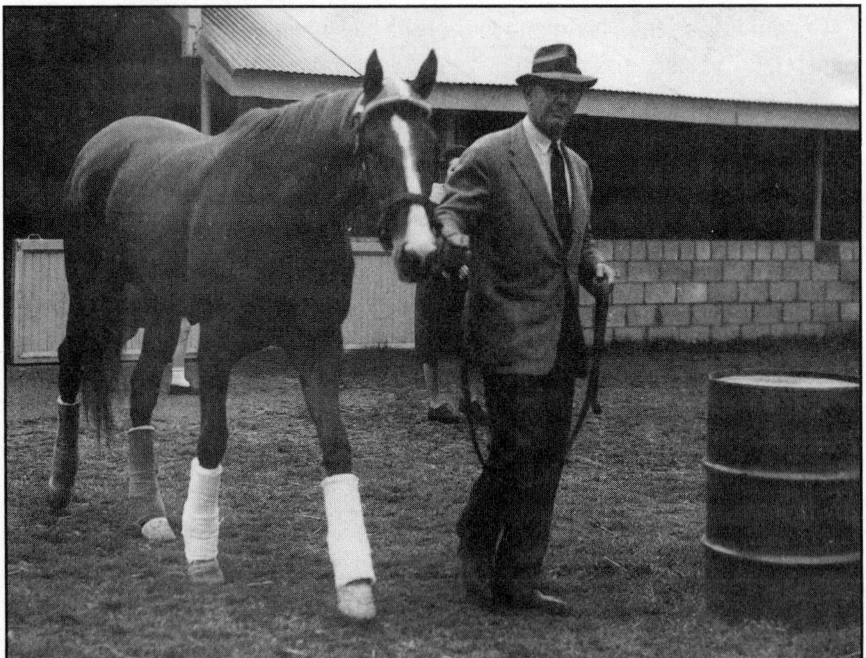

Moccasin with A.B. Hancock Jr., whose Claiborne Farm bred and owned her.

had produced a Nantallah filly named Thong, who would go on to further her dam's reputation and to establish her own successful family as the dam of stakes winners Thatch, Lisadell, King Pellinore, and Espadrille, and as the granddam of Nureyev, Number, Bound, Fairy Bridge (dam of Sadler's Wells), and others.

The maiden victory was the only time Moccasin didn't go off as the odds-on favorite. She was a very generous 7-1. In her next start she was odds-on at .30. That was eleven days later in an allowance at Saratoga. Running the same distance as in the maiden win, Moccasin hardly troubled herself to get to a full gallop this time, winning by the same margin of eight lengths in 1:04, two-fifths of a second faster than her maiden time.

Trotsek kept her at Saratoga for her first stakes, the $76,000 Spinaway, on August 25. Three days later on the final day of the Spa meet, another star-in-the-making, Buckpasser, a son of Tom Fool, would win the Hopeful Stakes to establish himself as the top juvenile colt in the land.

In the Spinaway, Moccasin prepared to do the same among fillies as she faced six others, including Swift Lady, winner of a division of the Astarita Stakes, plus Forefoot and Lyvette. In the first turn, Around the Roses gave a challenge and briefly took the lead before Moccasin quickly dismissed her and spurted to a four-length lead. She never relinquished it, galloping home to win by three and a half lengths. Although the victory was never in doubt, Moccasin still had to work a bit harder than she did in her first two efforts, which Hancock attributed to her working slower than normal before the race.

"We were so afraid she might work too fast that maybe she worked a little slow," he said in a post-race interview. "She has such good action she could be any kind of filly," the Claiborne Farm master continued, his excitement over the rangy chestnut filly evident. Moccasin reinforced Hancock's confidence in her next start, the Matron Stakes at Aqueduct.

The prestigious Matron was in its fifty-ninth running and with an added-money purse of $108,680 was its richest incarnation. Hancock had won the race ten years earlier with another brilliant filly, Doubledogdare, who went on to become a champion. Moccasin went out and simply took care of business. This time she allowed Calumet Farm's entrant, Another Love, to take the lead for about the first half-mile. Another Love came into the race off victories in the filly division of the National Stallion Stakes and also the Mermaid Stakes and was the only other filly in the twelve-horse field at odds of less than 10-1 — excepting Moccasin, of course, who was favored at 2-5. Another Love gave a good effort, but when Moccasin decided it was time to run, the other filly could not go with her and eventually faded to last. No other challenges were forthcoming, and Moccasin romped by six lengths in 1:11 3/5 for the six furlongs, even though she drifted out a little in the stretch as she strolled home. Lyvette, who went off as a 74-1 shot, finished second, followed by Shimmering Gold two more lengths back.

"Speed and a long stride," said Dr. Manuel Gilman, chief veterinarian for the New York Racing Association, to William Rudy of *The Blood-Horse*. "You don't see that combination too often."

After the Matron, Hancock indicated that Moccasin's next race would be the October 16 Alcibiades Stakes at Keeneland, Hancock's "home" track. After that he planned to put her away for the season.

"She has to be the champion now," he said after the Matron. "We want to win the Oaks next year." Hancock wasn't talking about just the Kentucky Oaks, either, but the Coaching Club American Oaks, as well.

Moccasin dominated her gender so easily not only through the speed and long stride Gilman spoke of, but also through her sheer size. Larger than most colts, Moccasin stood an impressive 16 hands, 1 3/4 inches, as measured by Gilman during her stay at Aqueduct. Her girth measured seventy-six inches, huge for a filly, especially a two-year-old; her cannon bone measured 8 1/4 inches around; her point of shoulder to point of hip, 47 inches; point of hip to point of hip, 27 inches; etc. While her size did not lend her the demure look most young fillies have — some observers said her legs were too rough — her brilliant chestnut color, her flashy blaze, and her kind disposition endeared her to horsemen and fans.

Her agreeable personality certainly did not come from her family, which had earned a reputation for producing talented but incorrigible runners. Chief among them were Moccasin's brothers, Ridan and Lt. Stevens. Ridan had a favorite groom and was known for going wild when other stable hands came near him, and, also, he would run off with exercise riders. Lt. Stevens could not stand training at two because of his recalcitrant nature and, like Ridan, would do his best to rid himself of exercise riders. Harry Trotsek delighted in Moccasin's gentle nature. Anyone could handle her, and she responded well to everything he asked of her in training. In training he worked mainly on controlling her natural speed.

"The first time I ever breezed her I knew she was a runner. She'd break watches if you'd let her and without effort. I took it very easy with her and gave her plenty of time to settle down. I didn't want her to become speed crazy. Once you know you have a horse that has speed, the big problem is to harness it and use it where it is needed most. In the races, I mean," Trotsek told the *Daily Racing Form* in 1965 in an interview on Moccasin's training regimen.

Surprisingly, Moccasin was caught napping at the start of her next race, an allowance prep a week before the Alcibiades, and broke in a tangle. Away last of seven in the six and a half-fur-

With trainer Harry Trotsek after winning the Gardenia Stakes.

long race, Moccasin was fourth after a half-mile, three and a quarter lengths back, but the fans that had made her the overwhelming favorite need not have worried. Moccasin steadily closed on the lead and firmly took over down the stretch to win by three lengths.

The Alcibiades, run at seven furlongs, Moccasin's first outing at that distance, presented no such problems. Only three other fillies could be found to take her on, so no pari-mutuel betting on the race was allowed. Moccasin won by fifteen lengths with "speed to spare."

Although the Alcibiades was supposed to be her final start for the season, she came out of the race in such good shape that Hancock decided to go on with her.

While Hancock, Trotsek, and Moccasin's fans were convinced already of her championship status, the connections of a two-year-old filly named Priceless Gem likely would have argued the point. Priceless Gem, trained by Hirsch Jacobs and owned by Jacobs' wife, Ethel, had been making a name on the East Coast with victories in the mile Frizette Stakes and in the Futurity, in which she bested Buckpasser. Priceless Gem and Moccasin seemed to be headed toward a meeting in the October 23 Selima Stakes at Laurel Park, but a few days before the race, Priceless Gem was withdrawn due to sore shins. That left the race easy prey for Moccasin.

Once again no wagering was allowed, and once again Moccasin toyed with outclassed opponents. In this case only four fillies showed up looking for second money, the best of the lot being Harbor View Farm's Swift Lady, winner of a division of the Astarita Stakes, second to Moccasin in the Spinaway, and third to Priceless Gem in the Frizette. But even Swift Lady's trainer, Burley Parke, stated he didn't think his filly had a chance to win. Swift Lady was the only other stakes winner to compete and ran to form, finishing second to Moccasin, who was never headed and won by five lengths. It was Moccasin's first attempt at a mile and one-sixteenth, and she ran strongly for most of it, swinging wide into the stretch before Larry Adams guided her back toward the rail and held her steady to the wire.

Adams was Moccasin's regular rider, having been aboard for all of her starts. Adams, a New Orleans native who got his start on the racetrack not as a hot walker but as a fry cook at Fair Grounds' track kitchen, rode his first winner in 1954 at age eighteen at Suffolk Downs in Massachusetts. In the winter of 1958, he fell on some ice at his hotel and broke the pitcher he was carrying. Shards from the pitcher severed a tendon in his knee. After he recovered, he needed longer stirrups. Adams found that the longer stirrups aided his balance, and his career took off. He rose quickly through the ranks, and in 1964 he rode 138 winners and earned $1.065 million. But Moccasin was the biggest horse of his career to that point.

Moccasin made her final start in the mile and one-sixteenth Gardenia Stakes at Garden State Park on November 6. A hoped-for meeting with Priceless Gem again failed to materialize, but Moccasin still had eight challengers to contend with, including Swift Lady, Adirondack Stakes winner Lady Dulcinea, stakes-placed Hula Girl, and Lady Diplomat, plus Frizette runner-up Lady Pitt and Schuyerville Stakes winner Prides Profile, who had deadheated to win a division of the Astarita. Moccasin carried herself with a regal air as she entered the paddock, and she stood quietly

Moccasin scored her eighth straight victory in the Gardenia Stakes.

while her rivals pranced and danced as they waited for the call to post. She broke from post seven and settled in third early, tracking leaders Lady Diplomat and Hula Girl. Adams asked Moccasin to pick up the pace leaving the backstretch, and she easily gained the lead and never relinquished it, finishing two and a half lengths in front of Lady Pitt. Moccasin's time of 1:44 2/5 was only two-fifths of a second off Queen Empress' stakes record.

Adams was wise not to push his filly for more, for she came out of the race with bucked shins, and Trotsek put her away for the winter.

The 1965 season had been a standout one for fillies and mares, harking back to the mid-1940s when Twilight Tear and Busher dominated not only their divisions but the boys as well. Moccasin and Priceless Gem had dominated in their category, with Priceless Gem defeating the boys, including two-year-old champion Buckpasser. Older mares Old Hat and Affectionately (1965 co-champion older females) bested their male counterparts as well. Old Hat defeated Roman Brother in the Michigan Mile and One-Eighth, while Affectionately, who also was named champion sprinter that year, won the Toboggan and Correction handicaps over males. Roman Brother, a four-year-old gelding by Third Brother, had won the Woodward Stakes, Manhattan Handicap, and Jockey Club Gold Cup, and was named Horse of the Year in the *Daily Racing Form* poll.

But both the Thoroughbred Racing Associations and *Turf and Sport Digest* awarded Horse of the Year to the two-year-old filly Moccasin for her undefeated, and mostly unchallenged, season. It was the first time a two-year-old filly had earned such an honor, and the first time since Native Dancer in 1952 that a two-year-old of either sex received racing's highest award. But like Moccasin's, Native Dancer's Horse of the Year title was shared; One Count received that honor in one year-end poll.

Also named champion two-year-old filly, Moccasin had ended her juvenile season with a record of eight wins in eight starts, with a combined margin of victory of fifty-one lengths, and earnings of $319,731.

Anticipation for her three-year-old season ran high, and even Hancock hinted at a possible Kentucky Derby start. "If she trains up to expectations, watch her in the Derby," he stated after

Moccasin was the first two-year-old filly Horse of the Year.

she received her championships.

As expected, Moccasin was the highest-rated filly on the Experimental Free Handicap, receiving 120 pounds, with Priceless Gem right behind her at 119. Buckpasser, also as expected, led the list at 126 pounds. The ratings were assigned by racing secretary Tommy Trotter, who didn't assign above-scale weight (greater than 126 pounds for males; 121 for fillies) to either Buckpasser or Moccasin. While Buckpasser would excel at three, indicating his rating should have been higher, Moccasin would not find her sophomore year quite as easy as her juvenile.

The spring of 1966 was not kind to either Buckpasser or Moccasin. Early on the Derby trail, Buckpasser had won the Everglades and Flamingo stakes at Hialeah and looked every bit like the leading contender he was. But he developed a severe quarter crack on the inside of his right front hoof in mid-March, and hopes of a Derby start for the colt quickly dissolved for owner-breeder Ogden Phipps and trainer Eddie Neloy.

Another three-year-old colt,

Graustark, who had won the Bahamas Stakes at Hialeah that winter, had taken over as the top Derby contender with strong works at Keeneland as he prepared for the April 9 Whitney Purse at the Lexington track. Moccasin also was training there for her first start since bucking her shins the previous November. Hancock had toned down his Derby pronouncements for the filly, especially with Graustark looking so good.

Moccasin was scheduled to run in the six-furlong Beaumont Purse, also April 9, but if fans were expecting her to pick up where she had left off, they were sorely disappointed. She broke well, but Adams quickly took her up, and Moccasin raced last of six in the early going. Observers noted that she didn't want to settle and seemed to be climbing as the field moved down the backstretch. Gradually she moved up before Adams set her down for the stretch run, but Moccasin had to go wide, and although she made up three lengths in the final sixteenth, she still finished fourth, one and three-quarters lengths back. The Keeneland crowd was stunned. Moccasin had been the overwhelming favorite, and she wasn't supposed to lose. Many who witnessed the race put the blame on Adams for riding her poorly, but when she returned a week later for the Ashland Stakes and showed little to finish sixth, a supposed bad ride wasn't the culprit. She was just dull. She had started slowly, giving the field a three- to four-length advantage, and hadn't done much after that. Hancock didn't think the bad break made a difference.

"If she were like she was last year, she would have won anyway. She just didn't run her race. Maybe it's the springtime — some fillies just don't run well in the spring," he said after the Ashland.

After some consideration, Hancock and Trotsek decided to forego the Kentucky Oaks and sent Moccasin to New York to contest the filly races there. She appeared at Aqueduct on May 17 in a six-furlong allowance with a new rider, Braulio Baeza. She also raced in blinkers for the first time to help her focus. Whether it was the change in scenery, the new rider, the new equipment, or a combination thereof, the old Moccasin seemed to return as she blasted a field of colts to win handily.

The excitement was short-lived, however, when eleven days later she finished third to

Marking Time and Around the Roses in the mile Acorn Stakes on a sloppy track. Moccasin came out of the race lame in her right hind leg but by the next morning seemed to be much better, although still "ouchy," and Hancock told reporters that it was probably just a muscle spasm or strain. Moccasin seemed to return in good order the next month with the mile and a quarter Coaching Club American Oaks on her schedule, but she weakened late in that race and finished fifth. Lady Pitt and Prides Profile, whom she had defeated in the Gardenia, were first and third, respectively.

Moccasin returned in August at Saratoga, this time in a division of the seven-furlong Test Stakes, and once again, she showed that she could still put together a devastating run. But just when it seemed she might be back, Moccasin came out of a half-mile work with a filling in her right rear ankle. X-rays revealed two fractures of a sesamoid bone. She was sent to Claiborne immediately, and Hancock announced plans to breed her the following spring.

However, Moccasin responded well enough to treatment and rest that she was returned to the

Moccasin defeating colts in the Phoenix Handicap at Keeneland.

track early the next year. Her four-year-old season was not spectacular, but it wasn't as uneven as her three-year-old campaign. She raced seven times, winning only once, against the boys in the six-furlong Phoenix Handicap at Keeneland, but she finished second in the Columbiana and Barbara Fritchie handicaps and third in the Ben Ali and Four Winds handicaps. Her only finish out of the money came in her final start when she ran fifth in the Equipoise Mile over a sloppy Arlington Park strip. Once again Moccasin was sent to Claiborne, but this time for good. She had completed three years of racing with twenty-one starts, eleven victories, six placings, and earnings of $388,075. She had put together one of the most dominant seasons ever at two, and now she would have the chance to pass on that brilliance.

In the spring of 1968, Moccasin was bred to a fellow Horse of the Year, the great Round Table, who was foaled at Claiborne and had returned there to stand at stud. The result of that mating was Indian, who became a minor stakes winner —

Moccasin with her first foal, Indian, a stakes winner by Round Table.

not exactly the result Hancock had hoped for. Still, he sent her to Round Table again, and in 1971, she produced a bay colt named Apalachee. He had his mother's precocity, earning champion juvenile honors in both England and Ireland in 1973. In England he won the Observer Gold Cup at two and was third in the English Two Thousand Guineas at three, and in Ireland he won the Gladness Stakes at three. At stud Apalachee would sire fifty-seven stakes winners, including Canadian champions Dance for Donna and Lubicon; Oaklawn Handicap winner K One King; and Alabama Stakes winner Up the Apalachee.

Moccasin's next foal was the unplaced Tom Rolfe filly Aztec, but Aztec produced her own stakes winner, Toltec, a son of L'Emigrant. After Aztec, Moccasin foaled two more colts, the first, Nantequos (by Tom Rolfe), who won the Whitehall Stakes in Ireland and the Chula Vista Handicap in California; the second, Brahms (by Round Table), captured the Railway Stakes in Ireland.

In 1978 Moccasin produced her second champion, Belted Earl, a chestnut son of Damascus. Racing in England and Ireland, Belted Earl won four of six races, including the 1981 Desmond Stakes and 1982 Greenlands Stakes, both in Ireland, and was named champion sprinter and champion older horse in that country. Then came two stakes-winning fillies. Scuff, by Forli, won three minor stakes but produced the grade II winner Ebros (by Mr. Prospector). Flippers, Moccasin's final foal, was a 1981 daughter of Belmont winner Coastal. She won the Golden Rod, Pleasant Hill, and Pocahontas stakes, all at Churchill Downs, and ran second in the Alcibiades and Monmouth Oaks. As a broodmare, Flippers produced the Santa Anita Oaks winner Hail Atlantis (by Seattle Slew), who, in turn, is the dam of stakes winner Stormy Atlantic and Mr. Katowice. Helstra, a winning daughter of Hail Atlantis, produced 2003 Puerto Rican multiple stakes winner Dr Arbatach.

After two consecutive barren seasons, Moccasin was pensioned in 1983 at the age of twenty, while her daughter Flippers was still a two-year-old in training. On July 1, 1986, Moccasin was euthanized due to the infirmities of old age and laid to rest in the Marchmont cemetery at Claiborne Farm.

Seven years after Moccasin's Horse of the Year season, the great Secretariat became the first two-year-old to earn that title outright, and twenty-five more years would pass before Favorite Trick received the title in 1997 for his undefeated juvenile season. But no other two-year-old filly, even the immortal Ruffian, can claim Moccasin's feat. She stands alone, still way out in front.

by Judy L. Marchman

<table>
<tr><td rowspan="7">Nantallah, 1953</td><td rowspan="4">Nasrullah, 1940</td><td rowspan="2">Nearco, 1935</td><td>Pharos, 1920</td><td>Phalaris
Scapa Flow</td></tr>
<tr><td>Nogara, 1928</td><td>Havresac II
Catnip</td></tr>
<tr><td rowspan="2">Mumtaz Begum, 1932</td><td>Blenheim II, 1927</td><td>Blandford
Malva</td></tr>
<tr><td>Mumtaz Mahal, 1921</td><td>The Tetrarch
Lady Josephine</td></tr>
<tr><td rowspan="4">Shimmer, 1945</td><td rowspan="2">Flares, 1933</td><td>Gallant Fox, 1927</td><td>Sir Gallahad III
Marguerite</td></tr>
<tr><td>Flambino, 1924</td><td>Wrack
Flambette</td></tr>
<tr><td rowspan="2">Broad Ripple, 1934</td><td>Stimulus, 1922</td><td>Ultimus
Hurakan</td></tr>
<tr><td rowspan="2">MOCCASIN</td><td>Hocus Pocus, 1928</td><td>Sir Gallahad III
Hazzaza</td></tr>
<tr><td rowspan="4">Gold Bridge, 1929</td><td rowspan="2">Golden Boss, 1920</td><td>The Boss, 1910</td><td>Orby
Southern Cross</td></tr>
<tr><td rowspan="7">Rough Shod II, 1944</td><td>Golden Hen, 1901</td><td>Chevele d'Or
Hazlehen</td></tr>
<tr><td rowspan="2">Flying Diadem, 1923</td><td>Diadumenos, 1910</td><td>Orby
Donnetta</td></tr>
<tr><td>Flying Bridge, 1911</td><td>Bridge of Canny
Gadfly</td></tr>
<tr><td rowspan="4">Dalmary, 1931</td><td rowspan="2">Blandford, 1919</td><td>Swynford, 1907</td><td>John o' Gaunt
Canterbury Pilgrim</td></tr>
<tr><td>Blanche, 1912</td><td>White Eagle
Black Cherry</td></tr>
<tr><td rowspan="2">Simon's Shoes, 1914</td><td>Simon Square, 1904</td><td>St. Simon
Sweet Marjorie</td></tr>
<tr><td>Goody Two-Shoes, 1899</td><td>Isinglass
Sandal</td></tr>
</table>

All Along

(1983)

In 1974 Nelson Bunker Hunt's great filly Dahlia pioneered a new era in international racing that reached an apex nine years later with All Along. Trained in France by Maurice Zilber, Dahlia had come to America the year before and annihilated her competition in the Washington, D.C., International at Laurel. The International, conceived by Laurel president John D. Schapiro in 1952, provided the only opportunity for racing fans in the United States to see their horses compete against stars from all over the world.

But that all changed in '74 when Dahlia crossed the Atlantic again to embark on a fall campaign consisting of the

All Along at Longchamp.

Man o' War Stakes at Belmont Park, the Canadian International Championship at Woodbine, and a return visit to Laurel for the International. She won the first two before losing the International to French longshot Admetus in a race in which the dawdling pace victimized her. As a result of her unprecedented accomplishment of winning two of the three big fall North American turf stakes, she became the first European-based runner to be voted champion American grass horse since the category was inaugurated in 1953.

Dahlia's feat opened the floodgates for a massive European influx over the next ten years during which European invaders Youth, Trillion, and April Run took home Eclipse Awards. Two others, Snow Knight and Perrault, captured Eclipse Awards the year after arriving and remaining to train in America. Another, Exceller, did not win a championship but became a major star in this country on both grass and dirt.

But Americans had seen only the tip of the iceberg. In 1983 the entire iceberg came crashing ashore in the form of a 16-hand, bay filly, bred in France, named All Along, who not only turned in one of the most remarkable strings of victories in racing history but also managed to strip away the title of grass horse to become the first European to be voted America's Horse of the Year. And she did it by defeating the best horses in Europe in the Prix de l'Arc de Triomphe in France and then journeying to North America, where she won the Rothmans International (formerly the Canadian International) at Woodbine, the Turf Classic at Aqueduct, and the Washington, D.C., International. And she did it all in the span of forty-two

Women of the 1980s

Sandra Day O'Connor in 1981 becomes the first woman to sit on the U.S. Supreme Court...Geraldine Ferraro is named Walter Mondale's vice presidential running mate in 1984. This is the first time a major American political party has nominated a woman for the vice presidency...Women earn almost 30 percent of all Ph.Ds awarded in the United States...In 1983 Sally Ride becomes the first U.S. woman astronaut in space as a crew member aboard *Challenger*...More than 600 women enter the first all-female triathlon (swim-bike-run) in California.

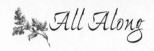

days. By winning all three races, she also earned a one million dollar bonus initiated by the host tracks.

By the end of 1983, All Along had become the most popular French female to grace the shores of America since Brigitte Bardot. And her timing was perfect, coming in between the great John Henry's 1981 and 1984 Horse of the Year campaigns. Old John was still trying to bounce back from the previous fall's ill-fated trip to the Japan Cup when All Along arrived to fill the void temporarily.

Daniel Wildenstein.

Americans were well aware of All Along's owner, Paris art dealer Daniel Wildenstein, who, along with Dahlia's owner, Nelson Bunker Hunt, dominated the international racing scene in the 1970s. Wildenstein had campaigned classic-winning fillies such as Allez France, Pawneese, Flying Water, and Madelia with trainer Angel Penna. But All Along's trainer, thirty-one-year-old Patrick-Louis Biancone, was a name they had never heard before.

In France, Biancone had become a man to be reckoned with. He burst on the racing scene in 1981, winning the Prix du Jockey-Club (French Derby) with Bikala at the unheard of age of twenty-nine. Americans would not have been quite so shocked at the young trainer's brazen attempt to sweep North America's three big fall turf stakes after winning the Arc had they known of his background and spirit of adventure. After becoming the European amateur champion rider in 1973 at age twenty-one, the third-generation horseman packed his bags and headed for the United States, where he went to work for LeRoy Jolley, trainer of 1975 Kentucky Derby winner Foolish Pleasure and later 1980 Derby winner Genuine Risk. The two years he spent with Jolley gave Biancone a feel for American racing and its emphasis on speed.

After winning the French

Derby with Bikala, Biancone was approached by Wildenstein, who was interested in purchasing one of his promising two-year-olds, Dear Patrick. The two hit if off, and after the close of the European flat season in December, Wildenstein sent Biancone four two-year-olds he had with Maurice Zilber, who had announced he was retiring from training. Biancone was already familiar with one of the four two-year-olds, a big, strapping daughter of the Round Table stallion Targowice named All Along, who had been bred by Wildenstein.

The sire had been chosen specifically for All Along's dam. According to Wildenstein in an interview with the *Thoroughbred Record*, "At the time, we had been feeling very strongly about

All Along traveled to Japan for the Japan Cup.

doing a certain type of inbreeding, matching the female line of the sire with the male line of the mare, and we tried to bring at least one or two bloodlines very close to each other. This has worked on Pawneese; it has worked on All Along; it has worked on quite a few others, but in this case here, we already had Abala, a half sister to All Along who had already shown some promise, who is bred along the same lines. This is one of the reasons we went to another Round Table colt. As a matter of fact, looking back at the family, we noticed that the only nick that has worked with the family is with the Round Tables."

All Along's dam, Agujita, won the Prix de Royaumont, and was a half sister to the classic-placed Autre Prince, second in the Prix Royal-Oak (French St. Leger). Her second dam, Argosy, was an unplaced daughter of the Hyperion stallion Coastal Traffic, out of a Prince Rose mare. The female family was a bit short on class until it stretched back to the great racing mare Brulette, the fifth dam of All Along. In England, Brulette won the Oaks, the Goodwood Cup, and the Jockey Club Gold Cup. In France she added the Prix du Cadran, which is the French version of the Ascot Gold Cup.

A month before joining Biancone, on November 10, All Along had dead-heated for a win with one of Biancone's fillies, Tarbelissima, in a maiden race at the tiny provincial track of Amiens, hardly the spawning ground of champions.

The Wildenstein stable, like the majority of stables in Europe, doesn't get going until March or April. But Biancone found a mile and a quarter race at Saint-Cloud in February that was perfect for All Along. "It was something we call a fake maiden race in France," Biancone recalled. "The race was for maidens and horses who hadn't earned a certain amount of money, let's say five thousand dollars. Being she dead-heated, she had to split the prize money and that qualified her for this race."

Biancone knew this was an unconventional spot, but he also knew he had to find a race for All Along. Earlier he had worked her in company with Tarbelissima to see how the two would fare again, and he was shocked when All Along beat her by ten lengths. "We may have something here," he thought.

He called Wildenstein and told him of his wish to run All Along at Saint-Cloud even though it was so early in the year. "If you think we should run, let's run," Wildenstein said. "Should I come for the race?"

"Sure, you should come; it shouldn't be any problem to win that race," Biancone answered.

When All Along won eased up by four lengths, no one realized at the time just whom she had beaten. Finishing second was a filly named Zalataia, who would go on to become a major stakes winner in France and the United States, eventually defeating John Henry in the 1983 Oak Tree Invitational Handicap, one day after All Along's victory in the D.C. International.

Finishing third at Saint-Cloud was Magic and Magic, trained by none other than Biancone's father, Pierre, for whom Biancone had worked prior to becoming a trainer.

A month after the Saint-Cloud race, Biancone ran All Along in the group III Prix Penelope, a mile and five-sixteenths race, also run at Saint-Cloud. Once again she drew off to win by four lengths, becoming the early favorite for the Prix de Diane (French Oaks). But All Along did have one Achilles heel, and that was deep, heavy ground. When the turf for the group I Prix Saint-Alary at Longchamp came up very soft, All Along, sent off as the 7-10 favorite, suffered her first defeat, settling for second behind the good filly Harbour.

Biancone, never one to train by conventional methods, decided to try for the English Oaks at Epsom only thirteen days later. With the great French rider Yves St. Martin replacing Biancone's apprentice rider, Serge Gorli, All Along was taken to the back of the pack, then made a brief move two furlongs out before fading to sixth, beaten almost six lengths by Time Charter. A heavy downpour earlier in the day hadn't helped her chances, and when she came out of the race in excellent shape Biancone and Wildenstein decided to take a chance and run her right back in the French Oaks eight days later. The same maneuver had proved successful for Wildenstein in 1976, when he won the English and French Oaks in the span of nine days with Pawneese.

But once again All Along was confronted with a soft course, and she could do no better than fifth. Following the French Oaks, she finally found good ground and defeated the colts in the group II Prix Maurice de Nieuil at Saint-Cloud, then came back after a two-month freshening to win the group I Prix Vermeille at Longchamp. That would be the last time she would ever run in a race for fillies. Her next stop was the Arc de Triomphe, which proved to be a disaster when she struggled home in fifteenth over very deep going.

The adventurous Biancone wasn't done yet. With the Arc taking so little out of her, he shipped All Along to Japan for the second running of the Japan Cup, and the first to which European horses were invited. When she struck the front in the stretch, she looked like a sure winner until her rider, Gary Moore, misjudged the finish line. He dropped his hands, easing up on the reins, and was nailed in the final strides by the American horse, Half Iced.

"It was frustrating," Biancone said. "But she ran a big race, and in this sport, you lose a lot more than you win, so you have to accept the defeats."

Wildenstein decided to keep All Along in training at four, and Biancone gave her the winter and spring off with the intention of having a fresh horse for the fall. But, as Biancone said, "(This) is when the headaches started."

No matter what he tried, he couldn't get All Along to return to form. "I mean she was a pain," he said. "For whatever reason, she was no good all spring. It happens sometimes with fillies. They just won't get in form."

He finally managed to get her ready for a race in June, entering her in the mile and a half La Coupe, a group III race at Chantilly. Carrying top weight of 127 pounds, she was sent off as the 6-5 favorite and finished third behind Zalataia. She followed that with a dismal seventh-place finish in the group I Grand Prix de Saint-Cloud.

By now Biancone was at his wit's end, and he began to doubt whether the filly would ever get back in form. He sent her to Deauville, the summer resort track on the Norman coast of France, and just let her unwind, jogging on the beach.

"We tried everything to get her mind back on racing, but she continued to work poorly," Biancone said. "It's not that she was difficult to train. She actually was very easy to train. She was the sweetest horse you'll ever meet in your life and was lovely to be around. The problem we had with her all spring was that she just wouldn't work fast. There was no halfway with her. She was either in great form or not in form at all, so it was always easy to tell how she was doing. She wouldn't do her job unless she was feeling perfect."

Biancone knew he had to run her in the group III Prix Foy at Longchamp on September 11 if she was going to make the Arc. He scheduled one final work for her, and she worked terribly. Biancone, watching with a friend of his, turned to him and said, "She just doesn't want to come back in form, and I'm not going to run her on Sunday in the Foy and look stupid."

All Along's career looked to be all but over. Then, on the Thursday before the Foy, a sudden transformation took place, and just like that she was back to her old self. "That morning she was a different horse," Biancone said. "Overnight her coat began to shine, and she started to perk up."

In the Foy she was blocked in the stretch, and jockey Freddy Head had to snatch her up and steer her to the outside. She closed liked a bullet but wound up second to Time Charter, beaten three-quarters of a length.

This had been her first race all year in which she was in form, and Biancone knew he would have a fresh horse for the big fall races. He already began thinking of the new bonus being offered in America and felt All Along would have a shot to sweep the three races if she ran big in the Arc.

After the Foy the Arc mount on All Along was in high demand. Head was to remain aboard, but while he and Biancone were in the jockey's room following the Foy, legendary British rider Lester Piggott approached Biancone and told him he wanted to ride All Along in the Arc.

"At the time, Piggott had a contract with Mr. Wildenstein to ride all his horses in England who were stabled with Henry Cecil," Biancone said. "I only had four or five for him. I went to dinner with Mr. Wildenstein and he said, 'Piggott wants to ride the mare in the Arc. What do you want to do?' I told him he has a contract with him, and he said, 'Well, if he wants to ride her, we better let him ride her.'

"I told Freddy I was sorry, but we have a contract with Lester and he's getting the mount. As it turned out, Sheikh Mohammed (bin Rashid al Maktoum of Dubai) was getting really big at the time and he offered Lester a large sum of money to ride Awaasif (who had finished third in the previous year's Arc). So, five days before the race, Lester dropped us to ride Awaasif. Freddy Head had already committed to ride Lovely Dancer, and here we are with no jockey."

Wildenstein was so upset he said Piggott would never again ride any of his horses. Cash Asmussen was already booked to ride Welsh Term, while veteran Joe Mercer remained loyal to Sailor's Dance, even though he was only in the race as a pace-setter for English Oaks winner Sun Princess. Biancone then thought of twenty-two-year-old Walter Swinburn, who at the age of nineteen had ridden Bikala for him. That same year, Swinburn made a big name for himself as the rider of the great Shergar. Also, his father, Wally, had ridden for Biancone's father

All Along winning the Arc de Triomphe in her native France.

in France. So, Biancone called Swinburn and offered him the mount on All Along. The match would prove perfect.

At first, however, things didn't look so promising when All Along drew post twenty-four. The morning of the race Biancone and Swinburn watched the tapes of the past six runnings of the Arc and concluded that Swinburn had to make his way to the inside and save ground as long as possible.

All Along broke cleanly, and Swinburn steered her toward the inside, taking up a position near the rear of the pack. Sailor's Dance did his job, cutting out the pace for seven furlongs, then gave way to Sun Princess, who led as they turned into the stretch. Paul Mellon's hard-knocking Diamond Shoal and King George VI and Queen Elizabeth Stakes winner Time Charter were in hot pursuit, with All Along still far back, waiting for an opening.

When the English horse Seymour Hicks drifted off the rail, Swinburn seized the opportunity and began his move up the inside. Diamond Shoal had dropped out of it, leaving Sun Princess, Time Charter, and

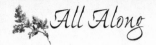

Walter Swinburn guiding All Along to victory in the Rothmans International.

Stanerra to battle it out. All Along was flying but needed something to open up in front of her. Just as Sun Princess kicked for home, All Along charged between her and a tiring Stanerra and shot through to win by a length. Her time of 2:28 over firm going was one-tenth of a second off the course record set by Detroit in the 1980 Arc.

After the Arc, Biancone told Wildenstein about his plan to try for the one-million-dollar bonus in North America. "I said she had come in form so late she should be able to hold her form for a while," Biancone recalled. "I told him if we go to Woodbine and we're beaten, we're beaten and the bonus is gone. But if we should win, the second leg should have a smaller field because of a $30,000 supplementary fee and might be easier. The third leg is an invitation, so that will be harder, but it's worth trying. Mr. Wildenstein was a great sportsman, and he said, 'Sure, let's try it; we have nothing to lose.' "

So, All Along embarked on her journey to conquer North America. At Woodbine ten opponents awaited her for the mile and five-eighths Rothmans International. The public bet her down to 8-5 favorite, with her main threat at 3-1 being Majesty's Prince, winner of the previous year's Rothmans and of the 1983 Man o' War Stakes and Sword Dancer Handicap. Also getting played at 5-1 was Nijinsky's Secret, who had scored in three major turf stakes in the United States and Canada before finishing a close third behind England's Tolomeo and John Henry in the Arlington Million. Fellow French invader Escaline, who had finished far up the track in the Arc, also was at 5-1. Others in the field were 1982 Rothmans runner-up Thunder Puddles, '82 Japan Cup winner Half Iced, and Arlington Handicap winner Palikaraki from the powerful Charlie Whittingham stable.

The only thing that worried Biancone was the weather. A week of rain had softened the turf considerably, but many regard Woodbine's turf course to be the best in North America, and when the sun shone brightly the day before the race the course dried enough for it to be labeled yielding.

Half Iced set a crawling pace for three-quarters, with fractions of :25 1/5, :51 1/5, and 1:16. Nijinsky's Secret put pressure on him all the way, with Thunder Puddles right behind. Swinburn had All Along back in tenth early, about ten lengths off the pace. He moved up steadily but felt the going was a bit too soft for the filly. The first time past the grandstand he moved out and found a firmer path. He continued to make progress around the far turn and moved up to fourth at the quarter pole, while still keeping his filly on that same path out toward the middle of the course. Once in the stretch she turned it on and led by a length and a half when she hit the eighth pole. Swinburn, knowing the ambitious schedule still ahead of her, took her under wraps and won in hand by two lengths over Thunder Puddles and the late-closing Majesty's Prince. Even under no pressure, she still came home her final eighth in :12 2/5.

With the low-profile Wildenstein remaining in France, his son Alec represented him at Woodbine. After the race Alec called his father, who had been at Longchamp earlier in the day watching his promising young star, Sagace, win the Prix du Conseil de Paris. Alec announced that All Along would be retired at the end of the year and bred to Great Nephew, a top stallion in England.

The day following the Rothmans, All Along was shipped to Belmont Park, where she took up residence in trainer Angel Penna's barn. The Turf Classic turned out to be as easy as Biancone had thought, even though a field of ten was entered. Her main threat looked to be the Charlie Whittingham-trained Erins Isle, winner of the Hollywood Invitational Handicap, San Juan Capistrano Invitational Handicap, and San Luis Rey Stakes, and second in the Man o' War Stakes. Rothmans runner-up Thunder Puddles was back for another try, along with Chem, winner of the Laurel Turf Cup, and Late Act, winner of the Louisiana Downs Handicap.

The only thing working against All Along, once again, was the turf course. Several days of rain had softened the course, but it was listed as yielding on race day. But yielding in this country in no way resembles some of the bog-like conditions she'd faced in Europe.

Longshot Sprink shot out to a clear lead early, but unlike her race in the Rothmans, All Along had "run" on her mind, and Swinburn let her settle in third, about six lengths off the pace. After fractions of :25 and

A win in the Turf Classic at Aqueduct added to All Along's fame.

:49 4/5, Sprink's jockey, Frank Lovato Jr., tried slowing the pace to a crawl. He got away with six furlongs in a snail-like 1:14 4/5, but Thunder Puddles, who had been tracking him in second, roared right on by and opened a length lead as they entered the far turn. Swinburn followed and was only a length and a half off the lead. Erins Isle also was making up ground.

Thunder Puddles tried to hold on desperately as All Along cruised up alongside nearing the quarter pole, but the filly totally outclassed him and quickly opened a clear lead. With Swinburn merely along for the ride, All Along opened a four-length lead at the eighth pole, then continued to draw away with every stride, as if she were in a workout. At the wire she was eight and three-quarters lengths in front, with Thunder Puddles holding off Erins Isle for second.

So far everything had gone exactly as Biancone had planned. The Turf Classic was a mere stroll in the park, and All Along came out of the race in excellent shape. She had held her coat well, and now it was on to the D.C. International to complete the unprecedented sweep.

All Along had become the darling of American racing fans. In a year that saw a forgettable Triple Crown won by three different horses — Sunny's Halo, Deputed Testamony, and Caveat — fans once again had a hero to follow. John Henry was still the marquee name, but the old gelding was attempting to return to form, having had only three starts at that point in '83.

Biancone sent All Along to Laurel, but as the race grew closer he could tell she was beginning to lose her form again. His only hope was that her class would get her through the final race.

"She was cooked," Biancone said. "But when an athlete looks unbeatable and has the opponents believing they can't beat you, they most often don't. We came to the race, and everybody was sure she was going to win — the owner was sure, the jockey was sure, and the groom was sure. The only one not sure was me. I know my horses, and I could see the pep was gone. She had done a lot of traveling and just wasn't herself. Fortunately, I was the only one to know that. But she was there, she was on a roll, and she had to keep going."

Biancone had no idea what to expect. After saddling All Along, he decided not to go up to the box, instead choosing to stand by the rail so he wouldn't be able to see most of the race.

"I was too nervous to watch the race," he said. "When my horses feel good, I feel good. When they don't feel tip-top, I don't feel that good. Everybody thought I was confident, because I was watching the race near the winner's circle. But they didn't know the real reason."

For the third straight time the course came up yielding after two days of intermittent rain. Fortunately, the rain stopped the night before the race, and cold winds and sunny skies Saturday morning helped dry out the course.

All Along went to the post the overwhelming 2-5 favorite against seven opponents. Majesty's Prince had returned after his third in the Rothmans,

Patrick Biancone and All Along after the Washington, D.C., International.

All Along and her filly by Dancing Brave.

as had Palikaraki, who finished fifth at Woodbine. The French-trained Welsh Term was persistent, coming back for more after finishing eighth at Woodbine and fourth at Aqueduct. Legitimate contenders from Europe posed new threats for All Along. Cormorant Wood, ridden by Steve Cauthen, was coming off a victory in the group I Champion Stakes at Newmarket, and Give Thanks had won the Irish Oaks. Also entered was C.V. Whitney's Hush Dear, who had beaten colts in the Tidal Handicap, then captured the Diana and Long Island handicaps.

With no speed in the race, the field bunched up immediately after the break, with seven lengths separating the first and last horse. Lovely Dancer set the early pace, with All Along back in sixth. After a half in :51 4/5, Welsh Term joined Lovely Dancer on the lead, with All Along creeping forward, now less than three lengths behind the leaders.

Down the backstretch Swinburn found himself in danger of being boxed. He decided he'd have none of this nonsense and let All Along roll. He broke out of the pack and charged to the lead nearing the half-mile pole. By the quarter pole she was already more than three lengths clear of the field and just kept pouring it on. At the eighth pole she was six in front, and the crowd was already standing and cheering. Swinburn could feel her tiring slightly and waved the whip at her, while vigorously hand-riding her the final furlong. All Along cocked her ears as she hit the wire three and a quarter lengths in front of Welsh Term. "Her class saw her through," Swinburn said afterward. "She's the equal of Shergar."

After the race a relieved Biancone greeted his champion, knowing how close she had come to losing her form, which had begun to show in the final furlong. Alec Wildenstein accepted the trophy, then discussed All Along's future with Biancone before flying back to France. The following morning Biancone announced she would remain in training as a five-year-old, with her ultimate goal being the inaugural Breeders' Cup Turf at Hollywood Park.

By winning all three races and the million-dollar bonus, All Along increased her career earnings to $2,441,955, making her the fourth-leading money winner of all time behind John Henry, Spectacular Bid, and the Venezuelan filly Trinycarol.

The coup had been completed. All Along had conquered America like no other European before her, and her accomplishments were rewarded with Eclipse Awards as the leading female turf horse and the big one, Horse of the Year. She had become the first female Horse of the Year since 1965 when Moccasin (who was given the award by the Thoroughbred Racing Associations) shared the honor with the traditional *Daily Racing Form/Morning Telegraph* selection, Roman Brother.

All Along began to feel the effects of her forty-two days of glory after she returned home to Chantilly. "When she came back to France, she laid down in her stall and slept for two straight days," Biancone said. "She just got up to eat and drink, then laid back down and went to sleep. It was like she was so happy to be back home in her own bed."

Biancone returned to the States that winter for the Eclipse Awards dinner and told everyone, "It can only happen in America that a foreign horse and an unknown French trainer can win the sport's greatest honor."

The road back for All Along was a long one. Once again she wouldn't return to form. Because the Breeders' Cup in November was the main goal, Biancone did not run her all spring and summer. In a brazen move, even for him, he brought her back to the races in the Turf Classic on September 22, more than ten months after her victory at Laurel, against a rejuvenated John Henry, who at the age of nine was having his greatest year ever. A mere shell of the filly America had seen a year earlier, All Along made a brief bid before finishing fourth to John Henry. But getting beaten only four and a quarter lengths by John Henry after such a long layoff certainly was no disgrace.

She returned to France for the Arc de Triomphe two weeks

ALL ALONG	Targowice, 1970	Round Table, 1954	Princequillo, 1940	**Prince Rose**, 1928	**Rose Prince** **Indolence**
				Cosquilla, 1933	Papyrus Quick Thought
			Knight's Daughter, 1941	Sir Cosmo, 1926	The Boss Ayn Hali
				Feola, 1933	Friar Marcus Aloe
		Matriarch, 1964	Bold Ruler, 1954	Nasrullah, 1940	Nearco Mumtaz Begum
				Miss Disco, 1944	Discovery Outdone
			Lyceum, 1948	Bull Lea, 1935	Bull Dog Rose Leaves
				Colosseum, 1937	Ariel Arena
	Agujita, 1966	Vieux Manoir, 1947	Brantome, 1931	Blandford, 1919	Swynford Blanche
				Vitamine, 1924	Clarissimus Viridiflora
			Vieille Maison, 1936	Finglas, 1923	Bruleur Fair Simone
				Vieille Canaille, 1930	Zionist Ficelle
		Argosy, 1950	Coastal Traffic, 1941	Hyperion, 1930	Gainsborough Selene
				Rose of England, 1927	Teddy Perce-Neige
			Prosodie, 1942	**Prince Rose**, 1928	**Rose Prince** **Indolence**
				Protein, 1936	Manna Brulette

later, but the ground was like a bog, and she ran a gutsy race to struggle home third behind her stablemate, Sagace, who was Europe's new king. Back across the Atlantic she came two weeks later for the Rothmans, her third overseas journey in a month. She rallied from far back to finish fourth, two and a quarter lengths behind Majesty's Prince, whom she had handled so easily on two occasions the year before. It was three weeks to the Breeders' Cup, and Biancone felt, despite the extensive traveling in a short period of time, she was just now returning to form.

He named Angel Cordero Jr. to ride All Along in the Breeders' Cup. Cordero, one of America's greatest jockeys, was an aggressive rider but was much more proficient in dirt races. He made a premature move from seventh and hit the front before they even reached the quarter pole. All Along continued on bravely, opening a length lead at the eighth pole, but despite running her final quarter in :24 flat, she was nailed right on the wire by 53-1 French invader, Lashkari.

All Along retired with nine victories in twenty-one starts, for earnings of $3,015,764, becoming the leading money-winning filly of all time. But it was her remarkable string of victories in the fall of 1983 that will remain etched in the memory as one of the greatest feats in the history of the sport.

All Along was sent to Three Chimneys Farm near Midway, Kentucky, to begin life as a broodmare.

All Along's first foal, Along All, by Mill Reef, won the group II Prix Greffulhe and group III Prix des Chenes and was second in the group I Grand Criterium. Her second foal, Allez Les Bleus, by Kris, produced the stakes-placed Golden Allez; and her third foal, All Dancing, by Dancing Brave, produced Asolo, second in the group II German St. Leger and third in the group I Prix Royal-Oak (French St. Leger). Her 1995 foal, Arnaqueur, by Miswaki, was a stakes winner in France and placed in a pair of group races.

At twenty-four, All Along was retired as a broodmare in November 2003 after producing thirteen foals.

Alec Wildenstein, whose father died in 2001 at age eighty-four, said of her retirement, "She was truly one of the great ones. My brother Guy and I appreciate the fine home Three Chimneys will provide her for the rest of her days. She deserves nothing less."

Biancone, who eventually left France to train in Hong Kong, returned to America to stay in 2000 and has become one of the nation's leading trainers. "I went to visit All Along last year and she looked great," he said. "She doesn't look her age at all. I remember I used to call her 'Cheval de Fer,' the Iron Horse. What can I say about her? She was, and still is, a truly remarkable filly."

by Steve Haskin

Lady's Secret

(1986)

Lady's Secret had done her part, turning in a dominating performance to win the one-million dollar Breeders' Cup Distaff with consummate ease and strengthening her candidacy for North American Horse of the Year for 1986. Now all that owner Eugene Klein and trainer D. Wayne Lukas could do was wait and see how the other leading contenders for racing's top honor would perform later that afternoon in the Breeders' Cup Classic. The Classic was the three-million-dollar finale of an event inaugurated at Hollywood Park in 1984 and held in 1986 for the first time at nearby Santa Anita Park in the Los Angeles suburb of Arcadia.

In the weeks that had led up to

Lady's Secret at Santa Anita.

the Breeders' Cup, Lukas talked with his son and chief assistant, Jeff, about possibly running Lady's Secret in the Classic. Victory in that race, where she would face the other Horse of the Year contenders, Turkoman and Precisionist, would assure her the title. She had held her own against males earlier in the year, though the Classic would be a tougher test.

The Distaff made more sense, even if the Lukases and Klein left it to someone else to upset Turkoman and Precisionist. "We need to win impressively," the elder Lukas said, "then sit back, watch the Classic, and hope." Interestingly, Pat Day, who rode Lady's Secret to her two and a half-length victory in the Distaff, would be aboard Turkoman, a long-striding son of Alydar.

Lukas' plan worked. Coming off a narrow loss to Crème Fraiche in the Jockey Club Gold Cup and, before that, posting a powerful victory over Precisionist in the Marlboro Cup Handicap, Turkoman unleashed a furious stretch rally in the Classic, but longshot Skywalker had stolen away from the field on the final turn and opened up an insurmountable lead. Precisionist, the previous year's sprint champion, showed his customary early speed but couldn't keep pace with Skywalker when it counted. Skywalker and Laffit Pincay won by a length and a quarter over Turkoman, the 8-5 favorite, with second betting choice Precisionist and Gary Stevens another length and a quarter back in third.

When the dust cleared from the Classic, there was no disputing that Lady's Secret deserved to wear the crown as Horse of the Year. She had earned it, winning a remarkable ten of fifteen starts, with three seconds, two thirds, and earnings of $1,871,053.

Though she continued to race in 1987, her Horse of the Year season was her finest. In 1986 she competed at five different tracks from California to New York, car-

Women of the 1980s

The Guerrilla Girls, a group of anonymous women activists fighting for gender and racial equality, is formed in reaction to discrimination in the art world...U.S. Supreme Court upholds affirmative action as a remedy for past job discrimination...Florence Griffith Joyner sets a world record in the 200-meter sprint at the 1988 Olympics.

ried a steadying 129 pounds while winning the Ruffian Handicap by eight lengths, and raced against males four times, never finishing worse than third and scoring a convincing win against the boys in the Whitney Handicap at Saratoga. All but two of her starts that season were against grade I company. Her nickname, the "Iron Lady," was well deserved.

But it would be a few years before the small filly, who was foaled in 1982, would realize her full potential, and the right team would come together to help her realize it.

In 1983 two heart attacks helped convince Eugene Klein, a former car salesman who owned the NFL's San Diego Chargers, to sell the team. He decided to invest in the Thoroughbred business instead, eventually selling the Chargers in 1984. Klein was as high-strung as a young Thoroughbred and wanted immediate action. He wasn't interested in buying mares and waiting for their foals to grow up and become racehorses. Klein hooked up with Lukas, the former Quarter Horse trainer whose increasingly strong stable was all about action; it had several divisions throughout the country, well stocked with expensive yearlings from the Keeneland and Saratoga sales. Klein received $50 million for selling the Chargers and spent that much or more at Thoroughbred auctions over the next several years. It got him the action he wanted.

Klein also purchased a small farm in the exclusive enclave of Rancho Santa Fe, just north of San Diego. He had an idyllic vision of watching young Thoroughbreds romping in the fields just outside his house while enjoying breakfast or lunch.

He called Lukas and asked him to buy a couple of foals and ship them to the farm. But Lukas tried to talk him out of it.

"The farm was on a pile of rocks, with a few avocado trees on the hills," Lukas remembered. "I told him, 'Gene, you'd be better off with mountain goats. It's too rocky for horses.' "

"I'm serious, Wayne," Klein insisted. "I want some babies."

Lukas had three young horses on the ranch he owned in Norman, Oklahoma, including a gray daughter of Secretariat out of the Icecapade mare Great Lady M. The pint-sized filly would later be named Lady's Secret. "Let me have them appraised," Lukas told Klein. "No, you just tell me what you think they're worth," Klein responded.

"I'll take $200,000 apiece," Lukas said. A deal was struck. In addition to Lady's Secret, Klein got a yearling daughter of What a Pleasure he named Gene's Lady. She won fourteen of eighty-nine starts, including ten stakes races, for Klein, earning $946,190. "He did pretty well in that deal," Lukas recalled, "though the third horse was a colt who died before he ever raced."

Jeff and Wayne Lukas.

Lukas had purchased the three horses from breeder Bob Spreen, a client from the trainer's Quarter Horse days who made the transition to Thoroughbreds with Lukas in the late 1970s. (By 1982, Spreen, a retired Cadillac dealer from the Southern California town of Downey, had decided to get out of the horse business.)

Lukas bought Great Lady M. for Spreen in the summer of 1978 — Lukas' first year of training Thoroughbreds exclusively. She caught Lukas' eye one morning at Atlantic City racecourse when he was there to saddle a turf runner named Effervescing — his first big horse — in the United Nations Handicap. He saw something he liked in Great Lady M., who earlier that year was running for a $35,000 claiming tag. Lukas sent Effervescing's co-owner, bloodstock agent Albert Yank, to the filly's barn to see if she was for sale. Yank came back with an affirmative answer, but Lukas was stunned that the price had nearly doubled. "You've got yourself a filly," Yank told him. "Write a check for $65,000."

"But she was running for $35,000 claiming," Lukas said.

"Wayne, it's the American way," Yank replied. "A little for me. A little for the groom. A little for everyone."

Lukas wrote the check, then shipped Great Lady M. to California, where she became one of the stars of his growing stable. The next year Great Lady M. gave Lukas his first Santa Anita Park stakes victory when she won the La Brea Stakes.

The year Lukas acquired her for Spreen, Great Lady M. ran in twenty races, winning five of them. In 1979 she raced nineteen times, winning four, and in 1980, as a five-year-old, she had fifteen starts, with another four victories. She won seven stakes races during her career and earned $332,008. Produced from the Young Emperor mare Sovereign Lady, Great Lady M. was a pure sprinter, never winning beyond seven furlongs. Lukas liked her heart and her desire to win. "She really laid it down when she raced," he remembered. She was also sound, running a total of fifty-eight times. "She passed on a lot of her soundness and toughness to Lady's Secret," Lukas said.

Though relatively new to Thoroughbreds, Lukas had developed some opinions about breeding. One of them involved Secretariat, the 1973 Triple Crown winner and two-time Horse of the Year who was at stud at Claiborne Farm near Paris, Kentucky.

"I thought Secretariat should be bred to fast horses," he said. "When his first foals hit the ground, he was not that precocious of a sire. My theory was they were breeding him to too many classic-type mares. I thought you had to breed him to speed."

Trained by Lukas, Terlingua, a lightning-fast filly who years later would produce champion sire Storm Cat, was a daughter of Secretariat out of Crimson Saint. "Crimson Saint was the fastest mare in the world," Lukas said.

Secretariat, of course, embodied speed, having scorched his way through the Triple Crown, highlighted by his thirty-one-length win in the Belmont Stakes in record time. He also set a track record in the Kentucky Derby, and though not credited with a record in the Preakness because of a teletimer malfunction, *Daily Racing Form* clockers were convinced his final time set a new mark.

Secretariat began his stud career in 1974, retiring as one of the greatest racehorses of all time and with a record syndication price and lofty expectations. His sire, Bold Ruler, led the general sire list on eight occasions while at Claiborne, and young Seth Hancock, who not long before had taken over running the farm after the death of his father, A.B. "Bull" Hancock Jr., put together a sensational group of mares to which Big Red would be bred. Secretariat, however, did not set the world on fire at stud. He never was able to measure up to his racetrack success.

When Great Lady M. was retired in 1981, Lukas recommended that Spreen breed her to

Secretariat. After she was confirmed in foal, Great Lady M. was sent to Lukas' farm in Oklahoma, where she gave birth to Lady's Secret on April 8, 1982.

Lady's Secret was small as a foal and as a racehorse; so small that when she began her racing career Lukas thought he might get lucky if he could develop her into a minor stakes winner.

Stabled with Jeff Lukas in New York, Lady's Secret made her racing debut on May 21, 1984, at Belmont Park. Sent off the 7-5 favorite and ridden by Angel Cordero Jr., she went right to the front and led throughout but was caught in deep stretch by Bonnie's Axe. Placing judges couldn't separate the two fillies and declared the race a dead-heat. That was the crowning achievement for Bonnie's Axe, who raced just one more time, finishing fifth.

For Lady's Secret it was only the beginning.

Competing against stakes company in her next start, Lady's Secret showed early speed but tired in the stretch to finish fifth in the Astoria at Belmont. Wayne Lukas then shipped her west, the first of many cross-country flights. Once again Lady's Secret forced the early pace but couldn't get a clear lead, tiring in the stretch to be fourth in the Landaluce Stakes, a grade III event at Hollywood Park named in honor of the unbeaten Lukas-trained filly who died near the end of her juvenile season in 1982.

Lukas then found a much easier spot, a restricted stakes named the Wavy Waves at Hollywood Park. Lady's Secret jumped out to an early lead, controlled the pace, and won clear by a length and a half, marking the first of her twenty-two stakes victories.

Lady's Secret raced four more times that year, winning her final start, the Moccasin Stakes at Hollywood Park on November 9. Lukas kept her out of the inaugural Breeders' Cup, thinking he had two better fillies for Klein, Fiesta Lady and Tiltalating, both of whom finished off the board in the Juvenile Fillies. Fran's Valentine finished first in the one-mile race but was disqualified and placed tenth after jockey Pat Valenzuela swung her out sharply at the top of the stretch, interfering with another runner in the race. The victory went to Outstandingly, who was named the two-year-old filly champion of 1984. Both Fran's Valentine and Outstandingly had enduring quality. Two years later in Lady's Secret's tour de force in the

Distaff, the two fillies finished second and third, respectively, behind the champ.

A few days after the Breeders' Cup, Great Lady M. was entered in the Keeneland November breeding stock sale, where she was consigned by Hurstland Farm and purchased for $2.7 million by Michael Stavola. Not bad for a former $35,000 claimer...and Lady's Secret, Great Lady M.'s first foal, had not yet realized her full potential.

Klein's racing stable jelled in 1984, soaring from less than $400,000 in purses won in 1983 to about $2.25 million. He and his wife, Joyce, were partners in the stable — though there was

Owner Eugene Klein leads Lady's Secret to the winner's circle.

never any doubt about who made the decisions — and they ranked third among all North American owners in purses won in 1984. That didn't include their co-ownership with Melvin Hatley of Life's Magic, who with her selection as 1984 champion three-year-old filly gave the Kleins their first Eclipse Award.

Lukas, meanwhile, enjoyed his best season yet in 1984, winning $5.8 million in purses and leading North American trainers in that category for the second year in a row. Before his reign at the top was over, the former Quarter Horse conditioner who earlier coached high school and college basketball in his native Wisconsin, would win ten consecutive money titles.

For both Klein and Lukas, the best was yet to come. And Lady's Secret was to play a big part.

Still concerned with her small size — she stood 15.1 hands and weighed 950 pounds — Lukas sent Lady's Secret to Bay Meadows in northern California to begin her 1985 campaign. She romped by four lengths in a minor stakes race on January 5 — the Hail Hilarious — so Lukas wheeled her right back a week later at the same track, but this time against colts at the same six-furlong distance. Never able to get a clear lead, Lady's Secret lost by a neck to the very good colt Bedside Promise, who went on to become a grade I winner and earner of nearly a million dollars.

Lady's Secret made two more starts in California that winter, losing both, then was sent east, stopping first at Oaklawn Park in Arkansas, where she won the Prima Donna Stakes by five lengths, going six furlongs. She then settled in with Jeff Lukas in New York, where she remained from April till October.

She had mixed success at first, finishing second in the Prioress, a grade III sprint in late April at Aqueduct and then being thoroughly outrun in the Comely, a grade III race at Belmont Park in which she was fourth, beaten eleven lengths by winner Mom's Command. It was Lady's Secret's worst finish since being thrashed by the top-class Folk Art going a mile and one-sixteenth the previous autumn at Santa Anita in the grade I Oak Leaf Stakes.

The Lukases then found a trio of easy spots at six furlongs to give Lady's Secret a boost in confidence. She won by daylight in all three races, the Bowl of Flowers at Belmont; the Regret Handicap at Monmouth Park in New Jersey; and the Rose at Belmont. None of the races were graded stakes, although the latter two were against older fillies and mares, and Lady's Secret was odds-on to win each one. Nevertheless, when the Saratoga season began, Lady's Secret was sitting on a three-race win streak and booming with confidence.

Mom's Command, a Top Command filly bred and owned by Peter Fuller and ridden by his daughter Abigail, was the clear-cut division leader after sweeping four big stakes at Belmont Park, including the series some referred to as the fillies triple crown — the Acorn Stakes, Mother Goose Stakes, and Coaching Club American Oaks. The CCA Oaks was run at a mile and a half in July. Mom's Command's next start would be at a much shorter distance, the seven furlongs of the Test Stakes at Saratoga on August 1. Lady's Secret also was being pointed for the Test, a grade II race that often served as a prep for Saratoga's grade I Alabama Stakes at a mile and a quarter. The Alabama was Mom's Command's major objective at Saratoga, but the Lukases decided Lady's Secret wasn't ready to go that distance and decided not to nominate her. Mom's Command would go on to win the Alabama.

Ridden by Jorge Velasquez, one of eight jockeys to partner with Lady's Secret to this point in her career, the gray filly showed a different dimension in the Test, allowing Mom's Command and another speedster, Majestic Folly, to duel on the front, while biding her time in fourth, a few lengths off the lead. Velasquez put Lady's Secret in gear on the turn for home, and she rallied to defeat Mom's Command by two lengths, completing seven furlongs on a good Saratoga track in 1:21 3/5. While thrilled with Lady's Secret's performance, Jeff Lukas said there were no plans to stretch her out beyond seven furlongs.

Eight days later, this time with Don MacBeth in the saddle, Lady's Secret took on older fillies and mares in the seven-furlong, grade II Ballerina Stakes. Once again she sat just off the early lead and rallied in the stretch to defeat Mrs. Revere by a nose in a very game effort. Now, Jeff Lukas said he was tempted to stretch the filly out, in the one-mile Maskette Stakes at Belmont, a grade I race for fillies and mares, three and up.

Reunited with Velasquez, Lady's Secret toyed with her seven opponents in the Maskette, going straight to the lead and clicking off rapid fractions of :22 2/5, :44 4/5, and 1:09 1/5 en route to a final clocking of 1:34 4/5. She opened up a four-length advantage at the top of the stretch and hit the wire five and a half lengths to the good of Dowery. As a three-year-old, she only had to carry 111 pounds.

Suddenly, the three-year-old filly championship many had conceded to Mom's Command was up for grabs. Jeff Lukas certainly felt the race was on. "We beat Mom's Command once," he told *The Blood-Horse*. "Maybe we can do it again."

Lady's Secret and Mom's Command were pointed toward Belmont's Rare Perfume Stakes for three-year-old fillies at one mile. Unfortunately, Mom's Command wrenched an ankle that led to her retirement and ended any chance of a rematch with Lady's Secret.

The Lukases switched gears after the injury and decided to stretch Lady's Secret out to nine furlongs, this time in the September 22 Ruffian Handicap, a grade I fixture that attracted several of the also-rans from the Maskette but also featured Lady's Secret's stablemate, Life's Magic, the reigning three-year-old filly champion. Lady's Secret romped again, taking the field wire to wire and winning by four lengths under 116 pounds, with Life's Magic a dull fourth in what was her sixth loss in a row. On the other hand, with seven consecutive victories, Lady's Secret was becoming the talk of the racing world.

With the 1985 Breeders' Cup scheduled at Aqueduct on November 2, Lady's Secret would have one more New York prep before going postward in the Distaff as part of an entry with Life's Magic and Alabama Nana. That final prep, the Beldame at Belmont, was a grade I race over the same mile and a quarter distance that the Breeders' Cup Distaff was then run (it was shortened to nine furlongs in 1988).

Once again Velasquez merely engaged cruise control. Lady's Secret was turning into a front-running machine, and in the Beldame she sizzled the first half-mile in :45 4/5 to gain a clear lead, then coasted around the expansive Belmont oval, winning by two lengths and covering the distance in 2:03 3/5. She carried 118 pounds and won as the 3-5 favorite.

Despite the eight-race winning streak for Lady's Secret and a seven-race losing streak for Life's Magic, Jeff Lukas was gaining confidence in Life's Magic as Breeders' Cup Day approached. Life's Magic had finished second in her final Breeders' Cup prep, the grade I Spinster at Keeneland.

Arriving from the West Coast, Wayne Lukas was stunned to see the wonderful condition the leggy Cox's Ridge filly was in. "Here it is November and she has dapples on her," the elder Lukas said.

But they also thought highly of the little gray Secretariat filly. In fact, they nearly entered Lady's Secret in the Classic. "We held out her (entry) card until one minute to nine o'clock, entry closing time," Wayne Lukas told *The Blood-Horse* in 1985. "Jeff and I went into a back room and had a last-minute summit meeting before we entered in the Distaff. We were thinking about rain, which was in the forecast, and we thought if it came up rain, Lady's Secret had a chance to win it all. She's a superior mud runner, and sending her on the lead in the mud would have horrified those colts, I thought."

Rain failed to materialize, however, though the 1985 Breeders' Cup was contested on a cold and blustery day at Aqueduct, a track that hosted the event only on this one occasion.

November 2, 1985, was a day to remember for Jeff and Wayne Lukas and Eugene and Joyce Klein. In the day's second race, the Juvenile Fillies, the Lukas-trained, Klein-owned duo of Twilight Ridge and Family Style ran first and second, earning $675,000 of the million-dollar purse.

Lukas and Klein pulled off another one-two finish in the Distaff, with the third member of the entry, the L.D. Mathis-owned Alabama Nana finishing fourth for Lukas. But it was Life's Magic getting first money over Lady's Secret, and it was no contest.

Velasquez took Lady's Secret out to an easy early lead, opening up five lengths early and recording fractions of :23 2/5, :46 4/5, and 1:11 2/5. But Aqueduct on Breeders' Cup day was no front-runner's paradise. All of the races run over the main track went to horses coming from off the pace, highlighted by Proud Truth's last-to-first victory in the Classic. Life's Magic also was the early trailer in the seven-horse Distaff line-up. She then made a strong move on the far turn, looping the field and taking dead aim on Lady's Secret. She took the lead from her stablemate at the top of the stretch and drew off under Angel Cordero Jr., winning by six and a quarter lengths. Lady's Secret held second by three lengths over California invader Dontstop Themusic, the second choice in the wagering.

After the race co-owner Klein

made a pitch for Life's Magic to win the Eclipse Award as top older filly or mare, despite a record of two wins from thirteen starts. Lukas, meanwhile, lobbied for Lady's Secret. Lukas said: "Lady's Secret I still consider to be the best three-year-old in training, period."

Eclipse Award voters gave Life's Magic the nod for her second consecutive championship. However, on the strength of her summer campaign, Mom's Command was voted three-year-old filly champion of 1985 over Lady's Secret. Both Lukas and the Kleins won Eclipse Awards as champion trainer and owner, respectively. It was the beginning of a three-year run for both parties in Eclipse Award voting. Family Style gave the Kleins a second Eclipse Award winner for 1985 as champion two-year-old filly.

Lukas and the Kleins topped the money list, too. Lukas became the first trainer to reach ten million dollars in earnings, finishing the year at $11,155,188 with a stable that had several divisions and made 1,140 starts during the course of the year. The Kleins won $5,451,201, far out-

Lady's Secret wins the Molly Pitcher.

distancing the $3.7 million won by Dennis Diaz' Hunter Farm, which campaigned Kentucky Derby winner Spend a Buck, who had a $2.6-million payday when he won the Jersey Derby — $600,000 in prize money and a $2-million bonus for winning a series of races in New Jersey along with the Kentucky Derby. Spend a Buck was voted champion three-year-old male and Horse of the Year despite being retired in late summer and not contesting the Breeders' Cup.

Lady's Secret had begun her three-year-old season modestly, shipped to Northern California for an easy spot in stakes company. She finished the year with an impressive ten wins from seventeen starts, with five seconds, and earnings of $994,349. Her previous year's earnings of $92,823 pushed her into the millionaire category. But the Iron Lady was just getting warmed up.

Lady's Secret had one additional start in 1985, the December 27, grade III La Brea Stakes at seven furlongs at Santa Anita. It was the opening race of the La Canada series that continued with the grade III El Encino Stakes in January and ended with the grade I La Canada in February. Lady's Secret was beaten a half-length in the La Brea by Savannah Slew, a filly owned by another relatively new owner, Allen Paulson. Paulson would go on to become the leading owner by money won in Breeders' Cup history.

But Lady's Secret had no problems in the mile and one-sixteenth El Encino or mile and one-eighth La Canada, racing to wire-to-wire victories in both. Chris McCarron rode Lady's Secret in all three races, but she was reunited with New York-based Velasquez when she won the Santa Margarita Handicap, the grade I race that serves as Santa Anita's winter championship event for fillies and mares. She wired the field over the nine furlongs, winning by two and three-quarters lengths. McCarron had opted to ride another filly in the Santa Margarita, Love Smitten, who wound up a well-beaten seventh. His reasoning was that Lady's Secret would be going east after the Santa Anita meeting, and he wanted to stay with a filly that he thought could win some big races in California.

Velasquez felt Lady's Secret was even better than she was during her 1985 winning streak. "Usually a horse hits a peak and then starts to descend," he told *The Blood-Horse* after the Santa Margarita. "But she just gets better and better."

Lady's Secret defeats males in the historic Whitney Handicap.

McCarron got a measure of revenge when trainer Eddie Gregson shipped Love Smitten to Oaklawn Park for the Apple Blossom Handicap, a grade I race on April 16 at a mile and one-sixteenth. Under the handicap conditions, Lady's Secret carried 127 pounds — two more than in the Santa Margarita. Love Smitten got in with a 119-pound assignment and got the perfect trip under McCarron, tracking Lady's Secret from the outset, taking a narrow advantage at the top of the stretch, and just outlasting her to win by a neck.

"Can you imagine a little filly carrying that much weight so successfully?" Velasquez said afterward. "The eight-pound difference beat Lady's Secret."

It was then on to New York for Lady's Secret, but this time there would be no confidence builders. In her eleven races during the remainder of the year, all but one were against grade I company, the exception being the grade II Molly Pitcher Handicap at Monmouth Park.

In the mile and one-sixteenth Shuvee Handicap at Belmont Park on May 17, the gray filly faced five others, including Claiborne Farm's Alydar filly Endear and the stakes winner Ride Sally. Away from the gate with customary quickness, Lady's Secret, ridden for the first time by Pat Day, led at every call to win by three and a half lengths over Endear.

Her facile victory convinced Lukas and Klein to test her against males in the Metropolitan Handicap nine days later. This bold move marked a pattern throughout the spring and summer in which Lukas, hoping to advance Lady's Secret's bid for Horse of the Year, would pit his star against males in stern handicap tests.

Lady's Secret was assigned 120 pounds for her Metropolitan engagement and faced seven rivals, including favored Turkoman, himself in the race for Horse of the Year. Lady's Secret led at the half and sustained her advantage into the stretch, when she was overtaken by Garthorn, who equaled the second-fastest running of the Metropolitan Mile and stretched his win streak to five. Love That Mac got a scant nose in front of the filly to finish second.

Lady's Secret barely had time to catch her breath when Lukas entered her in the June 8 Hempstead Handicap. Top-weighted at 128 pounds, she faced four others including her foes from the Shuvee, Endear and Ride Sally. Her high impost after her recent taxing effort in the Metropolitan possibly conspired to undermine her chances, for Endear overtook Lady's Secret at the top of the stretch to win the grade I event by an impressive six lengths.

A trip to the Jersey Shore for the Fourth of July weekend proved just the tonic for the muscular daughter of Secretariat. Stepping down to grade II status in the Molly Pitcher Handicap, Lady's Secret had no trouble in this race, grabbing the lead at the start and widening her margin at every call. She completed the mile and one-sixteenth in 1:41 1/5 and easily defeated Chaldea by six and a quarter lengths.

As Lady's Secret's popularity soared, Lukas plotted a busy schedule for his star. On August 2, Lady's Secret again took on older males, this time in the venerated Whitney Handicap at Saratoga. The field of seven included tough campaigners Ends Well, Skip Trial, King's Swan, and Cutlass Reality. Summer downpours had turned the track sloppy, but Lady's Secret paid no heed, skimming over the surface in her usual front-running fashion. She held off all challengers through the mile and one-eighth contest, crossing the wire four and a half lengths in front of Ends Well. Lady's Secret became the first female to win the Whitney since Gallorette in 1948.

Two weeks later Lady's Secret returned to Monmouth Park for the grade I Philip H. Iselin Handicap. Again the lone female in the field, Lady's Secret confronted her toughest competitor in Fred Hooper's champion Precisionist, who had won the Breeders' Cup Sprint at Aqueduct the previous year. However, it was longshot Roo Art who beat them both on a sloppy track. Ironically, though, Lady's Secret outsprinted the champion sprinter through the first three quarters and only gave way grudgingly in the final furlongs.

On August 30, Lady's Secret again faced her Iselin foe Precisionist, this time in the storied Woodward Stakes at Belmont. Precisionist had developed beyond mere sprinting dimensions during 1986 and had become regarded as perhaps the country's finest handicap horse. So the Woodward signaled a meeting between the best of both genders.

Getting off to her usual fast start, Lady's Secret led most of the way under Angel Cordero Jr., blazing a mile in 1:33 4/5. Chris McCarron was forced to go wide on Precisionist to avoid the tiring inside lane, and in an impressive display passed the stubborn Lady's Secret in the stretch. Precisionist drew off by four and three-quarters lengths, a margin that renewed debate about who should win Horse of the Year honors.

Despite her August exertions Lukas did not slacken the schedule for Lady's Secret. A week after her Woodward effort she returned in the Maskette Stakes, carrying 125 pounds. She won by seven lengths and completed the mile in 1:33 2/5, the fastest mile ever run at Belmont Park by a filly or mare. The Maskette marked her twentieth victory and pushed her earnings above $2 million.

Fifteen days later, Lady's Secret sealed her reputation as one of the best fillies ever with a devastating eight-length victory in the Ruffian Handicap at Belmont. Under 129 pounds, her highest impost, Lady's Secret set brisk early fractions and completed the mile and one-eighth in stakes-record time of 1:45 3/5.

"They ought to bronze Lady's Secret and put her right next to her daddy [Secretariat] in the paddock," an ebullient Lukas told the *New York Times*. "She just takes your breath away. She is mind boggling."

In the Beldame Stakes three weeks later, Lady's Secret completed her second consecutive sweep of Belmont's fall filly triple. This time, however, she showed little of her usual verve and style, managing to hold off the moderately regarded Coup de Fusil by just a half-length. Perhaps the Beldame's mile and a quarter exceeded the comfort zone of this brilliant miler. In any case, tenacity earned Lady's Secret the victory.

"She's a very competitive horse," regular rider Day told the *New York Times* afterward. "When the other horse came running behind us, she just dug in."

As October waned, debate raged in earnest about Horse of the Year candidates. Fred Hooper, owner of Precisionist, noted that his horse twice had finished ahead of Lady's Secret. Turkoman's trainer, Gary Jones, acknowledged Lady's Secret's superiority among her gender, but claimed she couldn't beat good colts. Jeff Lukas, meanwhile, argued that Lady's Secret's record spoke for itself.

Indeed as Breeders' Cup Day dawned November 1 at Santa Anita, the Lukases and Klein felt inordinately confident about their filly's chances both in the Distaff and in the larger race for Horse of the Year. Santa Anita, after all, had been the

Lady's Secret winning the Breeders' Cup Distaff.

scene of the filly's three consecutive stakes victories early in 1986.

With nearly 70,000 people watching, Lady's Secret took command of the Distaff from the start, getting the six furlongs in 1:10 and the mile in 1:34 4/5. She completed the mile and a quarter in 2:01 1/5 under regular rider Day while not fully extended. In her wake trailed Fran's Valentine, the disqualified winner of the inaugural 1984 Breeders' Cup Juvenile Fillies, and Outstandingly, the champion juvenile filly of 1984.

"She's the best that ever ran," Klein said after his filly's two and a half length victory. "There is no other Horse of the Year."

Added Lukas: "The Horse of the Year has to do something extraordinary. This filly has won the Fall Triple in New York two years running. She ran the fastest mile ever by a filly or mare at Belmont in the Maskette, then two weeks later carried 129 pounds to a stakes in the Ruffian. She raced in five stakes records during a seven-week period in August and September. Ask the handicap division to try that on for size."

Jockey Day described her as the best horse he had ever ridden, calling her a "mark of consistency all year."

Lady's Secret's emphatic Distaff victory stood in contrast to the defeats of other Horse of the Year contenders Precisionist and Turkoman in the Classic. When the votes were counted, the filly was the unanimous choice.

Sadly, Lady's Secret did not retain her form in 1987 and critics chastised Lukas and Klein for not retiring the Iron Lady after her Horse of the Year season.

In her first start as a five-year-old, in Gulfstream Park's Donn Handicap against males, Lady's Secret led early then stopped, finishing more than thirty-two lengths behind the winner. Lukas gave her three months off, then brought her back in an allowance race at Monmouth, her first allowance race ever. She won, then finished second in the Molly Pitcher before returning seventeen days later to capture another allowance race — her last victory.

Chris McCarron flew in from California to ride Lady's Secret in an August 10 allowance race at Saratoga, and admiring fans sent the gray off at 3-10. She broke first, but, shockingly, Lady's Secret bolted to the outside fence as she headed into the first turn and refused to run. McCarron pulled her up.

"She acted like she wanted to go back to the barn instead of being on the track," a shaken

McCarron was quoted as saying.

The New York stewards ordered Lady's Secret to show she could negotiate a turn before they would allow her to race again in New York. Lukas, who had planned to run her in the John A. Morris Handicap, announced her retirement instead. Lady's Secret left racing on a career low note but in the record books nevertheless as the leading North American-based female earner with a bankroll of $3,021,325. In all she had won twenty-five of forty-five starts.

Lady's Secret was headed for the auction ring and provided the hook for Fasig-Tipton Company's inaugural Night of the Stars sale in November 1987. However, when bidding stalled at $5.4 million, Klein retained ownership. She returned for the same sale the following year, this time in foal to Alydar, but again was bought back. Her Alydar offspring, a filly, topped the 1990 Saratoga yearling sale at $1.5 million. Sent to Japan and named Machikane Aida, she was unplaced in one start.

As a broodmare, Lady's Secret, like many great race mares, failed to replicate her talent. In all she produced a dozen foals, but only

Lady's Secret and her 1995 Seattle Slew filly.

four winners. She died of complications after foaling her last offspring, a General Meeting colt in 2003. By then Lady's Secret was living in California after being purchased from the Fares Farm dispersal at Keeneland some years earlier by John and Kim Glenney.

Lady's Secret was inducted into racing's Hall of Fame in 1992. Her trainer, himself inducted in 1999, has saddled many a winner since Lady's Secret's glory days but none of such sustained brilliance.

"She was known as the Iron Lady," Lukas said. "It was a title she earned by showing up every day and by not dodging anyone. She was a fierce little filly, not big or imposing, just a true competitor, ready at the bell."

by Ray Paulick

LADY'S SECRET	Secretariat, 1970	Bold Ruler, 1954	**Nasrullah**, 1940	**Nearco**, 1935	**Pharos** **Nogara**
				Mumtaz Begum, 1932	Blenheim II Mumtaz Mahal
			Miss Disco, 1944	Discovery, 1931	Display Ariadne
				Outdone, 1936	Pompey Sweep Out
		Somethingroyal, 1952	Princequillo, 1940	Prince Rose, 1928	Rose Prince Indolence
				Cosquilla, 1933	Papyrus Quick Thought
			Imperatrice, 1938	Caruso, 1927	Polymelian Sweet Music
				Cinquepace, 1934	Brown Bud Assignation
	Great Lady M., 1975	Icecapade, 1969	Nearctic, 1954	**Nearco**, 1935	**Pharos** **Nogara**
				Lady Angela, 1944	Hyperion Sister Sarah
			Shenanigans, 1963	Native Dancer, 1950	Polynesian Geisha
				Bold Irish, 1948	Fighting Fox Erin
		Sovereign Lady, 1969	Young Emperor, 1963	Grey Sovereign, 1948	**Nasrullah** Kong
				Young Empress, 1957	Petition Jennifer
			Sweety Kid, 1963	Olympia, 1946	Heliopolis Miss Dolphin
				Trustworthy II, 1956	My Babu Implicit Trust

Azeri

(2002)

The rain had been falling, quite heavily at times, for several days, but not even that was a concern. The filly was doing too well to think otherwise. No longer was she that callow, sparely made individual of a summer ago. Instead, she had matured into a sleek, robust athlete. There was a confidence about her, too, a quiet but unmistakable cool that had been collecting for weeks and weeks. As she stood alone in her stall, just hours shy of the foremost race of her young career, she exuded nothing but positive energy.

A no-name just a year earlier, she had become an overnight sensation, astonishing even those closest to her. She had not lost in several months, a spell that saw

Azeri at Churchill Downs.

her pile up a half-dozen stakes with consummate ease. This one, though — the $2-million Distaff at the Breeders' Cup World Thoroughbred Championships — would be the true test.

Despite her recent outright dominance, naysayers were not yet convinced of her ability. Some pundits thought she'd been beating up on small fields and the same ordinary rivals out west. Still others were pointing to California's tracks, claiming they were tailor-made for a horse of such innate speed. But how would Azeri fare, they asked, without a home-court advantage in unfamiliar weather against the toughest opponents she had seen all year long?

She answered decisively with a red-hot performance, a breathtaking display of excellence that went far beyond silencing her skeptics. On that brisk October day outside Chicago, Azeri's five-length runaway in the Breeders' Cup Distaff did more than certify her status as the best older female around. It climaxed a sensational campaign for the four-year-old chestnut, setting the stage for her coronation as North America's 2002 Horse of the Year.

Not since Lady's Secret in 1986 had the accolade gone to a female Thoroughbred, a surprise considering the fifteen-year interval featured some of the finest fillies and mares ever. Always, though, they were trumped by one of their male counterparts, be it a top handicap competitor or a battle-proven three-year-old. During the late eighties, for example, Personal Ensign ran thirteen races — mainly grade I stakes — and won every one of them, capping her impeccable career with a dramatic triumph in the 1988 Breeders' Cup Distaff. Still, she was overshadowed by Alysheba, whose big effort in the Breeders' Cup Classic that same afternoon helped clinch the title as the '88 Horse of the Year.

Women of the 2000s

Hillary Clinton becomes the only first lady to be elected to public office, as a U.S. senator from New York...CBS Broadcasting agrees to pay $8 million to settle a sex discrimination lawsuit by the E.E.O.C. on behalf of 200 women...A seventh grader, 12-year-old Michelle Wie, is the youngest player to qualify for an LPGA event.

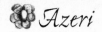

The incredible Argentine mare Bayakoa ran the table the following year, capturing seven grade I events throughout the land. By comparison, Sunday Silence won just five, but they included the Kentucky Derby, Preakness Stakes, and Breeders' Cup Classic. He was named 1989's Horse of the Year. In 1991 three-year-old Dance Smartly turned in a historic campaign, first overpowering males in a sweep of Canada's Triple Crown then invading Kentucky to take the Breeders' Cup Distaff. Dance Smartly ended her season undefeated. Black Tie Affair, the Breeders' Cup Classic winner, ended up with Horse of the Year.

Paseana, like Bayakoa a product of Argentina, dominated her division in 1992, taking five consecutive grade Is and later the Breeders' Cup Distaff. But it was not enough to outshine Horse of the Year A.P. Indy, whose résumé included the Santa Anita Derby, Belmont Stakes, and Breeders' Cup Classic. Inside Information was clearly the country's top distaffer in 1995, the very year Cigar went ten for ten and won Horse of the Year by a landslide.

Azeri, likewise, was simply stellar during her championship season. Her solid nine-race program in 2002 measured up just as well to those of her predecessors. Few of them, though, ever came so far so fast. A filly of ordinary breeding and average looks, Azeri progressed by leaps and bounds, meeting each new challenge with the poise of a pro. What she lacked in bloodlines and beauty, she offset with perfect conformation and mechanics, intelligence, and natural speed. Around the barn she was known lovingly as "Honeybear," yet her laid-back attitude belied an iron will on the track. The ingredients combined to create a single, redoubtable running machine.

Lithe and agile, Azeri would bound across the dirt rhythmically, her elastic stride letting her cover ground with great efficiency. More often than not, her rivals plainly could not keep up. By the end of 2002, the daughter of Kentucky stallion Jade Hunter was demonstrably the nation's best filly. Her blowout at the Breeders' Cup culminated a skein of seven graded stakes victories, making her unanimous selection for an Eclipse Award as North America's top older female a mere formality. But what enabled her to earn the sport's ultimate honor was more a matter of circumstance than accomplishment. Azeri simply picked an opportune year to shine her brightest.

"Usually there is a horse in the male division that stands out, and that didn't happen. That's how she got Horse of the Year," explained Laura de Seroux, the trainer behind Azeri's remarkable run. "I'm not downplaying it. That's how it happened. Our perfect script worked out."

Not even the most creative writers in Hollywood, though, could have dreamt up a story quite like Azeri's. Her early years, it turned out, were largely uneventful. Like many of the standouts bred by Allen Paulson, including Eclipse Award champions Ajina, Eliza, Escena, and two-time Horse of the Year Cigar, Azeri grew up at Paulson's posh Brookside Farms in the bluegrass near Versailles, Kentucky. She was soon sent to Brookside Farms South, located near Ocala in Florida, to begin serious preparation for life on the track and before long joined a group of other Paulson runners in the southern California barn of trainer Simon Bray. Minor physical ailments, however — the expected growing pains of a developing racehorse — precluded Azeri from racing at age two and through much of her three-year-old season, as well.

In August 2001 Azeri and a handful of stablemates were removed from Bray's care and transferred to de Seroux. With Paulson's death the previous summer, his racing and breeding interests had become the property of a trust headed by his youngest son, Michael. To help smooth the transition, Michael Paulson had sought the advice of Emmanuel de Seroux, a renowned bloodstock agent whose ties to the Allen Paulson stable dated back to 1984. Michael Paulson's eventual decision to switch trainers put the young, unraced Azeri in the hands of de Seroux's wife, Laura.

A lifelong horse nut, Laura de Seroux had learned the game under the wing of the eminent trainer Charlie Whittingham. Years of international travel, scouring the globe for potential acquisitions with husband Emmanuel, had given her a keen eye for distinguishing top-class equine athletes. By her recollection, however, Azeri hardly merited a second glance that lazy day she first stepped off the van, and for good reason. She sported nothing in the way of achievement, unlike Astra and Startac, a pair of first-rate turf competitors also involved in the move. In appearance Azeri was somewhat reedy and plain — "She's no beauty," de Seroux once remarked

— with no distinctive features aside from a peculiar white splotch on her rump. And although she carried the Paulson influence, her family tree was by many standards blue-collar.

In terms of pedigree, Azeri was far from a throwaway, but she was certainly not a standout. Her sire, Jade Hunter, was a son of the legendary stud Mr. Prospector. He had been heavily supported by Allen Paulson, first as a racing prospect in the late eighties and then as a stallion, and had responded with decent results. On the track Jade Hunter was good enough to win a couple of major Florida stakes, the Donn and Gulfstream Park handicaps. His breeding career got off to a fast start, as well, and fittingly, most of his best runners, including grade I winners Yagli, Stuka, and Diazo, were Paulson homebreds.

His appeal had its limits, however. By the time Azeri made it into the de Seroux barn, Jade Hunter was no longer considered a fashionable option. His annual progeny earnings had been steadily diminishing, excluding him from the roster of the nation's most prominent sires. His $10,000 stud fee was pocket

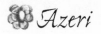

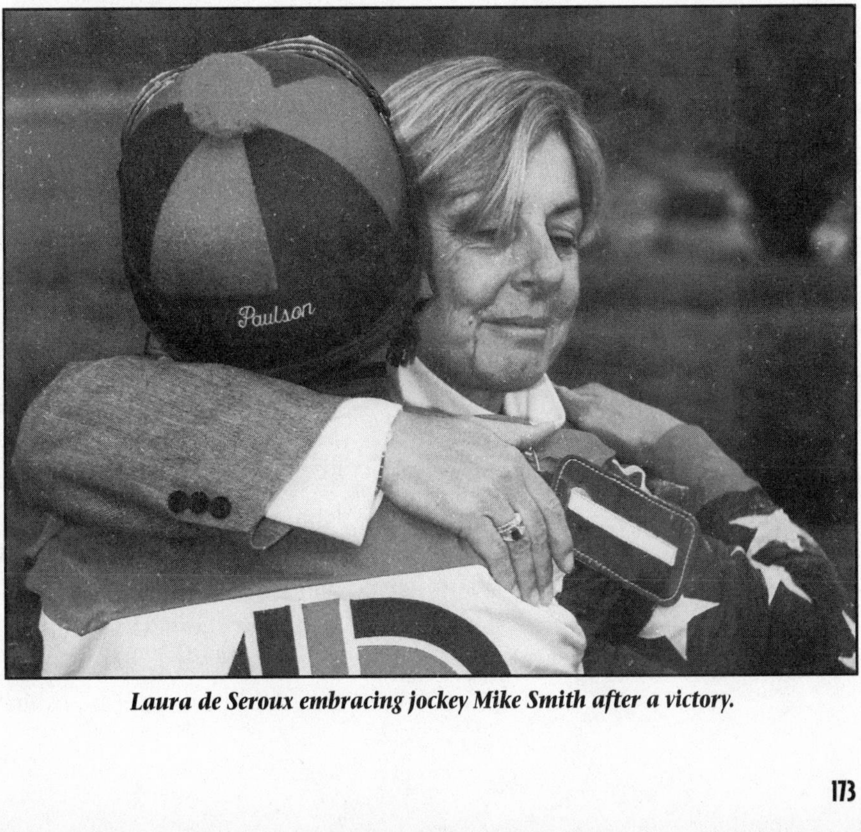

Laura de Seroux embracing jockey Mike Smith after a victory.

change compared to Kentucky peers such as Storm Cat ($500,000), A.P. Indy ($300,000), and Kingmambo ($200,000).

Azeri's maternal family wasn't anything to brag about, either. Zodiac Miss, her dam, had been a fair racehorse in Australia before Paulson brought her to California in 1993. She ran exclusively on grass throughout her career, never once beyond a sprint, and upon joining Paulson's high-profile band of broodmares showed more misfortune than promise. Her first foal, like Azeri a daughter of Jade Hunter, died in infancy. Zodiac Miss herself was killed alongside a newborn Theatrical filly when the pair were struck by lightning in 1999. Of her two remaining offspring, her only colt, a son of Paulson's French import Blushing John, never made it to the races. The other was Azeri.

As far as first impressions go, Azeri didn't make much of one, at least not to de Seroux. Azeri had shown up without reputation, just a modest three-year-old filly scheduled to be offered at a Keeneland auction that fall. It was just a matter of days, however, before de Seroux caught her first glimpse of Azeri's greatness.

De Seroux's training operation was more or less a spin-off of Narvick International, the successful worldwide bloodstock enterprise she and Emmanuel had headed for a decade and a half. When de Seroux finally established her stable in 1999, she set up shop at San Luis Rey Downs Training Center in the northern San Diego County town of Bonsall. Compared to the high-stress and often crowded backstretch environments of typical racetracks, San Luis Rey was basically a horse haven, ideal for the mental and physical stability of competitive Thoroughbreds.

"This is our little slice of heaven," de Seroux once said. San Luis Rey's low horse population and first-class feel gave it the look of a private training facility. Upon Azeri's arrival, the de Seroux barn itself boasted amenities galore, from its spacious tow ring and sand pens to the bevy of palm trees overlooking it all. An offshore breeze, steadily flowing in from the nearby Pacific Ocean, only added to the ambience.

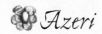

Into this serene atmosphere walked Azeri that August day back in 2001. De Seroux would later admit to curiosity as she watched the filly take her first spin around San Luis Rey's one-mile track the next morning. It had been an easy exercise, designed to give de Seroux a line on the Paulson stock. But Azeri's smooth motion had definitely caught her attention. When the filly came back days later and zipped through a routine half-mile workout, dusting a defenseless stablemate in the process, de Seroux need no further convincing — Azeri was for real.

About two months later the filly finally made her debut. It looked to be a nondescript weekday race at Santa Anita, pitting Azeri against eight fellow maidens at a distance of six furlongs. Clearly, no one else was in on the secret — at least not yet — for she left the starting gate a 17-1 outsider. Members of the de Seroux team, though, including Nuno Santos, Azeri's morning exercise rider, and stable foreman Dagmar Sykora, bet with both fists at the windows. They figured Azeri was a mortal lock to win. They were not disappointed.

A quick start put Azeri in a front-running duel up the backstretch and around the turn, resulting in a rapid half-mile of :43 2/5. That split alone would have exhausted a horse of lesser quality. Azeri, however, pushed right on through the heat, taking control under her own steam. Her lead only expanded through the stretch, eventually reaching six lengths as she galloped across the finish. Despite token encouragement from her jockey, Mike Smith, Azeri was still clocked in 1:08 4/5, demonstrating tremendous spark for a filly of such inexperience. It was a performance that foreshadowed a bright future. According to her trainer it also opened a world of tempting options.

"I had to exercise restraint not to jump her into a stake. That's how excited we were about her," de Seroux remembered. "I had to do it right and develop her."

Her next two outings were more of the same. Rather than ask Azeri to do too much too soon, de Seroux instead brought her along at a textbook pace. Azeri stepped up a level in her second start, easily taking a six and a half-furlong allowance at Hollywood Park. Because of her pedigree and conformation, it was thought that she would have little trouble stretching out around two turns, and she got her chance to prove it in her third race. The kickoff to her four-year-old campaign came in January 2002, when Azeri met five others going a mile at Santa Anita. As expected, she passed the test with flying colors, rushing to the lead with a quarter-mile to run before coasting in untouched.

Her progression could not have been any smoother. In the span of less than three months, Azeri had gone from a total unknown to an unbeaten filly of boundless promise. She had won three straight, each race longer than the one before it, against increasingly tougher competition. After two sprints she had learned to relax and ration her speed going a mile. And she had done every bit of it effortlessly.

It was time for the acid test. Well before Azeri had completed her hat trick, de Seroux had designated Santa Anita's grade II La Canada Stakes to be the chestnut filly's stakes bow. Azeri had leapt each new hurdle so far, and the La Canada, a nine-furlong event solely for four-year-old fillies, was the next reasonable step. Like a piece in an intricate puzzle, the race was a perfect fit. Naturally, the opposition would be Azeri's most challenging yet, led by the versatile Affluent and eastern distance specialist Summer Colony. Azeri would be facing rivals her own age, though, on a familiar track, and given the strength of her victory at a mile, the La Canada's one additional furlong didn't figure to pose a problem. Azeri was sharp and on the upswing. The timing was optimal. The La Canada, contested

Azeri en route to a record third victory in Oaklawn Park's Apple Blossom.

on de Seroux's fiftieth birthday, seemed custom-made for a blockbuster effort.

And it was — for Summer Colony. For Azeri, what could have gone wrong pretty much did, and her trouble stemmed from a bad break. Leaving post position four, Azeri rapped her left hind leg against the gate, hard enough to open a gash on the inside of her hock. The sloppy start cost her dearly, forcing her to play catch-up the rest of the way. She nearly pulled it off. A wide move on the final turn still gave her a shot to catch Summer Colony in the stretch. The adversity, however, was too much to overcome. Summer Colony, a daughter of Preakness winner Summer Squall, had successfully ventured west to claim her sixth victory in a row. Azeri's attempt to run her down had fallen a length short. Her exertion that afternoon left her weary for several days.

"She tried so hard to win that race, to overcome being so far back," de Seroux later recalled. "I was worried for the first couple weeks because she backed off the feed tub and she laid down in her pen and really slept a lot. That was the first time she acted like a race took anything out of her."

A month later Azeri rebounded with authority. What de Seroux, Paulson, and Smith had envisioned prior to the La Canada instead played out splendidly in the grade I Santa Margarita Invitational Handicap. As Santa Anita's most prestigious race for older females, the Santa Margarita appears on the résumés of a host of champions through the years. None of them, though, managed to win it after just four starts. Not Two Lea or Silver Spoon. Not Susan's Girl or Glorious Song. Not even Horse of the Year honorees Busher or Lady's Secret.

Azeri's triumph in the Santa Margarita was a milestone. Among her beaten opponents were Spain, winner of the 2000 Breeders' Cup Distaff, and Printemps, twice a champion in Chile. More importantly, it commenced a streak that would see Azeri string together no less than eleven graded stakes wins. Over the next year and a half, she would grow to become one of the most talked-about and admired Thoroughbreds in the world. Her emergence as a divisional force was meteoric, causing hardboots to shake their heads in disbelief. Racehorses in general, they knew, do not evolve with such acceleration.

But Azeri did. Nevertheless, her

breakthrough in the mile and one-eighth Santa Margarita was not picture perfect. As in her three previous races, Azeri's immaturity continued to manifest itself at the starting gate, where again, a somewhat clumsy beginning gave the rest first run at the lead. Unlike her early position in the La Canada, though, Azeri soon settled into a cozy spot along the rail and just off the pace. Rounding the far turn, Smith sent her after the leaders, and Azeri eventually wore down Spain passing the eighth pole. Striding powerfully away, she went on to win by three lengths. Within that final furlong, a star was born.

If the Santa Margarita legitimized Azeri as one of the most exciting prospects in the country, then the grade I Apple Blossom Handicap proved she could take her show on the road. The Apple Blossom was actually an afterthought, for de Seroux's original game plan had the filly taking a brief rest following the Santa Margarita. Azeri, however, gave her trainer every reason to keep pushing on. She had emerged from the race in full bloom, far from the wilt she had displayed in the days after the La Canada. It

Owner Michael Paulson with his champion.

was enough to earn Azeri an April trip east to Oaklawn Park in Arkansas.

In the mile and one-sixteenth Apple Blossom her competition again included Spain and Affluent, and her start was about as bad as they come. Azeri's first step from the gate was, in fact, a delayed hop, spotting the leaders an advantage of several lengths. But it was only a minor obstacle. After just a half-mile, she had already dragged Smith back into contention, then moved in on pacesetters Miss Linda and Spain around the final turn. Azeri soon brushed them aside and won by a length and three-quarters. Affluent, a daughter of Triple Crown legend Affirmed and herself a grade I winner on both dirt and grass, closed from last to finish second.

The outcome would be repeated twice more back in southern California, though the manner of Azeri's midyear triumphs at Hollywood Park took most everyone by surprise. De Seroux and Smith both agreed that Azeri's foibles at the gate were the result of simple greenness. They also believed that she was only one good start away from putting all the pieces together. It finally happened in Hollywood's grade I Milady Breeders' Cup Handicap. Breaking without a hitch — at long last — Azeri dashed straight to the front and never looked back. By the time she had reached the quarter pole, her pursuers were spent just trying to stay close. Smith hardly moved a muscle the entire way. Azeri eased through the stretch all alone, beating the late-running Affluent again by three and a half lengths.

"There's no words in my vocabulary that can describe her," Smith admitted following the Milady. "She just seems to be getting better every time she runs."

Even the competition had to acknowledge her talent.

"My filly ran great. The other filly's just too much," conceded Eddie Delahoussaye, Affluent's jockey. "She might be somethin' special."

The grade I Vanity Handicap confirmed that sentiment four weeks later. At face value the nine-furlong Vanity was a duplicate of the Milady — a quick start, solid fractions, and utter domination. Despite a 125-pound impost, Azeri outran Affluent once more, this time by three. Only two others had ever racked up the Santa Margarita, Apple Blossom, Milady, and Vanity in a single year, but Bayakoa and

Paseana were older, hard-bitten veterans when they each turned the trick. Azeri completed the sweep as a growing four-year-old filly. By the summer of 2002, her talent seemed unlimited. How far it would take her remained to be seen. But one thing was obvious — speed had become Azeri's principal weapon.

"That's when I realized she was on her way to becoming unbeatable," remarked de Seroux. "That's when it became clear to me that they were cooked if they tried to go with her and they couldn't catch her if they left her alone. How are you going to beat that?"

No one had the answer. When fall arrived, bringing with it the Breeders' Cup, Azeri's roll had hit six and her morale was sky-high. That August she had shouldered 126 pounds like a feather, winning Del Mar's grade II Clement L. Hirsch Handicap for pure fun. Back at Santa Anita she had gotten a real character builder in the grade II Lady's Secret Breeders' Cup Handicap in October. Forced through blistering fractions, Azeri still repelled a pair of speedy challengers and demoralized the Lady's Secret field, all beneath 127 pounds.

Contributing to the cause was the blessing of an ideal schedule. Still in the midst of maturation, Azeri was pushed at a cautious pace in the months leading up to the Breeders' Cup. Though she had been competing regularly since November, three of her most important races — the Apple Blossom, Vanity, and Clement L. Hirsch — were followed by valuable periods of downtime at San Luis Rey. Where some might have been depleted by a grueling, coast-to-coast campaign, Azeri instead was allowed opportunities to regroup and strengthen. The benefit was immeasurable. When she finally settled in at Arlington Park in Chicago, the site of the nineteenth Breeders' Cup, she was at an absolute peak.

The grade I Distaff would be her defining moment. Azeri notwithstanding, the lineup for the race was choice. Leading three-year-olds Farda Amiga, Imperial Gesture, and Take Charge Lady all showed up at the top of their game. Among the older fillies, Mandy's Gold and Summer Colony sported the best credentials.

But more stood in Azeri's path than just a slew of all-stars. Numerous critics, thus far not impressed with Azeri's work, had voiced opinions that the nine-furlong Distaff would expose her vulnerability. During Breeders' Cup week the skies had been uncooperative, dumping enough water throughout northern Illinois to take the zip off of Arlington's track. The wet surface, doubters said, would likely be Azeri's undoing. Additionally, the presence of frontrunner Imperial Gesture almost ensured the race would develop at a rapid tempo, and some thought that in the face of extreme pressure, Azeri would crack. To Smith in particular, the Distaff was about respect.

"Oh, without a doubt. That was all I had on my mind," the jockey later said. "I didn't want her to win. I wanted her to annihilate 'em. It was like a statement I wanted to make with her."

De Seroux, too, recognized that the implications were great. Since the Vanity in June, she and the rest of her team, including assistants Jeff Ford and Alex Hassinger, had been keeping a focused eye on the progress of the country's chief colts and geldings. As the months passed, they saw no clear-cut national leader among the three-year-olds or in the handicap division.

This, therefore, left Horse of the Year honors up for grabs. With six straight graded stakes wins to her credit heading into the Breeders' Cup, Azeri already held a strong hand. Even to be considered for Horse of the Year, though, she would have to come through in the Distaff, and she'd have to do it with fireworks. That day Azeri was a picture of composure on the track, her quirky lower lip flapping its usual eager beat as she neared the start. Neither dreary weather nor a crowd 46,118 strong could interrupt her focus. In those moments de Seroux knew the months of patience and sound judgment were about to pay off.

"It was the culmination of the whole year," she recalled. "On that day of the Breeders' Cup, I had never seen her saunter in the post parade the way she did. That was the finest she ever looked. It was the most composed she ever was. It was just everything I had planned and hoped for, and that all bespoke of what she did."

Sharing the conviction that Azeri was simply faster than anybody else out there, both de Seroux and Smith had settled on one basic strategy for the Distaff: Let her roll. As it was, the tactics gave the others no chance. Azeri rocketed from the gate, and within a quarter-mile, she had the field at her mercy. She sped around the muddy Arlington track, chased closely for seven furlongs by Imperial Gesture, and then it was over. Like so many times throughout the year, Azeri was dominance incarnate, powering under the wire five lengths in front.

The die had been cast. Azeri had done her part, gloriously racing her way into Horse of the Year contention. For the remainder of the afternoon, her connections could only wait and watch. Within hours the result of the $4-million Breeders' Cup Classic would dictate whether she had stood a chance.

"That's what made the whole rest of the day so interesting for us," remembered de Seroux. "The dream scenario unfolded."

Of the Classic contenders, War Emblem, Medaglia d'Oro, and Came Home — the cream of the Triple Crown crop — as well as the late-blooming four-year-old Evening Attire had all emerged as serious threats for the title. A victory by any one of them in the ten-furlong Classic, the richest race on the continent, was certain to lock up Horse of the Year. Their hopes were dashed before they even hit the stretch. By then, longshot Volponi had surprisingly blown the Classic wide open. His one-sided upset, at odds of 43-1, left the rest on the outside looking in. As night befell

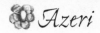

Singular in Chicago in the 2002 Breeders' Cup Distaff.

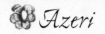

Chicago, Azeri had become a complete standout.

Her stats spoke for themselves. She had captured eight of nine races and earned $2,181,540, her only loss an unlucky runner-up finish. Over the entire year, in fact, just one horse had beaten her. She had won seven successive graded stakes — five of them grade I — at tracks in California, Arkansas, and Illinois, and there hadn't been a close call among the bunch. In some of her more impressive efforts, she had spotted substantial weight to her opponents and then beat them senselessly in spite of it. She had weathered everything thrown her way, from bad breaks and fast fractions to tough competition and foreign surfaces. And she had delivered her greatest performance on the biggest stage of them all, the Breeders' Cup. Hers was without question the single most outstanding season of any horse in North America, male or female.

Azeri had begun 2002 as a little-known rookie. By late October, she was the sport's headliner. The balloting for Horse of the Year reflected her superiority. Despite the fact that she never once stepped out of her division to defeat males — heretofore a tacit prerequisite — Azeri gar-

Wayne Lukas (right) with Smith and Paulson after the 2004 Apple Blossom.

nered 84 percent of the vote. War Emblem, the Kentucky Derby and Preakness hero, received the next highest total — about 5 percent.

Her magic would carry on the following year. Though it was unreasonable to expect Azeri to replicate her feats of 2002, she continued to add one win after another at age five, and with her success came inevitable comparisons. Her brilliance summoned such sacred names as Ruffian and Personal Ensign. Even those new to the sport understood they were witnessing a phenomenon.

By the fall of 2003, she had reeled off repeat victories in the Apple Blossom, Milady, Vanity, and Clement L. Hirsch, paving the way to her second Eclipse as the country's champion mare. Handed over to acclaimed trainer D. Wayne Lukas the following winter, Azeri launched yet another season in spectacular fashion, becoming the first in Oaklawn track history to win the Apple Blossom three years in a row. The effort left the six-year-old second only to Spain among North America's richest fillies

AZERI	Jade Hunter, 1984	Mr. Prospector, 1970	Raise a Native, 1961	Native Dancer, 1950	Polynesian Geisha
				Raise You, 1946	Case Ace Lady Glory
			Gold Digger, 1962	Nashua, 1952	Nasrullah Segula
				Sequence, 1946	Count Fleet Miss Dogwood
		Jadana, 1979	Pharly, 1974	Lyphard, 1969	**Northern Dancer** Goofed
				Comely, 1966	Boran Princesse Commene
			Janina, 1965	Match II, 1958	Tantieme Relance
				Jennifer, 1948	Hyperion Avena
	Zodiac Miss, 1989	Ahonoora, 1975	Lorenzaccio, 1965	Klairon, 1952	Clarion Kalmia
				Phoenissa, 1951	The Phoenix Erica Fragrans
			Helen Nichols, 1966	Martial, 1957	Hill Gail Discipliner
				Quaker Girl, 1961	Whistler Mayflower
		Capricornia, 1983	Try My Best, 1975	**Northern Dancer**, 1961	Nearctic Natalma
				Sex Appeal, 1970	Buckpasser Best in Show
			Franconia, 1976	Rheingold, 1969	Faberge II Athene
				Miss Glasso, 1961	Ratification Tulip

and mares of all-time.

Honors aside, however, Azeri's enduring imprint remains her incredible streak. For a female Thoroughbred it was an unprecedented run — eleven consecutive wins, all in graded stakes — and more than qualifies her as one of the best ever. As one of a select few to be named Horse of the Year, though, Azeri has forever secured her place among racing's pantheon of greats.

by Craig Harzmann

Past Performances

The following section includes the past performances of the ten female Horses of the Year profiled in this volume in chronological order. Miss Woodford's past performances were recreated using historical records from *The Blood-Horse* archives, and Azeri's past performances are complete through the June 4, 2004, Ogden Phipps Handicap, her most recent start at press time. The other past performances are copyrighted © 2000 by *Daily Racing Form* and are reprinted from the book *Champions* (published by DRF Press).

Miss Woodford

br.f. 1880, by Billet (Voltigeur)-Fancy Jane, by Neil Robinson

Lifetime record: 48 37 7 2 $118,270

Own.- Dwyer Brothers
Br.- Catesby Woodford and Ezekiel Clay (Ky)
Tr.- Frank McCabe

24Jul86	2Sar	fst	1	1:43¼	First Sweepstakes	1000	1	McLaughlinJ	115	*3.50	Miss Woodford 115^{4}, O'Fallon 98½, Joe Cotton 118	
8Jul86	3Mth	fst	1¾	3:07	3↑Monmouth Cup	1000	1	McLaughlinJ	122	*8.00	Miss Woodford 122^{3}, East Lynne 113½, Ten Booker 115	Drew away easily
3Jul86	3Mth	fst	1⅛	1:57	3↑Ocean S	1500	1	McLaughlinJ	115	-	Miss Woodford 115^{4}, Pontiac 120^{3}, Electric 102	In a canter
29Jun86	4Con	fst	1¼	2:08¾	Special Race	3000	2	McLaughlinJ	117	-	Troubador 118¾, Miss Woodford 117	
17Jun86	4Con	hy	1¾	3:07¼	3↑Coney Island Cup	1500	1	McLaughlinJ	118	10.00	Barnum 120^{dh}, Miss Woodford 118^{dh}	
7Jun86	4StL	fst	1½	2:35	3↑Eclipse S	10000	1	McLaughlinJ	117	*7.40	Miss Woodford 117^{1}, Volante 118^{4}, Alta 118	
31May86	2Jer	fst	1⅛	1:58½	3↑Harlem S	1000	1	McLaughlinJ	117	-	Miss Woodford 117^{1}, Pardee 118^{3}, Rowland 95	

19Sep85	3Con	fst	2	3:35	3↑Great Long Island S	2500	1	McLaughlinJ	111	-	Miss Woodford 111^{nk}, Binette 105, Caramel 111	
19Sep85	3Con	fst	2	3:37¼	Second Heat		1	McLaughlinJ	111	3.00	Miss Woodford $111^{1½}$, Binette 105, Caramel 111	
14Sep85	3Bri	fst	1¼	2:08	3↑Sweepstakes	3500	2	McLaughlinJ	115	-	Freeland 115^{4}, Miss Woodford 115^{3}, Modesty 115	
	Previously trained by James Rowe Sr.											
20Aug85	5Mth	fst	1¼	2:09½	Match Race	2500	1	McLaughlinJ	115	1.50	Miss Woodford 115^{hd}, Freeland 117	
18Aug85	5Mth	fst	1¼	2:09	3↑Special S	2000	2	McLaughlinJ	115	*1.60	Freeland 117^{hd}, Miss Woodford 115^{6}, Pontiac 118	
10Aug85	3Mth	fst	1½	2:36	3↑Champion S	2500	2	McLaughlinJ	115	*1.60	Freeland 118^{1}, Miss Woodford 115^{10}, Louisette 113	
6Aug85	4Mth	gd	1	1:43½	3↑Eatontown S	1500	4	McLaughlinJ	115	*3.00	Pontiac 118½ , Thackeray $111^{1½}$, Louisette 108	
28Jul85	4Mth	hy	1½	2:45½	3↑Freehold S	1500	1	McLaughlinJ	116	9.00	Miss Woodford116^{2}, Drake Carter115	
9Jul85	4Mth	fst	2	3:34	3↑Monmouth Cup	2000	1	McLaughlinJ	117	*3.50	Miss Woodford 117½ Drake Carter119^{4}, Boatman 119	
4Jul85	3Mth	hy	1⅛	1:59	3↑Ocean S.	1500	1	McLaughlinJ	115	*5.00	Miss Woodford 115¾ Goano 105¾, Louisette 113	
1Jul85	1Con	fst	7f	1:29¼	3↑Farewell S	1000	2	McLaughlinJ	115	5.00	Thackeray 106^{nk}, Miss Woodford 115^{1}, Louisette 101	
18Jun85	4Con	fst	1⅛	2:00	3↑Coney Island S	1500	1	McLaughlinJ	117	3.00	Miss Woodford 117^{1}, Wanda 98½, Louisette 113	
2Jun85	2Jer	gd	1⅛	1:58¾	3↑Alw	500	1	McLaughlinJ	117	3.00	Miss Woodford 117^{nk}, Pampero 108^{10}, Caramel 107	

20Sep84	3Con	fst	2	3:33	3↑Great Long Island S	2500	1	McLaughlinJ	107½	*3.00	Miss Woodford $107½^{3}$, Drake Carter 105^{6}, Modesty 92	
20Sep84	3Con	fst	2	3:31¼	Second Heat	2500	1	McLaughlinJ	107½	-	Miss Woodford $107½^{4}$, Drake Carter 105, Modesty 92	
18Sep84	3Con	fst	2½	4:28¾	Match	12000	1	McLaughlinJ	115	*.55	Miss Woodford 115^{10}, Drake Carter 115	
6Sep84	1Con	fst	7f	1:28¾	3↑Alw	500	1	McLaughlinJ	115	*.55	Miss Woodford 115^{4}, Buckstone 118^{3}, Mammonist 115	
9Aug84	3Mth	fst	1½	2:40¼	3↑Champion S	2000	1	McLaughlinJ	113	*.40	Miss Woodford 113^{4}, Drake Carter 115^{10}, Monitor 118	In a canter
7Aug84	4Mth	hy	1	1:47	2↑Eatontown S	1500	1	McLaughlinJ	113	*.45	Miss Woodford 113^{2}, Duchess 102^{20}, Little Minch 111	Under a pull
4Jul84	3Mth	hy	1⅛	2:01½	3↑Ocean S	1000	1	McLaughlinJ	113	*3.00	Miss Woodford 113^{4}, George Kinney 118^{2}, Aranza 115	Won pulling double
21Jun84	3Con	fst	1⅛	1:56½	3↑Coney Island S	750	1	McLaughlinJ	113	5.60	Miss Woodford 113^{1}, Kinglike $118^{1½}$, Miss Brewster 98	
12Jun84	2Con	hy	1½	2:18¾	3↑Alw	600	1	McLaughlinJ	111	5.30	Miss Woodford 113^{3}, RoyalArch 85	In a canter
10Jun84	2Con	fst	1½	2:40¾	3↑Alw	600	1	McLaughlinJ	113	-	Miss Woodford 113^{3}, Duke of Montalban 120^{8}, Chanticleer 98	
26Oct83	3Pim	fst	1⅝	2:57	3↑Pimlico S	5000	1	McLaughlinJ	107	*2.00	Miss Woodford 107^{3}, George Kinney 110^{2}, Iroquois 125	
17Oct83	3Wash	gd	1½	2:36¾	3↑District of Columbia S	2500	1	McLaughlinJ	105	12.35	Miss Woodford 105^{12}, Drake Carter 105^{4}, Eole 122	Won easily
4Oct83	3Jer	gd	1¾	3:13¼	3ⓣ ↑Hunter S	1000	1	McLaughlinJ	122	*4.50	Miss Woodford 122^{6}, Carnation 115^{dh}, Bella 115^{dh}	
29Sep83	3CD	fst	1½	2:37	3Lorillard Champion Stallion S	10575	1	McLaughlinJ	107	-	Miss Woodford 107^{20}, Slocum 107^{10}, Wandering 107	

PAST PERFORMANCES

13Sep83	3She	hy	1½	2:42	3Great Eastern H	5000	1	McLaughlinJ	110	12.35	Miss Woodford 1108, Referee 973, All Hands Around 97	
25Aug83	2Mth	gd	1½	2:36	3 ↑ Monmouth S	5000	5	Hughes	107	8.00	George Kinney 1121½, Eole 127nk, Iroquois 127	
21Aug83	3Mth	fst	1½	2:42	3 Ⓕ West End Hotel S	1000	1	McLaughlinJ	118	*4.00	Miss Woodford 1185, Caramel 1131, Carnation 116	
7Aug83	2Sar	gd	1	2:14¾	3 Ⓕ Pocahontas S	1000	2	McLaughlinJ	116	10.00	Empress 1081, Miss Woodford 1161, Blue Grass Belle 108	
26Jul83	2Sar	gd	1⅛	1:57½	3 Ⓕ Alabama S	800	1	McLaughlinJ	113	*5.60	Miss Woodford 1134, Bessie 1132, Vera 113	
10Jul83	3Mth	hy	1¼	2:20½	3 Ⓕ Monmouth Oaks	1000	1	McLaughlinJ	113	*5.30	Miss Woodford 1138, Carnation 1136, Caramel 113	Under a hard pull
21Jun83	3She	fst	1⅛	1:58¼	3 Ⓕ Mermaid S	800	1	McLaughlinJ	113	*5.35	Miss Woodford 1136, Carnation 113, Fairview 113	
5Jun83	2Jer	fst	1½	2:43½	3 Ⓕ Ladies S	1000	1	McLaughlinJ	113	2.00	Miss Woodford 1133, Carnation 1135, Fairview 113	
27Sep82	1CD	fst	6f	1:16	2 Ⓕ Blue Grass S	875	3	Stoval	102	*1.50	Queen Ban 1021, Bellona 1021, Miss Woodford 102	
14Sep82	3Lxt	fst	1	1:44	2Colt and Filly S	625	1	Stoval	102	*2.00	Miss Woodford 1021½, Vera 1022, Pike's Pride 102	
11Sep82	3Lxt	hy	6f	1:17¾	2 Ⓕ Filly S	800	1	Stoval	102	*2.00	Miss Woodford 1021, St. Martin filly 1026, Vera 102	
19Aug82	2Sar	fst	6	1:16	2 Ⓕ Misses' S	1575	1	Stoval	105	3.00	Miss Woodford 1052, War Dance-Tarantella filly 102nk, Pearl Thorn 10	
18Jul82	2Sar	fst	5f	1:03½	2 Ⓕ Spinaway S	1900	1	Stoval	103	*1.50	Miss Woodford 103hd, War Dance filly 953, Empress 100	
13Jul82	1Sar	hy	4f	0:53	2Flash S	2900	3	Stoval	107	5.00	George Kinney 1104, Empress 107½, Miss Woodford 107	
3Jul82	1Chi	hy	1	1:58½	2Nursery S	1950	2	Stoval	97	*1.00	Ascender 971, Miss Woodford 972, Lucky B. 100	
26Jun82	2Chi	hy	6f	1:20½	2 Ⓕ Ladies' S	1600	1	Stoval	97	2.50	Miss Woodford 971, Vis-a-Vis 97nk, Blue Grass Belle 97	

Imp

blk. f. 1894, by Wagner (Prince Charlie)–Fondling, by Fonso **Lifetime record: 171 62 35 29 $70,119**

Own.– Daniel R. Harness

Br.– Daniel R. Harness (Oh)

Tr.– P. Wimmer

9Nov01- 4Aqu	fst 1 1/16	:234:482 1:1421:474	2↑ Farmingdale H .8k	0 5	54¼	53½	44½	66¼	Odom	126	*1.50	92-10	Oom Paul1122Ben Mac Dhui1142Handicapper982	Poor effort	6
7Nov01- 1Aqu	fst 7f	:242:483 1:14 1:274	2↑ Oakdale H .8k	0 6	72¾	71½	62	51¼	Odom	126	2.60	83-12	Paul Clifford113hdShoreham1001Unmasked120hd	Closed gap	9
5Nov01- 4Aqu	gd 1 1/16	:243:50 1:491	2↑ Idlewild H .8k	0 2	1hd	2hd	2hd	2¾	Odom	126	*2.00	90-11	Potente110¾Imp1262St. Finnan115hd	Good try	5
26Oct01- 4MP	fst 2¼	:50 2:351 3:56	3↑ Morris Park 4.7k	0 3	32	46½	612	517	Bullman	121	7.00	90-05	GoldHeels1112Hernando111noWtrColor1113	Lacked condition	8
25Oct01- 6MP	fst 1¼	:5141:17 1:4222:072	3↑ Handicap 1045	0 1	12	12	13	14	Odom	122	5.00	91-10	Imp1224Advance Guard1264Rafaello1053	Never extended	4
22Oct01- 5MP	fst 1	:252:50 1:15 1:40	3↑ Handicap 660	0 1	1nk	1hd	1hd	1hd	Shaw	109	3.50	95-09	Imp109hdSt. Finnan1046Decanter1142	Driving	5
19Oct01- 3MP	fst *6f-EC	1:10	2↑ Handicap 885	0 7	8	78¾	73½	77	Bullman	116	15.00	86-09	Rockwater99½Roxane1091BelleofLxngton103½	Never a factor	10
6Sep01- 6She	fst 1½Ⓣ	:50 1:1612:08 2:332	3↑ Handicap 1445	0 1	1nk	45	48½	422½	Fairgood	110	3.50	81-00	Trigger97½Baron Pepper1022Maid of Harlem9220	Speed,quit	4
2Sep01- 4She	gd 1¼	:4911:1431:4042:07	3↑ Twin City H 6.3k	0 2	33	43	64¼	78½	Woods J	117	10.00	81-07	Herbert116hdTerminus108½Trigger951	Disliked going	10
24Aug01- 4Sar	my 1⅝	:51 1:45 2:522	3↑ Sar Cup 5k	0 2	23	315	325	338	Odom	122	2.60	--	Blues1138Baron Pepper11330Imp122	Disliked going	3
20Aug01- 3Sar	fst 1 1/16	:243:491 1:15 1:464	3↑ Alw 770	0 1	1hd	21	21½	26	Fairgood	111	*1.20	87-06	Roe Hampton1066Imp11112The Rhymer985	Poor ride	4
13Aug01- 4Sar	fst 1 70	:243:494 1:1611:452	3↑ Alw 790	0 2	21	21	21	1¾	Fairgood	113	*.90	--	Imp113¾Smoke11312Admonition110	Poor ride,much best	3
5Aug01- 4Sar	fst 1⅛	:4931:15 1:4031:531	3↑ Saratoga H 10k	0 5	4¾	42¼	34	53½	Odom	123	20.00	91-09	Rockton1162Water Cure1071Water Color115nk	Good try	11
Previously trained by C.E. Brossman,owned by Harness and Brossman															
23Nov00- 6Ben	fst 1 100	:252:50 1:1631:492	3↑ Handicap 445	0 1	1½	1hd	2hd	2no	Rutter	123	*.90	93-07	First Whip112noImp1234Asquith99no	Tired	4
14Nov00- 1Aqu	fst *7f	:232:483 1:14 1:252	2↑ Handicap 585	0 6	53¼	55¼	41	31	Rutter	126	*3.00	95-08	Bastile95hdTrumpet1171Imp1262	Hung	12
8Nov00- 4Aqu	fst 1½	:5011:17 2:0922:373	2↑ Alw 525	0 1	1¾	1½	2hd	21½	Burns T	123	*.50	108-06	McMeekin1171½Imp12312Compensation126	Saved ground	3
3Nov00- 4Emp	hy 1⅛	:5011:1511:4111:55	2↑ Wakefield H 1.4k	0 3	52¼	52¾	510	611¼	Burns T	126	4.00	--	James1121KingBarleycorn1062PinkCoat107no	Disliked going	6
1Nov00- 6Emp	sl 1 1/16	:243:483 1:15 1:474	2↑ Handicap 700	0 2	1hd	1hd	2½	21½	Burns T	128	2.00	--	McMeekin1131½Imp1282Herbert1061	Disliked going	5
25Oct00- 4Emp	sl 1 1/16	:25 :481 1:1411:47	3↑ ⒻMahopac H 1.1k	0 1	1½	11	11½	11½	Burns T	126	*.70	--	Imp1261½Kamara104hdOneck Queen951	Won easing up	4
22Oct00- 4Emp	fst 1¼	:4841:13 1:39 2:04	2↑ Emp City H 3.2k	0 1	1hd	1hd	1½	2hd	O'Conner	124	*1.60	--	Charentus106hdImp1241Pink Coat105no	Just missed	7

PAST PERFORMANCES

13Oct00- 5MP	fst	1¾	:49 2:08^{4}2:33^{3}2:58^3	3↑	Municipal H 3.9k	0	1	1½	1^2	$1^{1½}$	2^{hd}	Burns T	126	4.00	103-05	Ethelbert126^{hd}Imp126^{6}Maid of Harlem100^5	Gamely	5
22Sep00- 4Gra	fst	1⅛	:48^{4}1:14^{2}1:40^{4}1:53^4	2↑	Occidental H 2.3k	0	2	1^{hd}	$4^{¾}$	$7^{3¼}$	$7^{9¾}$	McJoynt	126	*3.00	86-07	PinkCoat102^{1½}JckPont116^{3}Chrntus103^{hd}	Tired under impost	9
15Sep00- 4Gra	fst	1½	:50^{2}1:17 2:08^{3}2:34^1	3↑	Second Spl 3.2k	0	1	1^1	1^1	1^1	1^1	Burns T	118	7.00	99-06	Imp118^{1}Kinley Mack126^{no}Ethelbert121^1	Handily	4
11Sep00- 4Gra	fst	1¼	:51^{2}1:17^{1}1:43^{1}2:08^1	3↑	First Spl 3.1k	0	1	1^1	1^1	1^{hd}	3^4	Odom	123	*.90	86-07	Kinley Mack126^{hd}McMeekin117^{4}Imp123	Speed,tired	3
3Sep00- 6She	fst	1$\frac{1}{16}$Ⓣ	:24^2:48^3 1:14^{3}1:46^4	3↑	Handicap 1120	0	1	$1^{1½}$	$1^{½}$	1^{hd}	$1^{1½}$	Odom	128	3.50	101-00	Imp128^{1½}Intrusive117^{1½}Maximo Gomez114^8	Gamely	6
4Aug00- 4Bri	fst	2¼	:50^{1}2:32^{3}2:57^{4}3:49^1	3↑	Brighton Cup 8.3k	0	1	1^4	1^6	$1^{1½}$	$2^{¾}$	Jenkins	121	8.00	135-00	Ethelbert124^{¾}Imp121^{10}Sidney Lucas109^{10}	Good try	4
1Aug00- 6Bri	fst	1⅛	:48^{3}1:14^{1}1:40 1:53	3↑	Alw 880	0	1	2^{hd}	2^{hd}	2^2	2^3	Clawson	121	*.70	104-00	Belle of Troy106^{3}Imp121^{2}Gonfalon106^{no}	Second best	5
25Jly00- 4Bri	fst	1	:24 :48^1 1:14^{2}1:40	3↑	Islip 2.5k	0	1	2^{hd}	2^{hd}	$3^{5½}$	$3^{5½}$	Mitchell	121	2.20	92-05	Ethlbrt126^{4}SkyScrpr107^{1½}Imp121	Speed,tired,pulled up lame	3
23Jly00- 2Bri	fst	1⅛	:47^{2}1:12^{2}1:39^{3}1:53	3↑	Alw 670	0	2	2^2	2^3	1^{hd}	$1^{1½}$	Mitchell	115	*.45	107-00	Imp115^{1½}Water Cure90^{2}Plucky95	Easily	3
7Jly00- 4Bri	fst	1¼	:47^{3}1:13 1:38^{2}2:04^3	3↑	Brighton H 11k	0	5	4^4	3^{nk}	3^1	3^2	Odom	129	8.00	102-03	Jack Point109^{1½}The Kentuckian109^{½}Imp129^3	Good effort	9
3Jly00- 4She	fst	1⅛	:50 1:14^{4}1:40^{4}1:54	3↑	Long Island H 2.5k	0	4	2^{hd}	1^{hd}	2^{hd}	2no	Odom	130	*2.20	95-08	Charentus99^{no}Imp130^{no}Greyfeld100^6	Driving	6
30Jun00- 4She	fst	1¾	:49^{1}2:05 2:32 2:59^1	3↑	Advance 5.3k	0	1	1^{20}	1^{30}	1^{30}	1^{30}	Odom	113	*.10	110-01	Imp113^{30}MaidofHarlem103^{8}PostHst95	Restrained throughout	3
23Jun00- 4She	fst	1	:24 :49 1:14^{4}1:40^4	3↑	Sheepshead Bay H 2k	0	3	$6^{4¼}$	$5^{4½}$	2^3	3^4	Tabor	133	6.00	87-09	Greyfeld91^{1}Bendoran121^{3}Imp133^{hd}	Tired under impost	10
20Jun00- 3She	fst	1$\frac{3}{16}$	:50^{1}1:15^{3}1:41^{3}2:00^3	3↑	Handicap 1270	0	1	1^2	$1^{1½}$	$1^{1½}$	$1^{1½}$	Tabor	131	*.80	98-09	Imp131^{1½}Col. Roosevelt101^{6}David Garrick113^5	Easily	4
16Jun00- 4She	fst	1¼	:49^{1}1:15 1:41^{1}2:06^4	3↑	Suburban H 10k	0	2	2^1	2^{hd}	4^2	$4^{10½}$	O'Conner	128	4.00	80-09	Kinley Mack125^{1½}Ethelbert130^{4}Gulden100^5	Speed,tired	10
13Jun00- 2Gra	fst	1¼	:50 1:15^{2}1:41^{3}2:08	3↑	Handicap 1080	0	1	1^2	1^3	1^3	$1^{1½}$	Tabor	126	*1.40	91-08	Imp126^{1½}Gulden99^{no}Lothario106^{no}	Easily	7
5Jun00- 4Gra	fst	1⅛	:49 1:14^{1}1:40^{4}1:54^1	3↑	Brookdale H 2k	0	2	$2^{½}$	2^{hd}	1^{hd}	2no	O'Connor	127	*.70	94-08	Jean Beraud127^{no}Imp127^{1½}Charentus101^{hd}	Gamely	4
30May00- 4Gra	fst	1$\frac{1}{16}$	:25 :49^2 1:14^{4}1:46^4	3↑	Parkway H 2.1k	0	1	1^{hd}	1^2	1^{hd}	1^2	O'Connor	124	*1.80	97-04	Imp124^{2}Kinley Mack127^{4}Survivor104^{hd}	Easily	6
26May00- 4Gra	hy	1¼	:49^{1}1:16^{1}1:43^{1}2:10	3↑	Brooklyn H 10k	0	4	3^2	$4^{1¼}$	$6^{1½}$	$6^{4¾}$	Clawson	128	8.00	76-15	Kinley Mack122^{1}Rafaello113^{¾}Herbert98^{hd}	Disliked going	9
15May00- 1MP	fst	6½f	:23^4:49^4 1:14^{3}1:21	3↑	Alw 590	0	3	3^1	3^1	$3^{½}$	$3^{1¾}$	Clay P	124	*.90	93-07	Vulcain113^{1}Unmasked103^{¾}Imp124^{1½}	Urged,not enough	6
9May00- 4MP	sl	7f	:24^4:51^1 1:16^{4}1:30¼	3↑	ⒻAlw 690	0	2	3^2	$3^{½}$	$4^{1¾}$	2^5	Vest	129	*.60	74-28	SparrowWing113^{5}Imp129^{no}StarChime106^{no}	Poor ride,outrun	5
5May00- 4MP	fst	1	:23^4:48^3 1:15 1:41¼	3↑	Metropolitan H 7.7k	0	7	$5^{1¾}$	3^2	2^2	3^3	Clawson	127	8.00	86-13	Ethelbert126^{3}Box121^{no}Imp127^{1½}	Driving	11
14Apr00- 5Ben	sl	7f	:24^2:49^4 1:16^{2}1:31	3↑	2nd Ben Spring H 1.1k	0	2	$3^{1½}$	4^3	$4^{3½}$	3^5	Clay	132	*1.10	85-13	Charentus112^{5}Boney Boy116^{hd}Imp132^{nk}	Impeded	4
2Apr00- 4Ben	gd	6f	:24^1:50 1:03 1:16^1	3↑	1st Bennings Spring H .9k	0	1	3^{nk}	3^{nk}	$4^{1¼}$	$3^{1½}$	Clay P	132	*1.20	91-09	Boney Boy106^{½}Charentus110^{1}Imp132^{hd}	Impeded½	7
30Sep99- 4Gra	fst	1¼	:49^{2}1:14^{1}1:41 2:07^3	2↑	Oriental H 2.5k	0	1	1^2	1^2	1^4	1^4	Clay P	128	*.50	94-08	Imp128^{4}Charentus106	Eased in stretch	2
23Sep99- 4Gra	fst	1½	:50 1:16 2:08 2:34	2↑	Second Spl 3.3k	0	1	1^2	1^3	1^5	$1^{1½}$	Clay P	124	3.50	107-04	Imp124^{1½}BenHolldy121^{10}ThBchlor118^{hd}	Eased final furlong	4
16Sep99- 4Gra	fst	1⅛	:49 1:14^{3}1:41^{1}1:54^2	3↑	Occidental H 2.3k	0	2	1^{hd}	2^{hd}	3^1	$5^{3¼}$	Clay P	129	3.50	95-06	Previous122^{hd}Charentus109^{1}Prince McClurg115^{hd}	Tired	7
12Sep99- 4Gra	gd	1¼	:49^{4}1:15 1:42 2:09^4	3↑	First Spl 3.5k	0	2	2^{nk}	1^{nk}	$1^{1½}$	1^2	Clay P	119	*1.60	83-11	Imp119^{2}May Hempstead112^{1½}Maxine119^{¾}	Restrained at end	6
4Sep99- 4She	gd	1¼	:49^{1}1:16 1:44 2:10	3↑	Twin City H 6k	0	1	1^{hd}	2^{hd}	6	8	Clay P	130	4.00	- -	Previous114^{4}Bangle120^{1½}Bannockburn126^1	Disliked footing	9
1Sep99- 6She	fst	1¼Ⓣ	:49 1:14^{1}1:40^{1}2:07^1	3↑	Turf H 1.7k	0	1	1^3	1^4	1^2	1^2	Clay P	128	3.00	100-00	Imp128^{2}Decanter117^{3}Bon Ino97^3	Never threatened	6
30Aug99- 4She	fst	1	:24^2:48^2 1:14^{1}1:40^1	3↑	Ocean H 1.5k	0	1	1^{hd}	1^{hd}	1^{hd}	1^{hd}	Clay P	123	8.00	94-09	Imp123^{hd}Charentus109^{2}Batten112^{hd}	Driving	9
26Aug99- 3She	fst	6f	:23^2:47^3 1:13^2	3↑	Fall H 1.5k	0	1	2^{hd}	2^{hd}	2^1	$3^{3½}$	Clay	124	5.00	91-10	Previous111^{½}Batten114^{3}Imp124^2	Outpaced	7
31Jly99- 5Bri	fst	1	:24^1:48^2 1:14^{1}1:40^3	3↑	Islip 2.3k	0	2	3^1	2^1	2^{hd}	1^{hd}	Clay	111	1.80	95-05	Imp111^{hd}Firearm113^{2}Peep o' Day111^4	Just up	4
24Jly99- 3Bri	hy	1$\frac{1}{16}$	:25 :50^2 1:16^{2}1:50	3↑	Handicap 775	0	1	2^{nk}	4^1	$3^{4½}$	4^6	Clay P	124	3.50	79-15	Kirkwood104^{1½}Maxine114^{4}Tamor98^{½}	Poor ride	4
18Jly99- 3Bri	fst	1	:25 :50^1 1:16 1:41^2	3↑	Handicap 735	0	1	1^1	$1^{½}$	$1^{½}$	$1^{½}$	Clay P	126	*1.00	91-08	Imp126^{½}Charentus106^{5}Cambrian105^2	Driving	4
11Jly99- 4Bri	fst	6f	:23^2:48^1 1:01^{2}1:14^4	2↑	Flight H 1.8k	0	5	5^3	$6^{5¾}$	$6^{6¼}$	4^4	Clay P	126	6.00	88-08	Firearm108^{2}Bendoran126^{2}Swiftmas115^{hd}	Finished fast	6
6Jly99- 4Bri	fst	1¼	:49^{1}1:14^{3}1:40 2:05^2	3↑	Brighton H 9.9k	0	1	1^1	1^1	1^1	1^1	O'Leary	115	8.00	110-02	Imp115^{1}Ethelbert107^{1}Bangle112^{nk}	Mild drive	7
3Jly99- 3She	fst	1⅛	:50 1:14^{4}1:40^{1}1:53	3↑	Handicap 1080	0	1	1^1	1^1	1^{hd}	3^2	Turner N	126	*3.50	98-04	Tragedian106^{2}Survivor107^{hd}Imp126^4	Driving	7
29Jun99- 4She	hy	1⅛	:49 1:15 1:41^{1}1:54^1	3↑	Long Island H 2k	0	1	1^1	1^{hd}	1^{hd}	$3^{4½}$	O'Leary	119	2.60	89-06	Bangle109^{3}Maxine113^{1½}Imp119^5	Dueled,tired	5
24Jun99- 4She	fst	1	:23^2:47^1 1:12^{3}1:39^4	3↑	Sheepshead Bay H 1.5k	0	2	2^5	3^5	$3^{3¼}$	$7^{8¼}$	Taral	125	3.50	88-06	Fly by Night108^{¾}Azucena98^{2}Bendoran123^{hd}	Weakened	9
20Jun99- 4She	fst	6f	:23^4:47^2 1:00 1:13^2	3↑	Coney Island H 1.5k	0	4	4^7	$4^{5½}$	2^3	$2^{1½}$	Taral	128	*3.50	93-10	Bendoran118^{1½}Imp128^{2}St. Cloud122^{nk}	Second best	12
17Jun99- 4She	fst	1¼	:49^{2}1:14^{1}1:39^{3}2:05^4	3↑	Suburban H 10k	0	3	3^1	1^1	1^3	1^2	Turner N	114	6.00	96-06	Imp114^{2}Bannockburn112^{3}Warrenton114^{nk}	Never threatened	13
14Jun99- 2Gra	fst	1⅛	:49^{4}1:15^{1}1:41 1:53^4	3↑	Handicap 1100	0	1	1^2	1^3	1^4	1^3	Clawson	126	3.20	101-06	Imp126^{3}Pirate M.97^{1}Warrenton125^1	Never extended	6

8Jun99- 2Gra	fst	1 1/16	:24 :49 1:15^{2}1:49	3↑ (F)Alw 700	0	4	2^1	1^1	1^½	1^{1½}	Taral	123	3.50	90-08	Imp123^{1½}Gaze98^{3}Azucena106^½	Easily 7
5Jun99- 5Gra	fst	1 1/16	:25^1:50^3 1:15^{2}1:48^3	3↑ Handicap 875	0	2	2^1	3^{1½}	3^3	3^{4½}	Mitchell	122	4.00	87-07	Intrusive112^{3}Charentus110^{1½}Imp122^2	Weak handling 9
27May99- 4Gra	fst	1¼	:49^{1}1:14^{2}1:39^{2}2:06^1	3↑ Brooklyn H 10k	0	5	5^{3½}	6^{2¼}	1^5	1^5	Clayton	110	15.00	--	Banastar110^{3}Lanky Bob105^{1}Filigrane98^2	Outrun 16
23May99- 6MP	fst	1⅛	:50^{2}1:15 1:41 1:53^3	3↑ Handicap 850	0	2	2^{hd}	2^{hd}	1^1	1^1	Taral	125	*2.00	89-05	Imp125^{1}Glonoine108^{hd}Jefferson108^3	Handily 8
18May99- 5MP	fst	6½f	:24 :49 1:14 1:20^2	3↑ Claremont Hwt H 1.5k	0	3	1^{nk}	1^1	1^1	3^½	Taral	119	*3.50	100-01	Kinnikinnick124^{½}Dr. Eichberg106^{hd}Imp119^1	Good effort 8
16May99- 4MP	fst	7f	:24 :49^2 1:14^{1}1:26^3	3↑ New Rochelle H 1.6k	0	5	3^{1¼}	4^1	2^{nk}	2^2	Taral	112	5.00	102-01	Previous113^{2}Imp112^{2}Kingdon112^{no}	Good try 10
13May99- 5MP	fst	1 1/16	:26 :51 1:15^{3}1:47^1	3↑ Handicap 900	0	9	4^¾	2^{nk}	2^½	2^¾	O'Connor	113	4.00	95-04	Don D'Oro128^{¾}Imp113^{6}Free Lance105^½	Second best 10
11May99- 6MP	my	1	:25^1:50^1 1:16 1:43	3↑ Handicap 880	0	1	2^2	2^2	2^5	4^{2¾}	Taral	117	*1.60	84-10	Don D'Oro122^{2}Twinkler98^{½}Charentus107^{nk}	Tired 6
9May99- 4MP	fst	*6f-EC	:23^1:47 :58 1:09	3↑ Toboggan H 2.1k	0	4	2^½	6^{3¼}	6^{3½}	8	McGlone	120	8.00	--	Banastar116^{¾}Sanders121^{3}Octagon130^3	Pulled up 10
6May99- 4MP	fst	1	:24^2:49 1:14 1:39^4	3↑ Metropolitan H 8.2k	0	5	5^{2¼}	4^{1¾}	4^2	4^3	McGlone	112	6.00	100-00	Filigrane102^{2}Ethelbert106^{hd}Sanders110^1	Outrun 14
12Apr99- 5Ben	fst	1 1/16	:25^4:50^1 1:16^{1}1:50^3	3↑ Handicap 350	0	1	1^2	1^4	1^3	1^3	McGlone	126	1.60	--	Imp126^{3}Alice Farley116^{1}Double Dummy109^{hd}	Cantering 5
8Apr99- 5Ben	sl	1 100	:25 :51 1:19^{4}1:52^2	3↑ Handicap 335	0	2	1^{hd}	2^{1½}	4^3	4^{12}	Scherrer	126	*.50	--	Beau Ideal100^{2}Imperator104^{6}Alice Farley114^4	Weakened 5
15Nov98- 3Lak	hy	1 1/16	:25¼ :52 1:19 1:53½	3↑ Handicap 400	0	1	1^5	1^{12}	1^6	1^8	McNickle	116	1.40	68-27	Imp116^{8}Macy114^{2}Al Fresco97	Galloping 3
14Nov98- 3Lak	hy	6f	:26¼ :52½ 1:05 1:17½	3↑ Handicap 400	0	1	2^{nk}	2^{nk}	2^½	2^3	McNickle	125	*.60	81-29	O'Connell117^{3}Imp125^{5}Timemakr111^3	Carried wide by winner 6
8Nov98- 4Lak	gd	1⅛	:50 1:14½ 1:42 1:55¾	Handicap 400	0	1	1^¾	1^3	1^1	1^5	McNickle	112	1.40	88-14	Imp112^{5}Macy116^{3}Storm King99^2	Easily 5
5Nov98- 4Lak	hy	1 1/16	:25¼ :50¾ 1:16½ 1:52¾	3↑ Handicap 400	0	1	2^¾	2^3	2^4	3^5	Ellis	115	*.90	67-25	Macy111^{3}Storm King97^{2}Imp115^5	Dull effort 4
29Oct98- 4Lak	hy	1 100	:25¼ :50¼ 1:15¾ 1:46¼	Alw 400	0	1	1^2	1^2	1^{nk}	2^{1½}	Sheppard	119	3.00	--	Macy104^{1½}Imp119^{8}Storm King96^¾	Second best 5
12Oct98- 3Haw	sl	7f	:25½ :50 1:15¾ 1:29	3↑ Dash 1.3k	0	2	1^½	1^{1½}	1^{2½}	1^1	Rutter	118	*.60	--	Imp118^{1}May W.102^{4}Lady Ellerslie97^6	Hand ride 5
1Oct98- 4Hrm	gd	6f	:23¼ :47¾ 1:01 1:13	2↑ Speed 1.5k	0	3	2^4	2^5	2^3	1^{2½}	Rutter	115	*.60	96-10	Imp115^{2½}Frank Bell92^{3}Traverser113^{2½}	In hand 5
28Sep98- 4Hrm	gd	1 70	:24¾ :49¾ 1:15¼ 1:44½	Alw 400	0	1	1^5	1^8	1^3	1^1	Rutter	119	*.70	94-15	Imp119^{1}Dare II94^{7}Carnero94^5	Easily 4
19Sep98- 4Hrm	gd	7f	:25 :49¾ 1:15¼ 1:27¾	3↑ Austin 1.7k	0	1	1^{nk}	1^{hd}	1^{1½}	1^{2½}	Rutter	119	3.50	92-16	Imp119^{2½}Hugh Penny108^{2}Found95^{no}	Easily 9
17Sep98- 3Haw	hy	1⅛	:53 1:19 1:47¼ 2:01½	3↑ Monadnock 1.1k	0	1	1^2	1^5	1^{1½}	1^2	McNickle	114	*.95	--	Imp114^{2}Hugh Penny114	Easily 2
12Sep98- 3Haw	fst	1⅛	:49¾ 1:14¾ 1:40½ 1:53	3↑ Alw 500	0	1	1^2	1^6	1^5	1^2	McNickle	109	1.80	--	Imp109^{2}Crocket99^{10}John Bright107^2	Eased up 5
8Sep98- 3Haw	gd	1	:26 :51 1:16½ 1:42	4↑ Alw 500	0	2	2^½	1^{nk}	2^1	2^5	Conley	111	4.50	--	Hugh Penny111^{5}Imp111^{6}David104^2	Good try 5
3Sep98- 5Hrm	fst	1 70	:25 :50¼ 1:15¾ 1:44	Alw 400	0	2	2^{hd}	2^1	3^{3½}	4^{10½}	Sheppard	112	9.00	85-07	Storm King98^{1}David Tenny112^{1½}What Next100^8	Stopped 4
1Sep98- 3Hrm	fst	6f	:24 :48¾ 1:01 1:13¾	3↑ Alw 400	0	3	3^2	3^4	3^{4½}	3^{4¾}	Sheppard	109	4.50	88-07	Eugenia Wickes104^{4}Flora Louis98^{¾}Imp109^2	Driving,lost whip 7
30Jly98- 5Hrm	hy	6f	:24¾ :50¼ 1:03¾ 1:17¼	3↑ Alw 400	0	2	2^5	2^3	2^4	2^5	Thorpe	112	*1.00	70-36	Mary Black105^{5}Imp112^{50}Storm King117^{100}	Good try 4
23Jly98- 30WP	fst	1¼	:48¼ 1:13¼ 1:39 2:04½	3↑ Wheeler H 5.4k	0	3	4^4	5^6	4^{4¾}	7^{21¼}	Reiff L	115	15.00	--	Algol107^{5}Goodrich107^{½}Pink Coat109^¾	No threat 10
16Jly98- 50WP	fst	1	:24½ :48¾ 1:13½ 1:39	3↑ Alw 400	0	3	1^{nk}	1^{nk}	2^{hd}	2^2	Caywood	109	*.70	--	Azucena97^{2}Imp109^{8}Miss Gussie97^{nk}	Wide,careless ride 5
11Jly98- 50WP	fst	6½f	:24 :49 1:13¾ 1:17	3↑ Alw 500	0	3	2^2	2^2	3^{1¾}	4^{2½}	Turner N	112	*1.00	--	Satsuma109^{nk}Algol117^{1½}Abuse119^¾	Dull 5
9Jly98- 20WP	fst	1⅛	:48¼ 1:14 1:39¼ 1:51¾	4↑ Alw 595	0	1	1^{1½}	1^2	1^{1½}	1^{1½}	Caywood	112	1.30	--	Imp112^{1½}Macy117	Best 2
5Jly98- 30WP	fst	1 1/16	:25 :50¼ 1:15¾ 1:46	3↑ Alw 600	0	1	1^1	1^{2½}	1^2	1^3	Caywood	110	*.55	--	Imp110^{3}The Devil100^{10}The Roman110	Easily 3
2Jly98- 30WP	fst	1⅛	:49½ 1:14¼ 1:39¼ 1:51¾	3↑ Oakwood H 2.4k	0	1	1^¾	1^{1½}	1^{nk}	3^{1½}	Caywood	118	7.00	--	Fervor103^{no}What Er Lou108^{1½}Imp118^6	Faltered late 6
22Jun98- 1She	gd	6½f	:23^2:49 1:15^{3}1:22^1	3↑ HiW H 845	0	4	3^3	4^3	5^{4½}	6^8	McCafferty	135	6.00	78-16	Swiftmas120^{1}Hanlon106^{½}Mainstay112^3	Eased up late 10
18Jun98- 4She	gd	1¼	:51 1:16 1:41^{2}2:08^1	3↑ Suburban H 10k	0	6	4^{nk}	2^1	3^1	6^{10½}	Clawson	102	5.00	73-14	Tillo119^{½}Semper Ego106^{hd}Ogden109^3	Faltered 11
13Jun98- 2Gra	gd	1⅛	:51 1:16 1:41¾ 1:55½	3↑ Handicap 875	0	1	1^{1½}	1^{1½}	1^{1½}	1^1	Spencer	108	2.00	93-10	Imp108^{1}Havoc126^{1½}Knight of the Garter93^4	Tiring 5
3Jun98- 5Hrm	fst	6f	:24½ :48½ 1:01 1:14¼	3↑ Handicap 400	0	2	2^1	2^{2½}	2^{1½}	1^{1½}	Martin W	124	*.50	90-17	Imp124^{1½}Dave Waldo108^{¾}Cherry Leaf95^5	Driving 6
30May98- 5Hrm	sl	1 1/16	:25 :51¼ 1:18½ 1:51½	3↑ Memorial Day H 1.9k	0	1	1^4	1^6	1^3	1^{10}	Caywood	118	*.80	70-31	Imp118^{10}Dr. Sheppard109^{25}Goodrich100	Won eased up 3
24May98- 5Hrm	gd	1	:26 :49¾ 1:16½ 1:44	3↑ Alw 500	0	1	1^1	1^{1½}	1^{2½}	1^¾	Turner N	105	*.25	73-21	Imp105^{¾}Frank Thompson94^{6}J.H.C.110^{12}	Won eased up 4
21May98- 6Lak	hy	1⅛	:52 1:18¾ 1:45¾ 1:59¼	3↑ Handicap 400	0	1	1^3	1^5	1^8	1^6	Turner N	117	*.50	70-29	Imp117^{6}Moncreith105^{5}Banquo II105^{10}	Won eased up 4
18May98- 5Lak	hy	1 1/16	:24¾ :50½ 1:16¾ 1:54½	4↑ Alw 400	0	1	1^{15}	1^{25}	1^{20}	1^6	Turner N	102	*.17	63-29	Imp102^{6}Kirk108^{no}Arrezzo102^{10}	Won pulled up 4
21Oct97- 5Hrm	fst	6f	:23½ :48 1:00½ 1:13¾	3↑ Alw 400	0	2	3^{1¾}	3^{2¼}	4^4	4^9	Clay	104	7.00	--	Timemaker105^{2}May W102^{3}Abuse112^4	Showed little 4
19Oct97- 6Hrm	fst	7f	:23¾ :48½ 1:14½ 1:27	2↑ Alw 400	0	1	1^{nk}	1^{nk}	2^{nk}	6^7	Everett	104	7.00	--	Mav W102^{¼}Lieber Karl94^{3}Gath119^{no}	Dueled.tired 7

PAST PERFORMANCES

Date-Race	Cond	Dist	Fractions	Race			Calls				Jockey	Wt	Odds		Company Line	Comment / Field
16Oct97-5Hrm	fst	6f	:24¼ :48½ 1:01¼ 1:13¼	2↑ Speed .6k	0	1	2nk	32¾	41	41½	Everett	105	30.00	--	May W102noGath117no D Flora Louise871½	Impeded stretch 5
Placed third through disqualification																
12Oct97-3Hrm	hy	5½f	:25¾ :52 1:05¾ 1:12¾	3↑ Alw 400	0	4	32¾	313	312	316	Clay	99	3.00	--	Gath1146B & W10210Imp9912	Disliked going 4
9Oct97-5Hrm	fst	5½f	:23 :48½ 1:01 1:07¼	2↑ Alw 400	0	1	31	32¾	41¼	45	Clay	102	4.50	--	Flora Louise881Charm1074Judge Wardell88hd	Good effort 5
18Sep97-4Hrm	gd	6f	:24½ :49½ 1:01¼ 1:13½	2↑ Alw 400	0	3	44	44¼	21½	21	Connolly	105	4.00	--	Harry Duke1071Imp1052½The Swain1076	Driving 8
15Sep97-4Hrm	fst	6f	:24 :48½ 1:01¾ 1:14½	3↑ Handicap 400	0	2	41¼	43¼	31½	46½	Clay	115	*1.60	--	Laureate110½Preston983Simmons983	Poor ride 5
11Sep97-5Hrm	fst	6f	:24 :48½ 1:00½ 1:13¼	2↑ Alw 400	0	1	12½	1½	1nk	11½	Clay	108	4.50	--	Imp1081½HrryDuk109½Prsbytrn885	Rated,drew away cleverly 5
9Sep97-5Hrm	fst	7f	:24½ :49¾ 1:14½ 1:26¾	3↑ Alw 400	0	1	11	1¾	1nk	1no	Clay	104	6.00	--	Imp104noThe Swain104½Macy1011½	Tired,well ridden 5
2Sep97-4Hrm	fst	6f	:23½ :47½ 1:00¾ 1:13	3↑ Alw 400	0	1	11	11	1½	1½	Clay	97	*1.40	--	Imp97½Harry Duke105.5¾Abuse11310	All out drive 4
30Aug97-5Hrm	fst	7f	:22¾ :47 1:12½ 1:26¼	2↑ Alw 400	0	1	18	16	12	11	Clay	97	*1.10	--	Imp971Fretful1046Irene Woods1094	Tiring 5
28Aug97-5Hrm	fst	6f	:23¾ :48½ 1:00¼ 1:12¾	2↑ Alw 400	0	1	13	11½	1nk	2½	Clay	99	8.00	--	Flora Louise85½Imp991½Timemaker110hd	Driving 5
24Aug97-3Hrm	fst	6½f	:23½ :48¾ 1:13¼ 1:19¾	2↑ Alw 400	0	3	2½	2¾	3nk	34½	Clay	103	8.00	--	Timemaker1081½Irene Woods1103Imp103hd	Used,tired 5
19Aug97-4Hrm	fst	1	:24 :48 1:13½ 1:40	Alw 400	0	2	2½	2hd	21½	35½	Woods J	89	7.00	--	Lady Callahan892½Serrano963Imp89hd	Appeared lame 4
16Aug97-3Hrm	fst	1	:24 :49 1:13¾ 1:39¾	Alw 400	0	2	2hd	2hd	21½	37½	Caywood	102	1.60	--	Lady Callahan981½Dunois986Imp10210	Dueled,tired 6
13Aug97-4Hrm	fst	7f	:24¼ :49 1:14½ 1:27¾	3↑ Alw 400	0	1	1¾	12	11½	15	Burns T	97	5.00	--	Imp975Greyhurst1042½Nimrod1072	Handily 7
11Aug97-6Hrm	fst	6f	:24¼ :48¼ 1:01¼ 1:13¾	3↑ Alw 400	0	6	57¾	46	53	53	Hicks J	95	8.00	--	IreneWoods1091½LadyCallahn95noThDuc105no	Never a threat 11
29Jly97-4Oky	fst	7f	:23¾ :48¼ 1:14¼ 1:27	Ohio Selling 1k	0	1	1hd	2½	2hd	33½	Everett	97	8.00	--	Taluca1031½Remember Me902Imp971	Gave way 6
27Jly97-4Oky	hy	6f	:24½ :49 1:16½	Press 1.5k	0	1	2½	21	22	21	Piggott	103	2.50	--	Abe Furst1081Imp1035Eugenia Wickes103	Driving,no match 3
17Jly97-6Oky	hy	6½f	:25 :50¼ 1:16½ 1:23½	3↑ Alw 300	0	6	66½	614	611	717½	Reiff C	103	3.00	--	Box984Arlington1064Geyser1063	Bad start 7
8Jly97-5Oky	fst	1	:25¼ :50 1:15½ 1:43	Ⓕ Alw 350	0	1	1½	11	12	1hd	Reiff C	104	2.50	--	Imp104hdPerformance1041½BelleBramble1078	Tiring,held on 5
1Jly97-1Oky	fst	6f	:24½ :49¼ 1:14½	3↑ Inaugural Dash .5k	0	2	42	42½	31½	42½	Burns T	98	4.00	--	Panmure101hdGeyser1061Boanerges1131½	No threat 7
29Jun97-5Lat	fst	1	:24½ :48¾ 1:14¼ 1:41¾	Clm	0	3	2½	1nk	32	45	Everett	97	3.50	--	LordZeni1041½Viscount932AbFurst1021½	Stopped in stretch 6
24Jun97-5Lat	fst	1	:24½ :49 1:15 1:41¾	Handicap 500	0	2	2no	11	12	21	Burns T	97	5.00	--	Donna Rita951Imp972Boanerges1142	Second best 4
14Jun97-4Lat	fst	1	:24½ :48½ 1:13¾ 1:41¼	3↑ Alw 300	0	2	2½	2½	21	53½	Burns T	102	3.00	--	Cavalero1071½FredBarr102.51JoClrk100no	Stopped in drive 8
10Jun97-4Lat	fst	6f	:24¼ :49 1:14¼	3↑ Milldale 1.5k	0	6	52¼	33	44½	62½	Nutt	111	20.00	--	Taluca101.51Byron McClelland112½Pete114hd	No threat 8
8Jun97-5Lat	gd	6f	:24¼ :49 1:14½	3↑ Alw 300	0	1	11	11	1½	2hd	Nutt	106	*1.40	--	Geyser97hdImp1062Orimar973	Speed,just missed 8
1Jun97-4Lat	fst	6f	:24½ :48¾ 1:14	3↑ Handicap 480	0	1	11	12	11½	11½	Everett	104	10.00	--	Imp1041½Byron McClelland1061Sangamon100hd	Cleverly 8
29May97-5Lat	fst	6f	:24¼ :48½ 1:13¾	3↑ Alw 350	0	2	22	2½	21	2½	Burns T	100	15.00	--	Pete109½Imp1001Sharon1103	No match 10
26May97-6Lat	gd	6f	:24½ :49 1:14	3↑ Clm	0	3	41	55½	31½	512	Hill J	103	8.00	--	J.A. Gray1091½Balk Line108.5hdW C T10910	Bid,tired 10
18May97-4Nwp	fst	6f	:24 :48¾ 1:01¾ 1:14½	Ⓕ Alw 250	0	2	22	41½	31	4nk	Sheedy	115	5.00	--	Suisun105noHer Excellency115noTrimuda105no	Driving 8
15May97-4Nwp	fst	7f	:23¾ :48¾ 1:15¼ 1:28½	3↑ Clm 1500	0	1	11	12	1½	21	Sheedy	105	*2.00	--	Irksome1051Imp105½Miss Ross105½	Stopped when challenged 9
13May97-1Nwp	gd	6f	:25 :50 1:03 1:16¼	Alw 250	0	3	21	11	11	1½	Sheedy	109	2.00	--	Imp109½Box1092Myth1062	Handily 6
7May97-1Nwp	fst	5f	:24 :49 1:02	Alw 250	0	3	64½	44½	43	31	Knapp	112	3.00	--	Lady Juliet1071Her Excellency107hdImp1123	Good try 9
4May97-4Nwp	hy	7f	:25 :51½ 1:19½ 1:34¼	3↑ Clm 1400	0	1	12	12	12	12	Hill J	104	3.50	--	Imp1042J H C1026Banquo II986	Handily 8
1May97-2Nwp	sly	1	:27¼ :54 1:20¼ 1:46½	3↑ Alw 250	0	1	13	11	2½	26	Chenault	86	1.60	--	Skate1046Imp863Jamboree1083	Used,tired 8
29Apr97-6Nwp	fst	6f	:23½ :48½ 1:01½ 1:14½	3↑ Clm 1200	0	1	11	12	13	13	Reiff C	105	*2.50	--	Imp1053J. Walter100nkGooding1111	Easily 8
19Apr97-4Nwp	gd	6f	:23¾ :48 1:01½ 1:14¾	3↑ Alw 300	0	1	35	36	55	49	Hill J	100	10.00	--	Flotow1053Winker1055Abe Furst1101	Outrun 6
16Apr97-3Nwp	hy	1 50	:25¼ :51¼ 1:17¼ 1:50	3↑ Clm 1500	0	1	11	1½	2½	33½	Reiff C	101	2.50	--	John Sullivan103½Parson1043Imp1018	Weakened 6
14Apr97-1Nwp	hy	6f	:25 :50½ 1:05 1:19¾	Ⓕ Alw 250	0	2	1hd	13	12	15	Hill J	115	*.70	--	Imp1155Adalid1158Carlotta C.1156	Much best 8
10Apr97-3Nwp	sl	1	:25½ :52 1:20¾ 1:50¾	Ⓕ Queen City Oaks 1.3k	0	1	12	2hd	1½	49	Reiff C	112	12.00	--	Faunette107hdNannieL'sSister1121Panchital1128	Stopped 5
8Apr97-1Nwp	hy	6f	:25 :50½ 1:04 1:19	Alw 300	0	3	2½	24	36	54½	Scherrer	102	*.90	--	Vengeance104½Suydam1072Cynthia II1021	Stopped 6
1Apr97-4Nwp	fst	1	1:41¾	Alw 300	0	0	1	1	1	33½	Scherrer	107	3.50	--	Winker109½Vengeance1043Imp107	9
25Jly96-5Lat	sl	5½f	:25 :51½ 1:11¾	Ⓕ Alw 400	0	3	1hd	1½	1nk	36	Sherrin	115	*2.50	--	Truelight1121Lady Keith1005Imp115no	Quit badly 6

24Jly96- 2Lat	hy 5f	:26 :53¼	1:06¾	ⒻAlw 300	0	1	1½	12½	15	12½	Sherrin	112		*1.30	--	Imp1122½Black Heart105.51Carlotta C112no	Never extended	13
14Jly96- 5Lat	sly 5f	:25¾ :51¼	1:04	ⒻAlw 400	0	1	12	12	12	13	Sherrin	107		*2.00	--	Imp1073Carlotta C1072Pouting1074	Easily	8
9Jly96- 5Lat	hy 5f	:26 :52¼	1:05½	ⒻAlw 400	0	2	1½	1hd	12	21	Sherrin	107		7.00	--	Mertie Reed1071Imp1071Adowa1103	Tiring badly	9
7Jly96- 4Lat	sl 5f	:25 :49¾	1:01¾	ⒻClipsetta 2.5k	0	4	43	54½	34½	48½	Van Kuren	110		15.00	--	Midlight105½EugeniaWcks1188BllBrmbl115hd	Never a threat	9
23Jun96- 3Oky	hy 5f	:25 :50	1:04	Alw 400	0	1	1½	2hd	21	22	Thorpe	112		*1.20	--	Orion1152Imp1125Red115hd	Second best	6
15Jun96- 3Oky	gd 5f	:24¼ :49¼	1:03	Alw 400	0	3	54¼	1no	2½	41	Snedeker	110		6.00	--	Burlsqu1131ChrryLf108noOron113no	Taken up,altered course	8
12Jun96- 3Oky	gd 5f	:24 :48½	1:02½	Alw 400	0	2	31	2½	21	22	Snedeker	108		3.00	--	Eugenia Wickes1072Imp1083Cavalero110hd	Outrun	7
2Jun96- 1Oky	fst 5f	:24¼ :49	1:01¾	ⒻAlw 400	0	1	1hd	11½	11	2½	Thorpe	115		3.00	--	White Frost105½Imp1156Charina1052	Used in pace	6
26May96- 4Oky	sl 4f	:24½	:50¾	ⒻSapphire 2.5k	0	2		32	32	33	Perkins	115		4.00	--	Cleophus1202Amiable1151Imp1151	No threat to winner	5
22May96- 1Oky	sl 4f	:25	:50¾	ⒻMd Sp Wt	0	4		12	15	11	Snedeker	110		2.50	--	Imp1101Dulcenea1055Scarf Pin1055	Urged at end	8

Beldame

ch. f. 1901, by Octagon (Rayon d'Or)–Bella–Donna, by Hermit

Lifetime record: 31 17 6 4 $102,570

Own.– A. Belmont
Br.– August Belmont (Ky)
Tr.– A.J. Joyner

19Aug05- 4Sar	fst 1¾	:51 2:08 2:3413:004	3↑	Sar Cup 7.5k	1	1	12	1hd	21½	21½	O'Neill F	121	w	3.60	84-11	Caughnawaga1271½Beldame1213Cairngorm113	Gamely	3
8Aug05- 4Sar	fst 1	:244:483 1:13 1:392	3↑	Delaware H 2.6k	1	1	1hd	31	46	52½	O'Neill F	122	w	3.20	89-13	MollyBrnt1132DollySpnkr108noCrngorm109hd	Fast pace,tired	7
31Jly05- 4Sar	sl 1¼	:4741:1321:41 2:07	3↑	Saratoga H 10k	8	6	65¼	51½	44	33½	O'Neill F	120	w	4.50e	86-15	Caughnawaga1193WaterLight108½Beldm1208	Wide,game at end	9
8Jly05- 4Bri	sly 1¼	:4821:1311:3912:044	3↑	Brighton H 25k	4	4	42½	44	36	39	O'Neill F	125	w	3.20	81-12	Artful1031Ort Wells1258Beldame1253	Impeded first turn	7
5Jly05- 4Bri	fst 1	:243:483 1:1311:381	3↑	Brighton Mile 3.8k	1	1	11½	11½	1½	2¾	O'Neill F	121	w	*.80	98-08	OrtWells126¾Beldame1217Delhi1268	Sulked when challenged	4
24Jun05- 4She	hy 1⅜	:4941:1511:4112:204	3↑	Advance 15k	3	1	11½	11½	1hd	2no	O'Neill F	121	w	*.20	84-14	Agile111noBeldame12150Graziallo126	Just missed	3
15Jun05- 4She	fst 1¼	:4841:1331:3932:052	3↑	Suburban H 20k	3	2	23	22	11½	11	O'Neill F	123	w	3.50	96-07	Beldame1231Proper1094First Mason118¾	Easily	11
8Jun05- 4Gra	hy 1¼	:49 1:1441:4132:073	3↑	Standard 5.8k	2	2	2nk	2hd	1hd	11	O'Neill F	121	w	*.70	89-15	Beldame1211Cairngorm11110MajorDaingerfld128	Dueled,best	3
5Jun05- 3Gra	fst 1 1/16	:24 :48 1:1331:47	3↑	Handicap 1405	7	1	1½	11½	1nk	21½	O'Neill F	126	w	4.00	93-08	Garnish1071½Beldame1264Kehailan1024	Second best	12
4May05- 4Bel	fst 1	:253:49 1:413	3↑	Metropolitan H 12k	4	3	33	33½	72	915	O'Neill F	122	w	4.00	--	DHSysonby107DHRace King975Colonial Girl1114	Tired	12
Previously owned by N. Bennington;previously trained by F. Burlew																		
24Sep04- 4Gra	fst 1½	:50 1:1532:0732:352	3↑	Second Spl 5.7k	4	1	12	13	16	15	O'Neill F	112	w	*.55	88-10	Beldame1125Broomstick1101McChesney121hd	Easing up	4
19Sep04- 4Gra	fst 1¼	:4841:14 1:4022:06	3↑	First Spl 5.9k	2	1	14	13	12	11½	O'Neill F	114	w	*1.00	97-06	Beldame1141½Caughnawaga1263Stalwart11710	Easily	5
7Sep04- 4She	fst 1⅜	:49 1:1421:4022:193		September 4.8k	4	2	11½	12	13	12½	O'Neill F	123		*1.20	97-05	Beldame1232½Graziallo122¾Ort Wells1261	Easily	4
30Aug04- 4She	fst 1⅛	:49 1:1411:4021:53		Dolphin 3.6k	3	1	12	12	13	14	O'Neill F	126	w	*.14	96-09	Beldame1264Ormonde's Right1143Aurumaster1052		4
Repelled stretch challenge																		
20Aug04- 4Sar	sly 1¾	:50 2:0822:36 3:034	3↑	Sar Cup 10k	5	1	16	15	14	14	O'Neill F	108	w	*1.80	71-21	Beldame1084Africandr126½ThPckt1262	Never fully extended	5
4Aug04- 4Sar	fst 1⅛	:49 1:14 1:4021:533		ⒻAlabama 5k	1	1	15	16	18	16	O'Neill F	124	w	*.05	89-08	Beldame1246Dimple1164Ishlana116	Easing up late	3
6Jly04- 4Bri	fst 1	:241:48 1:1231:38	3↑	Test H 5k	1	3	21½	22	22	21	O'Neill F	115	w	1.40	99-07	Hermis1331Beldame1155Dainty1034	Off slowly,poor ride	5
30Jun04- 2She	gd 1	:242:48 1:13 1:392	3↑	ⒻAlw 1140	2	1	16	16	14	12	O'Neill F	111	w	*.35	92-05	Beldame1112Lux Casta1105Hortensia1013	Bumped at start	6
22Jun04- 4She	fst 1⅛	:4831:14 1:41 1:542		ⒻMermaid 6.3k	6	1	13	15	16	17	O'Neill F	126	w	*.60	89-11	Beldame1267Little Em1112½Possession1113½	Easing up	6
9Jun04- 4Gra	sly 1 1/16	:24 :50 1:1731:523		ⒻGazelle 4.6k	4	1	12	13	15	110	O'Neill F	124	w	*.17	67-27	Beldame12410Graceful1211Little Em1135	Easily	5
1Jun04- 1Gra	sly *6f	:234:481 1:11	3↑	ⒻAlw 1220	3	3	32	21	11	11	O'Neill F	106	w	*.50	88-17	Beldame1061Mamie Worth1155Graceful1016	Easily	8
21May04- 4MP	1	:243:50 1:1531:411		ⒻLadies 5.6k	4	1	11½	1½	14	1¾	Hildebrand	121	w	*.60	87-10	Beldame121¾Audience1215Marjoram12110		4
Bolted before start and returned to stable area,won asing up																		
5May04- 4MP	fst 1	:242:48 1:1421:40	3↑	Metropolitan H 13k	9	7	73¼	77	45	34	Brennan A	98	w	20.00	89-09	Irish Lad1232Toboggan1032Beldame98½	Gamely	17
15Apr04- 4Aqu	fst 7f	:24 :494 1:1411:27	3↑	Carter H 8.7k	5	1	11	11	11¼	12	O'Neill F	103	w	7.00	96-09	Beldame1032Peter Paul985Wotan1001½	Speed in reserve	17
5Nov03- 5Aqu	sly 6f	:251 1:154		Handicap 880	0	2	11½	11½	11	14	O'Neill F	121	w	1.70	90-11	Beldame1214Harangue1221Palette1056	Easily	5

PAST PERFORMANCES

Previously owned by A. Belmont;previously trained by J. Hyland

3Oct03- 3MP	fst *6f		1:10^{2}	Nursery H 7.6k	0 2 5^{1¾} 6^{2¼} 6^{1½} 4^{2¼}	Cochran H	116 w	15.00	89-11	Race King114^{1½}Grenade115^{hd}Divination108^{¾}	Finished fast12
28Sep03- 3MP	gd *6f		1:10^{1}	ⒻMatron 7k	0 4 5^{7½} 4^{4½} 4^{3½} 3^{2}	Cochran H	123 w	6.00e	90-07	Armenia112^{hd}For Luck109^{2}Beldame123^{½}	Fast finish 8
2Sep03- 3She	gd *6f		1:12^{4}	ⒻGreat Filly 17k	0 2 3^{2½} 2^{½} 2^{½} 1^{hd}	Bullman	116wb	15.00	76-20	Beldame116^{hd}Ocean Tide116^{no}Mineola116^{6}	Dueled,just up15
22Aug03- 5Sar	fst 5½f	:23^{2}:47	1:00^{2}1:07	Alw 740	0 11 7^{5¾} 5^{5} 7^{7¾} 6^{8}	Bullman	114 w	9.00	87-00	Hamburg Belle114^{1½}Long Shot117^{1½}Race King117^{2}	Bad start11
1Jly03- 4She	fst 5f		1:01^{2}	ⒻVernal 4.9k	0 3 1^{1} 1^{1} 1^{2} 1^{1}	Bullman	107 w	*.90e	85-15	Beldame107^{1}Monsoon107^{hd}Tepee107^{hd}	Gamely13
10Jun03- 3Gra	my 5f	:24^{4}:50	1:03	ⒻClover 2.6k	0 12 7^{6¼} 7^{2½} 3^{2} 2^{1½}	Minder	112 w	*2.50	81-20	Contentous112^{1½}Bldm112^{½}Mordll112^{4}	Bad start,fast finish12

Regret

ch. f. 1912, by Broomstick (Ben Brush)–Jersey Lightning, by Hamburg **Lifetime record: 11 9 1 0 $35,093**

Own.– H.P. Whitney
Br.– H.P. Whitney (NJ)
Tr.– J. Rowe

25Sep17- 1Aqu	fst 7f	:23^{4}:47^{2}	1:11^{2}1:24^{1}	2↑ Handicap 764	2 1 1^{2} 1^{2} 1^{3} 1^{3}	Robinson F	127 w	*.08	101-09	Regret127^{3}Ima Frank109	Speed in reserve 2
10Jly17- 4Aqu	gd 1$\frac{1}{16}$	:24^{1}:48	1:15^{2}1:45^{2}	3↑ ⒻGazelle H 3.1k	6 1 1^{2} 1^{3} 1^{3} 1^{3}	Loftus J	129 w	*.17	96-11	Regret129^{3}Bayberry Candle123^{hd}Wistful105^{1}	Won eased up 6
25Jun17- 4Aqu	fst 1⅛	:47	1:12^{2}1:36^{3}1:49^{2}	3↑ Brooklyn H 5.8k	3 1 1^{2} 1^{1} 1^{1½} 2no	Robinson F	122 w	3.60e	103-04	Borrow117^{no}Regret122^{1}Old Rosebud120^{1}	Overconfident ride11
31May17- 3Bel	fst 5½f-Str		1:04^{2}	3↑ ⒻAlw 880	2 1 1^{1} 1^{3} 1^{5} 1^{8}	Robinson F	128 w	*.17	97-09	Regret128^{8}YankeeWitch118^{½}Admiration106^{1½}	Won pulling up 5
18Aug16- 3Sar	fst 1	:25 :49	1:14 1:39^{2}	3↑ Alw 710	4 1 1^{1½} 1^{3} 1^{2} 1^{1½}	Keogh F	108 w	*.07	90-10	Regret107.5^{1½}Flittergold115^{4}Polroma104^{1½}	5
	Under restraint throughout										
31Jly16- 4Sar	fst 1¼	:50	1:14^{4}1:40 2:05^{1}	3↑ Saratoga H 4.8k	6 1 1^{1} 2^{nk} 2^{1½} 8^{16}	Notter J	123 w	*.90	78-10	Stromboli121^{1½}EdCrump123^{1½}FriarRock107^{hd}	Set pace,tired 8
17Aug15- 4Sar	gd 1	:25 :49	1:15^{1}1:42	Saranac H 1.4k	2 1 1^{2} 1^{1} 1^{2} 1^{1½}	Notter J	123 w	*.33	77-21	Rgrt123^{1½}TrlbyJury114^{3}LdyRoth106^{1}	Under stout restraint 8
8May15- 5CD	fst 1¼	:48^{3}1:13^{3}	1:39^{2}2:05^{2}	Ky Derby 14k	2 1 1^{½} 1^{½} 1^{1½} 1^{2}	Notter J	112 w	*2.65	90-09	Regret112^{2}Pebbles117^{2}Sharpshooter114^{1}	Won easing up16
22Aug14- 3Sar	hy 6f	:24^{1}:49^{1}	1:16^{2}	Hopeful 10k	2 2 5^{6½} 6^{6¾} 3^{1½} 1^{½}	Notter J	127 w	*1.60	76-27	Regret127^{½}AndrewM.114^{3}Pebbles130^{4}	In heavy going,gamely11
15Aug14- 3Sar	sl 6f	:23 :47^{1}	1:13^{2}	Sanford Mem 3.4k	1 3 1^{1} 1^{2} 1^{1½} 1^{1½}	Notter J	127 w	*.80e	91-17	Regrt127^{1½}Solly113^{2}DnhDo107^{5}	Under restraint throughout 8
8Aug14- 3Sar	fst 6f	:23 :47	1:11^{3}	Sar Spl 4.1k	8 1 1^{3} 1^{½} 1^{2} 1^{1}	Notter J	119 w	*1.60e	100-03	Regret119^{1}Pebbles122^{3}Paris122^{no}	Speed in reserve 8

Twilight Tear

b. f. 1941, by Bull Lea (Bull Dog)–Lady Lark, by Blue Larkspur **Lifetime record: 24 18 2 2 $202,165**

Own.– Calumet Farm
Br.– Calumet Farm (Ky)
Tr.– B.A. Jones

28Aug45- 6Was	fst 6f	:22^{1}:45^{2}	1:10^{2}	3↑ Alw 5000	3 1 2^{1½} 2^{4} 4^{7½} -	Dodson D	117 w	1.80	- -	FightingDon110^{3}Occupy116^{5}MyTetRambler111^{1½}	Bled,eased 5
1Nov44- 7Pim	fst 1$\frac{3}{16}$	:48^{1}1:12^{2}	1:37^{2}1:56^{3}	3↑ Pim Spl 25k	2 1 1^{3} 1^{4} 1^{4} 1^{6}	Dodson D	117 w	*.65	99-12	Twilight Tear117^{6}Devil Diver126^{10}Megogo120	Galloping 3
21Oct44- 6Lrl	my 1¼	:48^{1}1:14	1:41^{4}2:08^{3}	Maryland H 16k	4 1 1^{1} 2^{3} 4^{6½} 4^{15½}	Dodson D	130 w	*.15e	51-40	Dare Me109^{7}Miss Keeneland110^{2½}Aera106^{6}	Quit badly 6
12Oct44- 6Lrl	fst 1⅛	:47^{2}1:23^{1}	1:40 1:53^{1}	3↑ ⒻQueen Isabella H 11k	4 1 1^{6} 1^{6} 1^{5} 1^{5}	Dodson D	126 w	*.15e	82-23	Twilight Tear126^{5}Good Morning118^{2}Legend Bearer108^{3½}	8
	Never extended										
2Oct44- 5Bel	fst 5½f-W	:22^{4}:45^{2}	1:03^{2}	3↑ ⒻHandicap 3480	3 1 2^{hd} 1^{½} 1^{2½}	Arcaro E	126 w	*.40e	97-08	Twilight Tear126^{2½}Tellmenow118^{¾}Cocopet114^{5}	5
	Bore out,impeded runner-up str										
8Aug44- 6Bel	fst 1¼	:47^{1}1:11^{2}	1:37^{2}2:03^{3}	ⒻAlabama 23k	1 1 1^{½} 1^{1} 1^{1½} 2^{¾}	Haas L	126 w	*.05	81-14	Vienna114^{¾}Twilight Tear126^{5}Thread o' Gold117^{1¼}	Faltered 4
22Jly44- 6Was	fst 1¼	:48 1:12	1:37^{2}2:03^{3}	Classic 79k	1 1 1^{1} 1^{2} 1^{3} 1^{2}	Haas L	114 w	*.10e	92-08	TwlghtTr114^{2}OldKntuck119^{4½}Pnsv126^{5}	Saved ground,handily 5
17Jly44- 3Was	fst 1	:23^{3}:47^{1}	1:11^{2}1:36^{1}	Alw 5000	2 1 1^{2} 1^{2} 1^{3} 1^{1¼}	Haas L	117 w	-e	97-11	Twilight Tear117^{1¼}Pensive122^{2}Appleknocker110^{1}	Easily 4
	Nonwagering event										
6Jly44- 6Was	fst 7f	:23 :45^{3}	1:09^{3}1:22^{3}	Skokie H 11k	5 2 1^{1} 1^{2} 1^{3} 1^{1½}	Haas L	121 w	*.30e	103-10	TwilightTear121^{1½}Sirde114^{2½}ChallengM106^{5}	Speed to spare 7
28Jun44- 6Was	fst 6f	:22^{2}:45^{3}	1:10^{3}	ⒻPrincess Doreen 11k	1 2 2^{1} 2^{2½} 2^{hd} 1^{1½}	McCreary C	121 w	*.40	98-09	TwilightTear121^{1½}BellSong110^{6}HrrtSu114^{nk}	Altered course 6

27May44-6Bel	gd	1⅜	:48^1 1:13^3 1:40 2:21	ⒻC C A Oaks 17k	1	1	1^2	1^3	1^3	1^4	McCreary C	121	w	*.10	66-27	Twilight Tear121^{4}Dare Me121^{3}Plucky Maud121^2	Easily	6
17May44-6Bel	fst	1	:23^3 :46^4 1:11^2 1:37	ⒻAcorn 14k	9	4	4^2	2^1	$1^{1\frac12}$	$1^{2\frac12}$	McCreary C	121	w	*.20	89-13	TwilightTear121$^{2\frac12}$Whirlabout121^{6}Evrgt121^1	Speed to spare	10
10May44-6Pim	fst	1 1/16	:23^4 :48 1:12^3 1:45^1	ⒻPim Oaks 18k	5	1	$1^{1\frac12}$	1^1	$1^{1\frac12}$	1^3	McCreary C	121	w	*.30	92-19	Twilight Tear121^{3}Plucky Maud121^{3}Everget121^5	In hand	5
3May44-6Pim	fst	6f	:22^1 :45^3 1:11^3	Rennert H 7k	10	3	2^2	$2^{\frac12}$	1^3	$1^{1\frac12}$	McCreary C	118	w	*.40e	95-17	TwilightTear118$^{1\frac12}$Glctc108^{3}IdlGft112.5^2	As rider pleased	10
25Apr44-6Pim	sl	6f	:22^4 :47^4 1:14	Alw 4000	3	2	2^{hd}	1^1	$1^{\frac12}$	$1^{1\frac14}$	McCreary C	117	w	*.50e	83-35	TwilightTear117$^{1\frac14}$GrampsImage114^{5}Jmm114^6	Rated,drew away	5
17Mar44-5TrP	sly	6f	:22^1 :45^3 1:12^2	ⒻAlw 1800	5	3	3^7	$3^{6\frac12}$	$2^{\frac14}$	1^3	McCreary C	118	w	*.30	88-29	Twilight Tear118^{3}Lassie Sue120$^{1\frac12}$Cuban Bomb106^2	Handily	7
10Mar44-6TrP	fst	6f	:23 :46^4 1:11^4	Alw 1800	7	1	1^1	1^1	1^4	1^2	McCreary C	117	w	*.25	91-16	Twilight Tear117^{2}Comenow119$^{2\frac12}$Surrogate122^{nk}	Easily	7
29Feb44-6Hia	fst	6f	:23 :46^2 1:12^1	3↑ Leap Year H 5k	4	5	$4^{2\frac14}$	$3^{\frac12}$	3^1	3^2	Smith FA	101	w	9.00	86-23	Mettlesome116^{1}Adulator112^{1}Twilight Tear101^{hd}	Held well	8
8Nov43-6Pim	sly	1 70	:24^1 :49 1:15^3 1:47^2	ⒻAlw 5000	4	1	1^5	1^2	1^1	$1^{2\frac14}$	Thompson B	120	w	*.50e	74-28	Twilight Tear120$^{2\frac14}$Miss Keeneland120^{8}Red Wonder111^{10}		5
	Speed in reserve																	
27Oct43-6Pim	my	1 1/16	:23^4 :48^1 1:14 1:48^2	ⒻSelima 24k	5	3	1^1	$1^{1\frac12}$	1^{nk}	2^1	Thompson B	119	w	*1.20e	75-27	MissKeeneland111^{1}TwilightTear119$^{1\frac12}$Whrlbout122^6	No match	8
20Oct43-5Pim	fst	1 70	:24^1 :49 1:14^3 1:45^4	ⒻAlw 2500	6	1	$1^{1\frac12}$	1^2	1^1	1^2	Thompson B	115	w	*.40e	82-21	TwilightTear115^{2}MissKenlnd109^{6}MyMlch106^1	Speed to spare	6
16Oct43-7Pim	sly	6f	:23 :48^1 1:15^3	ⒻAlw 2500	1	4	1^{nk}	2^{hd}	2^{hd}	$3^{2\frac12}$	Smith FA	117	w	*1.05e	72-21	Red Wonder111^{no}Countess Wise114$^{2\frac12}$Twilight Tear117^{nk}		8
	Used in pace,lost ground																	
3Jly43-6Was	fst	6f	:22^4 :46^4 1:13^1	ⒻArl Lassie 34k	3	6	2^2	2^2	1^3	$1^{2\frac12}$	Jemas N	113	w	*1.00e	85-14	TwilightTear113$^{2\frac12}$MissKeeneland113^{2}MusicHall110^4	Easily	15
25Jun43-1Was	fst	5½f	:22^4 :47^3 1:00^3 1:07^3	ⒻMd Sp Wt	6	5	$6^{8\frac12}$	4^5	2^1	$1^{\frac34}$	Eads W	115	w	*1.60	87-17	Twilight Tear115$^{\frac34}$Letmenow115^{1}Durazna115^3		12
	Slow into stride,drawing clear																	

Busher

ch. f. 1942, by War Admiral (Man o' War)–Baby League, by Bubbling Over

Lifetime record: 21 15 3 1 $334,035

Own.–L.B. Mayer

Br.– Idle Hour Stock Farm Co (Ky)

Tr.– G. Philpot

2Jan47-7SA	fst	6f	:22^3 :45^4 1:10	4↑ ⒻAlw 7500	2	6	6^3	6^6	$5^{6\frac12}$	5^5	Westrope J	118	w	*1.00	92-12	Miss Doreen114^{2}Monsoon114$^{1\frac14}$Going With Me111^1		6
	Dwelt,under urging at finish,worked seven furlongs;Previously trained by G.M. Odom																	
6Oct45-7Hol	fst	1 1/16	:23 :46^3 1:11^1 1:43^4	3↑ ⒻVanity H 27k	2	4	4^9	2^5	$1^{1\frac12}$	1^2	Longden J	126	w	*.35e	93-09	Busher126^{2}Canina114^{4}Paula's Lulu113^{hd}	Speed in reserve	9
29Sep45-7Hol	fst	1⅛	:46^2 1:11 1:37^1 1:50^1	Hol Derby 57k	13	6	$6^{4\frac34}$	$4^{\frac34}$	$1^{\frac12}$	$1^{1\frac12}$	Longden J	123	w	*.65	94-09	Busher123$^{1\frac12}$Mano'Glory112^{1}QuickRewrd121^2	Bumped 1st turn	14
15Sep45-7Hol	fst	1	:22^3 :46 1:11^2 1:37^3	Will Rogers H 30k	1	3	$3^{\frac12}$	4^3	$3^{\frac12}$	2^{hd}	Longden J	123	w	*.35	93-11	Quick Reward112^{hd}Busher123$^{\frac12}$War Allies110^3	Driving	14
3Sep45-7Was	fst	1¼	:46^3 1:10^3 1:36^1 2:01^4	3↑ Wash Park H 57k	4	3	3^3	1^3	1^3	$1^{1\frac12}$	Longden J	115	w	*1.40	101-12	Busher115$^{1\frac12}$Armed120^{1}Take Wing112^5	Driving	13
29Aug45-7Was	gd	1	:23 :45^3 1:10^4 1:37^4	3↑ ⒻMatch Race 25k	1	2	1^{hd}	2^{nk}	1^{hd}	$1^{\frac34}$	Longden J	115	w	*.50	89-21	Busher115$^{\frac34}$Durazna115	Inside,vigorous ride	2
18Aug45-7Was	fst	1⅛	:46^3 1:12 1:37^3 1:51^2	3↑ ⒻBeverly H 32k	6	6	$5^{7\frac12}$	$3^{4\frac12}$	$3^{2\frac12}$	$3^{3\frac34}$	Longden J	128	w	*.40e	87-14	Durazna116$^{2\frac12}$Letmenow102$^{1\frac14}$Busher128^4	No threat	8
4Aug45-7Was	fst	1¼	:49^1 1:14 1:39 2:03^4	3↑ Arlington H 54k	2	1	1^2	1^1	1^3	$1^{4\frac12}$	Longden J	113	w	*1.10	91-12	Busher113$^{4\frac12}$Take Wing110^{no}Sirde114^{no}	Speed in reserve	8
25Jly45-6Was	fst	1	:23^3 :47 1:11^2 1:37^2	ⒻCleopatra H 26k	9	4	2^{hd}	1^2	1^2	$1^{4\frac12}$	Bailey W	126	w	*.90	91-18	Busher126$^{4\frac12}$Twosy116^{2}War Date122$^{2\frac12}$	Speed in reserve	9
4Jly45-6SA	fst	1 1/16	:22^4 :46^1 1:10^3 1:43	3↑ ⒻS Margarita H 53k	2	5	5^6	4^4	3^{nk}	$1^{1\frac12}$	Longden J	126	w	*.75e	97-09	Busher126$^{1\frac12}$Whirlabout123$^{\frac12}$Canina117^2	Easily	10
23Jun45-6SA	fst	1⅛	:46 1:11 1:37^2 1:50	S Anita Derby 54k	8	4	$3^{2\frac12}$	1^{hd}	1^3	$2^{\frac12}$	Longden J	121	w	*.55	93-09	Bymeabond119$^{\frac12}$Busher121^{1}Best Effort126^5	Wide turn	8
9Jun45-6SA	fst	1	:22^3 :45^4 1:10^1 1:36^3	San Vicente 27k	4	4	$4^{3\frac12}$	$2^{1\frac12}$	1^{hd}	$1^{1\frac14}$	Longden J	121	w	*.60e	95-10	Busher121$^{1\frac14}$Sea Sovereign121^{7}Bismarck Sea121^2		8
	Impeded by riderless horse																	
2Jun45-6SA	fst	7f	:23 :45^4 1:10^4 1:23^3	ⒻS Susanna 27k	1	2	$2^{\frac12}$	1^1	1^6	1^7	Longden J	121	w	*.15	94-15	Busher121^{7}Mist115$^{\frac12}$Glory Time115^2	As rider pleased	7
26May45-5SA	fst	6f	:22^4 :46^3 1:12	ⒻAlw 4000	6	5	1^{hd}	1^3	1^5	1^5	Longden J	121	w	*.20	89-19	Busher121^{5}Glory Time115^{4}Mist115$^{3\frac12}$	As rider pleased	8
	Previously owned by E.R. Bradley;previously trained by J.W. Smith																	
14Oct44-6Lrl	sl	1 1/16	:23^3 :47^4 1:14^1 1:49^3	ⒻSelima 29k	3	4	3^2	2^3	$1^{1\frac12}$	1^3	Arcaro E	117	w	*.90	69-34	Busher117^{3}Ace Card119$^{2\frac12}$Gallorette114^4	Off slowly	10
23Sep44-4Bel	fst	6f-WC	:22^2 :45^1 1:09^2	ⒻMatron 27k	12	1		$5^{1\frac34}$	1^{hd}	1^{nk}	Arcaro E	119	w	*1.40	94-11	Busher119^{nk}Twosy115$^{1\frac14}$Price Level123^4	Driving	12
19Sep44-5Bel	fst	6f-WC	:22^2 :44^3 1:08^3	ⒻAlw 3500	9	5		$4^{2\frac12}$	$3^{\frac14}$	2^{hd}	Woolf G	119	w	*1.00e	98-05	Nomadic108^{hd}Busher119^{2}Thine108$^{2\frac12}$	Fast finish	12

30Aug44- 6Bel	fst 6f-WC	:22^4:46	1:11^3	Ⓕ Adirondack H 10k	11	4		31½	31¼	12	Arcaro E	123	w	*2.20	88-18	Busher123^{2}War Date114½Leslie Grey116^{nk}	Bobbled start	12
16Aug44- 6Bel	fst 6f	:22^2:46^2	1:12^1	Ⓕ Spinaway 18k	7	12	1111	96¼	74¼	43¾	Zufelt F	114	w	*1.20e	85-12	Price Level115^{2}½Ace Card119^{nk}Safeguard111^1	Fast finish	12
2Aug44- 3Bel	fst 5½f-W	:22^4:45^4	1:04^2	Ⓕ Alw 3000	7	2		2½	11	14½	Young S	115	w	8.25	92-09	Bushr115^{4}½ScotchPlns115^{1}¼Conn'sGrl110¾	Speed in reserve	7
30May44- 2Bel	fst 4½f-W	:23 :46^3	:52^4	Ⓕ Md Sp Wt	12	1		21½	1hd	1½	Atkinson T	115	w	*2.25e	91-09	Busher115½Pin Up Girl115^{hd}Faint Heart115^{hd}	Driving	13

Moccasin

ch. f. 1963, by Nantallah (Nasrullah)–Rough Shod II, by Gold Bridge

Lifetime record: 21 11 2 4 $388,075

Own.– Claiborne Farm
Br.– Claiborne Farm (Ky)
Tr.– H. Trotsek

17Jun67- 9AP	sly 1	:22^2:45^1	1:10^{3}1:37	3↑ Equipose Mile 43k	2	4	47½	44¼	69	59½	Fires E	115		2.20	68-29	Renewed Vigor111^{1}½Estreno II111½Errante II114^{4}½		7
	Flattened out in drive																	
24May67- 8AP	fst 7f	:23^1:46	1:10^{3}1:23	3↑ Ⓕ Four Winds H 21k	4	6	45	67¼	45½	31	Fires E	121	b	*1.10	89-17	MssMoon120^{hd}MstySwords111^{1}Moccsn121^5	Wide,strong finish	7
22Apr67- 6Kee	fst 1$\frac{1}{16}$	:24^1:47^3	1:11^{4}1:45	3↑ Ben Ali H 23k	3	2	21½	2hd	32	31¼	Fires E	116	b	*1.30	80-17	FrancisU.119^{nk}SwiftRuler120^{1}Moccsn116^{1}½	Lacked response	6
8Apr67- 6Kee	fst 6f	:21^3:45^1	:57^1 1:09^3	3↑ Phoenix H 23k	1	6	43½	22	2hd	11	Knapp K	114	b	3.30	95-15	Moccsn114^{1}CountryFrnd114^{4}¼GlbrtB.114^{hd}	Wore down leader	7
25Feb67- 8Bow	fst 7f	:22^3:44^2	1:08^{4}1:21^4	3↑ Ⓕ Barbara Fritchie H 59k	5	8	4nk	32	3½	2nk	Broussard R	120	b	*.60	104-05	Holly-O117^{nk}Mccsn120^{2}½LdyDplmt111^{2}¾	Bobbled leaving gate	13
15Feb67- 8Hia	fst 7f	:23 :45^2	1:10 1:23	3↑ Ⓕ Columbiana H 33k	4	3	1½	15	13	2hd	Hartack W	117	b	*2.40	94-16	Mac'sSparkler115^{hd}Moccasin117^{1}½StraightDeal122½	Failed	14
6Feb67- 9Hia	fst 6f	:22 :44^4	1:10^3	4↑ Alw 5500	3	8	52¼	65¼	46	31¾	Baeza B	114	b	*1.00	89-14	FleetAdmiral116¾GoldenButtons113^{1}Moccasin114¾	Steadied	12
4Aug66- 8Sar	fst 7f	:22^3:45	1:10 1:23^2	Ⓕ Test (Div 2) 24k	8	2	2hd	23	22	11½	Baeza B	118	b	*.90	93-13	Moccasin118^{1}½Native Street124^{2}Politely112¾	Going away	10
25Jun66- 7Aqu	fst 1¼	:47^{2}1:12	1:38^{2}2:05	Ⓕ C C A Oaks 119k	2	2	22	42¼	55	59¼	Broussard R	121	b	2.40	64-17	LadyPitt121¾[D]GentleRain121^{nk}PridesProfile121^8	Weakened	10
28May66- 7Aqu	sly 1	:22^4:45^2	1:10^{2}1:36	Ⓕ Acorn 59k	7	4	22	21	2hd	34½	Broussard R	121	b	*1.40	83-18	Marking Time121^{2}½Around the Roses121^{2}Moccasin121½	Tired	11
17May66- 7Aqu	fst 6f	:22^2:45^3	1:10^2	Alw 10000	5	5	21½	21	1hd	11½	Baeza B	112	b	*1.10	91-19	Moccasin112^{1}½Imam115^{1}Bold Tactics115^{nk}	Bore out,handily	6
16Apr66- 6Kee	fst 6f	:21^3:45	1:10	Ⓕ Ashland 30k	3	9	54½	66½	66½	66¼	Adams L	121		*.30	87-12	Justakiss121^{nk}PridsProfl121^{1}½ChmpgnWomn118^2	Away slowly	9
9Apr66- 7Kee	fst 6f	:21^4:45^2	1:10^1	Ⓕ Alw 10000	6	5	67½	66½	55	41¾	Adams L	121		*.20	90-14	Stealaway115¾Dutch Maid110^{hd}Justakiss121^1		6
	In close entering stretch																	
6Nov65- 8GS	fst 1$\frac{1}{16}$	:23^4:47^1	1:12^{1}1:44^2	Ⓕ Gardenia 183k	7	3	35	31	11½	12½	Adams L	119		*.30	83-21	Moccasin119^{2}½Lady Pitt119½Prides Profile119^{nk}	Cleverly	9
23Oct65- OLrl	fst 1$\frac{1}{16}$	:24^4:49^1	1:14^{4}1:45^4	Ⓕ Selima 93k	1	1	12	13	14½	15	Adams L	119		-	88-15	Moccasin119^{5}SwiftLady119½Drryll114¾	Scored well in hand	5
	Run between 6th and 7th races. No wagering.																	
16Oct65- 6Kee	fst *7f		1:25^4	Ⓕ Alcibiades 37k	2	3	1½	14	18	115	Adams L	119		-	94-16	Moccasin119^{15}Chalina119^{no}Hurry Star119^{20}	Speed to spare	4
	No wagering.																	
9Oct65- 4Kee	fst 6½f	:23 :46^3	1:11^{3}1:18	Ⓕ Alw 7500	1	7	76	43¼	1hd	13	Adams L	119		*.10	88-14	Moccasin119^{3}Fanrullah107^{4}½Strawshy107^{1}½	Drew out easily	7
11Sep65- 7Aqu	fst 6f	:22^3:46^4	1:11^3	Ⓕ Matron 108k	3	2	2½	2hd	14	16	Adams L	119		*.40	85-20	Moccasin119^{6}Lyvette119^{2}Shimmering Gold119^1	Easily	12
25Aug65- 7Sar	fst 6f	:22 :45^1	1:11	Ⓕ Spinaway 76k	7	1	2hd	11	14	13½	Adams L	119		*.30	93-10	Moccasin119^{3}½Swift Lady119^{no}Forefoot119^{hd}	Much the best	7
17Aug65- 6Sar	fst 5½f	:21^4:45^2	:57^3 1:04	Ⓕ Alw 5500	1	3	1½	11	15	18	Adams L	119		*.30	97-11	Moccasin119^{8}IndianSunlite119^{6}RoyalTantrm119^{3}½	Galloping	7
6Aug65- 4Sar	fst 5½f	:22^1:46	:58 1:04^2	Ⓕ Md Sp Wt	9	2	11½	11½	14	18	Adams L	119		7.90	95-13	Moccasin119^{8}Lady Dulcinea119^{6}Ultra Quest119^2	Easily	12

All Along

b. f. 1979, by Targowice (Round Table)–Agujita, by Vieux Manoir

Lifetime record: 21 9 4 2 $3,015,764

Own.– Daniel Wildenstein
Br.– Dayton Ltd. (FR)
Tr.– Patrick–Louis Biancone

10Nov84- 6Hol	fm 1½Ⓣ	:49^{1}1:13^1	2:01^{1}2:25^1	3↑ BC Turf-G1	7	7	73¼	1½	11	2nk	Cordero A Jr	123		3.20	94-00	Lashkari122^{nk}AllAlong123½Ram122½	Failed to hold winner	11
21Oct84- 7WO	gd 1⅝Ⓣ	:49^{1}1:39^1	2:04^{4}2:42^4	3↑ Rothmans Int'l-G1	5	8	812	63¾	34	42¼	Swinburn WR	123		*.75	84-15	Majesty'sPrince126^{2}JckSld126^{no}EsprtduNord126^{nk}	Bid,hung	9
7Oct84♦ Longchamp(Fr)	sf *1½ⓉRH		2:39	3↑ Prix de l'Arc de Triomphe-G1						38	Swinburn WR	127		2.90e		Sagace130^{2}Northern Trick120^{6}All Along127¾		22

PAST PERFORMANCES

				Stk550000							Progress into 7th 2½f out,mild late gain.Sadler's Wells 8th	
22Sep84- 8Bel	fm 1½Ⓣ	:48^{4}1:13 2:01^{3}2:25^{1}	3↑	Turf Classic-G1	1 4 4^{3} 3$^{2\frac{1}{2}}$ 3^{3}	4$^{4\frac{1}{4}}$	Swinburn WR	123	1.80	94-10	JohnHenry126^{nk}Win126^{4}Majesty's Prince126^{hd} Flattened out	6
12Nov83- 8Lrl	yl 1½Ⓣ	:51^{4}1:17^{3}2:08^{4}2:35	3↑	DC Int'l-G1	6 6 5$^{2\frac{1}{2}}$ 1$^{3\frac{1}{2}}$ 1^{6}	1$^{3\frac{1}{4}}$	Swinburn WR	124	*.40	44-56	AllAlong124$^{3\frac{1}{4}}$WelshTerm127$^{2\frac{3}{4}}$Majsty'sPrnc127^{hd} Ridden out	8
29Oct83- 8Aqu	yl 1½Ⓣ	:49^{4}1:14^{4}2:09 2:34	3↑	Turf Classic-G1	10 3 3$^{6\frac{1}{2}}$ 2^{hd} 1^{4}	1$^{8\frac{3}{4}}$	Swinburn WR	123	*.90	71-29	AllAlong123$^{8\frac{3}{4}}$ThunderPuddles126$^{1\frac{1}{2}}$ErinsIsl126^{1} Ridden out	10
16Oct83- 9WO	yl 1⅝Ⓣ	:51^{1}1:42 2:45	3↑	Rothmans Int'l-G1	5 10 8^{11} 4$^{2\frac{1}{2}}$ 1$^{1\frac{1}{2}}$	1^{2}	Swinburn WR	123	*1.65	75-25	AllAlong123^{2}ThundrPuddls126$^{\frac{3}{4}}$Mjsty'sPrnc126^{nk} Drew clear	11
2Oct83♦ Longchamp(Fr)	fm*1½ⓉRH	2:28	3↑	Prix de l'Arc de Triomphe-G1 Stk635000		1^{1}	Swinburn WR	127	17.30e		All Along127^{1}Sun Princess120^{nk}Luth Enchantee120^{no}	26
											Rated in midpack,rail bid 2f out,led 100y out. Time Charter 4th.	
11Sep83♦ Longchamp(Fr)	sf *1½ⓉRH	2:40^{3}	3↑	Prix Foy-G3 Stk39600		2$^{\frac{3}{4}}$	Head F	120	6.00		Time Charter127$^{\frac{3}{4}}$All Along120$^{\frac{1}{2}}$Great Substence126^{2}	11
											Rated in 7th,lacked room 2f out,angled out,gaining late	
3Jly83♦ Saint-Cloud(Fr)	gd *1$\frac{9}{16}$ⓉLH	2:34^{4}	3↑	Grand Prix de Saint-Cloud-G1 Stk276000		7$^{7\frac{3}{4}}$	Starkey G	131	5.75		Diamond Shoal134$^{\frac{3}{4}}$Lancastrian134$^{\frac{3}{4}}$Zalataia129$^{\frac{3}{4}}$	9
											Tracked in 3rd,weakened 1½f out,bled.Lemhi Gold 4th.	
12Jun83♦ Chantilly(Fr)	fm*1½ⓉRH	2:24^{2}	4↑	La Coupe-G3 Stk44200		3$^{2\frac{3}{4}}$	Starkey G	127	*1.20		Zalataia124^{2}Flower Prince123$^{\frac{3}{4}}$All Along127^{6}	8
											Tracked leader,led 2f out,headed and faded 150y out	
28Nov82♦ Tokyo(Jpn)	fm*1½ⓉLH	2:27	3↑	Japan Cup-G1 Stk940000		2^{nk}	Moore GW	117	5.20		Half Iced121^{nk}All Along117^{nk}April Run121^{1}	15
											Closed well	
3Oct82♦ Longchamp(Fr)	sf *1½ⓉRH	2:37	3↑	Arc de Triomphe-G1 Stk637000		15^{21}	Starkey G	120	17.00		Akiyda120^{hd}Ardross130$^{\frac{1}{2}}$Awaasif120^{hd}	17
											Raced in midpack to 3f out,weakened quickly	
12Sep82♦ Longchamp(Fr)	fm*1½ⓉRH	2:29^{3}		ⒻPrix Vermeille-G1 Stk191000		1$^{1\frac{1}{2}}$	Starkey G	128	7.30		All Along128$^{1\frac{1}{2}}$Akiyda128^{hd}Grease128$^{\frac{3}{4}}$	13
											Tracked in 3rd,led 2½f out,ridden out.Zalataia 6th.	
14Jly82♦ Saint-Cloud(Fr)	gd *1$\frac{9}{16}$ⓉLH	2:46^{3}	3↑	Prix Maurice de Nieuil-G2 Stk95600		1$^{\frac{1}{2}}$	Gorli S	113	5.20		All Along113$^{\frac{1}{2}}$No Attention128^{3}Arc d'Or128^{2}	12
											Close up,led 1f out,held well	
13Jun82♦ Chantilly(Fr)	sf *1$\frac{5}{16}$ⓉRH	2:16^{4}		ⒻPrix de Diane-G1 223000		5$^{5\frac{3}{4}}$	Gorli S	128	13.00		Harbour128^{2}Akiyda128^{2}Paradise128$^{\frac{3}{4}}$	14
											Tracked in 4th,led briefly 1½f out,weakened 170y out	
5Jun82♦ Epsom(GB)	fm 1½ⓉLH	2:32^{1}		ⒻEnglish Oaks-G1 Stk220000		6$^{5\frac{3}{4}}$	St. Martin Y	126			Time Charter126^{1}Slightly Dangerous126$^{1\frac{1}{2}}$Last Feather126$^{\frac{3}{4}}$	13
											Toward rear,brief bid 2f out,one-paced late.Awaasif 4th	
23May82♦ Longchamp(Fr)	sf *1¼ⓉRH	2:20		ⒻPrix Saint-Alary-G1 Stk127000		2^{4}	Gorli S	128	*.70		Harbour128^{4}All Along128$^{1\frac{1}{2}}$Perlee128^{nk}	8
											Well placed in 3rd,led 2f to 1f out,no chance with winner	
27Mar82♦ Saint-Cloud(Fr)	sf *1$\frac{5}{16}$ⓉLH	2:23^{2}		ⒻPrix Penelope-G3 Stk51000		1^{4}	Gorli S	123			All Along123^{4}Paradise123^{1}Charmer123^{1}	11
											Strong run to lead 1f out,ridden clear	
27Feb82♦ Saint-Cloud(Fr)	hy *1¼ⓉLH	2:24^{1}		ⒻPrix Mirska Alw18800		1^{4}	Gorli S	123			All Along123^{4}Zalataia123^{1}Magic and Magic123^{1}	13
											Tracked in 3rd,led 2f out,easily;Previously trained by Maurice Zilber	
10Nov81♦ Amiens(Fr)	sf *1 50ⓉRH			ⒻPrix d'Hornoy Mdn7200		1^{nk}	Vache S	119			DHAll Along119DHTarbelissima118^{nk}Vitilla121^{1}	12
											Tracked leader,dueled 1f out,gamely.Time not taken.	

Lady's Secret

gr. f. 1982, by Secretariat (Bold Ruler)–Great Lady M., by Icecapade **Lifetime record: 45 25 9 3 $3,021,425**

Own.– Mr. and Mrs. Eugene V. Klein
Br.– R.H. Spreen (Okla)
Tr.– D. Wayne Lukas

10Aug87- 1Sar	sly 1⅛	:47^{1}1:11^{3}1:36^{1}1:49^{2}	3↑	Alw 45000	2 0 - - -	-	McCarron CJ	117	*.30	- -	Kamakura115^{11}The Watcher122$^{2\frac{1}{4}}$Jack of Clubs119$^{2\frac{1}{2}}$ Bolted	5
21Jly87- 8Mth	fst 1$\frac{1}{16}$	:23^{1}:46^{2} 1:11 1:43^{2}	3↑	ⒻAlw 25000	1 2 1$^{\frac{1}{2}}$ 1$^{3\frac{1}{2}}$ 1^{9}	1^{7}	McCarron CJ	119	*.10	88-18	Lady'sSecret119^{7}BriefRemarks115^{nk}ShaknBy115$^{\frac{3}{4}}$ Easy score	6
4Jly87-10Mth	fst 1$\frac{1}{16}$	:23^{1}:46^{1} 1:10 1:42	3↑	ⒻMolly Pitcher H-G2	3 2 2$^{1\frac{1}{2}}$ 2$^{\frac{1}{2}}$ 2^{hd}	2^{2}	McCarron CJ	125	*.30	93-10	ReelEasy112^{2}Lady'sSecret125$^{\frac{3}{4}}$Cattonc117^{nk} Best of others	8
13Jun87- 8Mth	sly 6f	:22^{2}:44^{4} 1:09^{4}	3↑	ⒻAlw 25000	5 1 2^{hd} 1$^{\frac{1}{2}}$ 1^{1}	1$^{3\frac{1}{2}}$	Cordero A Jr	122	*.30	91-14	Lady'sSecret122$^{3\frac{1}{2}}$Nick'sNag115^{6}BriefRmrks115^{8} Ridden out	5

PAST PERFORMANCES

14Mar87-10GP	fst	1⅛	:4621:11 1:3611:484 3♠	Donn H-G2	2	1	12	43	618	632½	Day P	120	*.80	55-18	LittleBoldJohn111noSkipTrl1186WsTms1174½	Fin. after½	7
1Nov86-5SA	fst	1¼	:4611:10 1:3442:011 3♠	ⒻBC Distaff-G1	5	1	14	14	14	12½	Day P	123	*.50	83-13	Lady's Secret1232½Fran's Valentine1232Outstandingly123¾		8
		Ridden out															
12Oct86-8Bel	fst	1¼	:4611:10 1:3522:013 3♠	ⒻBeldame-G1	4	1	15	11	1½	1½	Day P	123	*.05	90-13	Lady's Secret123½Coup de Fusil1231¾Classy Cathy11823½		4
		Drifted,ridden out															
21Sep86-8Bel	fst	1⅛	:4541:0931:3411:464 3♠	ⒻRuffian H-G1	5	2	1½	13½	16	18	Day P	129	*.50	93-12	Lady's Secret1298Steal a Kiss1092¼Endear1196	Handily	6
6Sep86-8Bel	fst	1	:231:454 1:0941:332 3♠	ⒻMaskette-G1	5	1	11	11½	14½	17	Day P	125	*.30	98-10	Lady's Secret1257Steal a Kiss1091¾Endear120no	Handily	6
30Aug86-8Bel	fst	1⅛	:4531:0921:3341:46 3♠	Woodward-G1	4	1	11½	12½	2hd	24¾	Cordero A Jr	121	1.40e	92-14	Precisionist1264¾Lady'sScrt1215½PrsonlFlg1105¾	2nd best	5
16Aug86-9Mth	sly	1⅛	:4641:1031:3531:484 3♠	Iselin H-G1	1	1	11½	1hd	1hd	33½	Day P	120	*1.20	86-16	Roo Art1172¼Precisionist1251¼Lady's Secret1206	Gave way	5
2Aug86-8Sar	sly	1⅛	:4631:1041:3631:494 3♠	Whitney H-G1	2	1	12½	13	12½	14½	Day P	119	*1.30e	86-22	Lady's Secret1194½Ends Well1163¼Fuzzy110nk	Ridden out	7
5Jly86-9Mth	fst	1 1/16	:23 :46 1:0911:411 3♠	ⒻMolly Pitcher H-G2	4	1	1½	1½	13½	16¼	Day P	126	*.20	99-13	Lady's Secret1266¼Chaldea1142¼Key Witness1121½	Easily	8
8Jun86-8Bel	my	1⅛	:4441:0941:3531:483 3♠	ⒻHempstead H-G1	4	2	1hd	1hd	22½	26	Day P	128	*.40	78-16	Endear1156Lady's Secret1281½Ride Sally12413	2nd best	5
26May86-8Bel	fst	1	:232:454 1:0911:333 3♠	Metropolitan H-G1	4	1	2hd	1hd	1½	31¼	Day P	120	5.30	96-11	Garthorn1241¼LoveThatMac117noLady'sSecrt120nk	Held well	8
17May86-8Bel	fst	1 1/16	:233:461 1:1011:414 3♠	ⒻShuvee H-G1	3	1	11	11	13	13½	Day P	126	*.70	93-15	Lady's Secret1263½Endear1156¼Ride Sally1251	Easy score	6
16Apr86-9OP	fst	1 1/16	:231:454 1:1011:402 4♠	ⒻApple Blossom H-G1	4	1	13	1hd	2½	2nk	Velasquez J	127	*.40	99-16	LoveSmitten119nkLady'sSecret1276Sefa'sBeauty1226	Failed	7
23Feb86-8SA	fst	1⅛	:4621:10 1:3431:47 4♠	ⒻS Margarita H-G1	1	1	11½	11	11½	12¾	Velasquez J	125	*1.60	94-11	Lady'sSecret1252¾Johnica1201¼DontstopThemusc1222	Easily	9
9Feb86-8SA	fst	1⅛	:4641:11 1:3631:494	ⒻLa Canada-G1	3	1	1½	11½	11½	11¼	McCarron CJ	126	*.50	80-16	Lady'sSecret1261¼Shywing1194NorthSider1181¾	Hard ridden	6
18Jan86-8SA	fst	1 1/16	:222:452 1:0931:414	ⒻEl Encino-G3	8	3	1½	13	12½	12	McCarron CJ	124	*.80	92-12	Ldy'sScrt1242Shywng1194ShrpAscnt119nk	Lugged into stretch	10
27Dec85-8SA	fst	7f	:222:45 1:0931:222	ⒻLa Brea-G3	1	3	1hd	1½	2hd	2½	McCarron CJ	124	*.80	87-16	SavannahSlew119½Lady'sSecret1243AmbraRidge1142½	Gamely	7
		Previously owned by E.V. Klein															
2Nov85-5Aqu	fst	1¼	:4641:1121:3642:02 3♠	ⒻBC Distaff-G1	1	1	14	11	21½	26¼	Velasquez J	119	*.40e	80-10	Life's Magic1236¼Lady's Secret1193Dontstop Themusic1231¼		7
		Ducked out start															
13Oct85-8Bel	fst	1¼	:4541:1021:36 2:033 3♠	ⒻBeldame-G1	4	1	1½	12	13	12	Velasquez J	118	*.60	80-19	Lady'sSecret1182Isayso1232¾KamikazeRick1182¼	Ridden out	5
22Sep85-8Bel	fst	1⅛	:4621:0941:3431:472 3♠	ⒻRuffian H-G1	3	1	11½	14	15	14	Velasquez J	116	*.30e	90-17	Lady's Secret1164Isayso1152¼Sintrillium118hd	Ridden out	6
7Sep85-8Bel	fst	1	:222:444 1:0911:344 3♠	ⒻMaskette-G1	6	1	1½	11	14	15½	Velasquez J	111	*1.00e	91-14	Lady's Secret1115½Dowery117noMrs. Revere117¾	Ridden out	8
9Aug85-8Sar	fst	7f	:214:441 1:0911:223 3♠	ⒻBallerina-G2	4	3	21½	2hd	1½	1no	MacBeth D	117	*.90e	89-19	Lady'sSecret117noMrs.Revere1162¾SolarHalo116¾	Driving	9
1Aug85-8Sar	gd	7f	:221:444 1:09 1:213	ⒻTest-G2	9	1	42½	31½	1hd	12	Velasquez J	121	10.10	94-13	Lady'sScrt1212Mom'sCommand124nkMjstcFolly118½	Driving	10
6Jly85-6Bel	fst	6f	:22 :451 1:111 3♠	ⒻThe Rose 54k	6	1	32	3nk	12	14¾	Velasquez J	116	*.40	86-20	Lady'sScrt1164¾FoolishIntentions115¾ProudClarioness115nk		6
		Ridden out															
22Jun85-9Mth	fst	6f	:221:443 1:093 3♠	ⒻRegret H 49k	6	1	11½	11½	12½	13½	Antley CW	114	*.40	92-16	Lady'sSecret1143½FurashFolly1182Nck'sNg1202½	Ridden out	6
26May85-5Bel	fst	6f	:222:444 1:09	ⒻBowl of Flowers 55k	6	1	1½	1hd	14	17	Velasquez J	121	*.50	97-13	Lady'sSecret1217RideSally114nkIndinRomnc1143	Ridden out	7
11May85-8Bel	fst	7f	:22 :443 1:0911:221	ⒻComely-G3	1	4	43	45	47½	411	Cordero A Jr	121	6.30	80-12	Mom'sCommnd1214½MajestcFolly1131¾ClocksScrt1214¾	Tired	9
28Apr85-8Aqu	fst	6f	:222:451 1:10	ⒻPrioress-G3	5	1	21	21½	21½	21¼	Velasquez J	118	*1.30	90-21	ClocksSecret1151¼Lady'sSecret1185RideSally1122	Gamely	8
16Apr85-9OP	fst	6f	:214:45 1:10	ⒻPrima Donna 76k	7	2	32½	3½	11½	15	Velasquez J	123	*.80	90-18	Lady'sSecret1235TakeMyPictur1232Lt.A.J.1121¾	Ridden out	9
23Feb85-8GG	fst	6f	:213:442 :573 1:10	ⒻVallejo 43k	1	3	1½	1½	1hd	21½	Baze RA	122	1.90	87-16	SavannahSlew1141½Lady'sScrt1226SprtdMdm1143½	Game try	7
30Jan85-8SA	fst	7f	:221:444 1:0941:232	ⒻS Ynez-G3	6	1	2hd	1hd	2hd	53¾	Valenzuela PA	122	7.40	79-17	Wising Up119¾Rascal Lass1222Reigning Countess119¾	Hung	9
12Jan85-8BM	fst	6f	:222:444 :572 1:101	Determine 44k	7	1	2½	1hd	2hd	2nk	Baze RA	115	*1.10	88-21	Bedside Promise113nkLady'sScrt1151½[D]SantaRosaPrince115no		8
		Gamely															
5Jan85-8BM	fst	6f	:222:45 :573 1:10	ⒻHail Hilarious 43k	5	3	31½	1hd	13	14	Baze RA	120	*.70	89-16	Lady's Secret1204Missadoon1125Bloomer Miss115no		7
		Bumped start,wide into str															
9Nov84-9Hol	fst	6f	:221:453 :58 1:111	ⒻMoccasin 61k	8	1	1hd	2½	1½	1½	McCarron CJ	120	*1.90	- -	Lady's Secret120½Neshia1131Lotta Blue1173	Driving	9
20Oct84-8SA	fst	1 1/16	:224:454 1:1021:423	ⒻOak Leaf-G1	6	1	13	1½	36	516¼	Sibille R	115	7.10	72-13	FolkArt1174½Pirate'sGlow1156½WaywardPirate1153½	Tired	6
8Oct84-8SA	fst	7f	:22 :443 1:1011:233	ⒻAnoakia-G3	11	1	12½	13½	12	3hd	Black K	120	6.10e	82-16	WaywardPirate120hdPrt'sGlow117noLdy'sScrt1201¼	Weakened	11

8Aug84- 8Dmr	fst 6f	:22	$:45^{1}$	:58	$1:11^{1}$	Ⓕ Junior Miss 53k	3	1	2^{hd}	1^{hd}	$2^{2 1/2}$	4^{6}	Valenzuela PA	122	3.00e	76-21	Doon's Baby $117^{2 1/2}$ Fiesta Lady 117^{3} Trunk $117^{1/2}$	Weakened 6
23Jly84- 3Hol	fst 6f	$:21^{4}$	$:44^{3}$	$:57^{2}$	1:11	ⒻⓇ Wavy Waves 46k	5	1	$1^{1/2}$	1^{2}	1^{2}	$1^{1 1/2}$	Valenzuela PA	117	2.20	82-18	Lady's Secret $117^{1 1/2}$ Full o Wisdom $115^{1/2}$ Neshia $117^{2 1/4}$	Driving 6
7Jly84- 8Hol	fst 6f	$:21^{3}$	$:44^{4}$	$:57^{1}$	1:10	Ⓕ Landaluce-G3	13	1	2^{hd}	$2^{2 1/2}$	2^{5}	4^{9}	Valenzuela PA	116	21.40e	78-18	WindowSeat $114^{6 1/2}$ RaiseaProspctor 119^{1} FulloWsdom $114^{1 1/2}$	Tired 13

Azeri

ch.m. 1998, by Jade Hunter (Mr. Prospector)-Zodiac Miss (Aus), by Ahonoora (GB)

Lifetime record: 20 15 3 0 $3,419,820

Own.- Allen Paulson Living Trust
Br.-Allen E. Paulson (Ky)
Tr.-D.Wayne Lukas

As of press time, Azeri is still in training.

19Jun04	9Bel	fst	1 1/16	:45⅗	1:10	1:41⅗	3 ↑ Ⓕ Ogden Phipps H	300000	4	$1^{1/2}$	1^{hd}	2^{hd}	4	4	DayP	123	*.80	- Sightseek $120^{3 1/4}$, Storm Flag Flying $117^{6 1/2}$, Passing Shot 116^{2},	Tired 4
31May04	9Bel	fst	1	:46	1:10	1:35⅗	3 ↑ Metropolitan H	750000	6	$3^{2 1/2}$	$3^{1/2}$	$5^{1 1/4}$	$6^{2 3/4}$	$8^{6 3/4}$	DayP	117	5.80	82 Pico Central (Brz) 119¾, Bowman's Band 114^{2}, Strong Hope $119^{1 1/2}$,	Empty stretch 9
01May04	8CD	fst	7f	:22⅗	0:45	1:22⅗	4 ↑ Ⓕ Humana Distaff H	280250	4	2^{1}	$2^{1 1/2}$	-	2^{hd}	2^{hd}	SmithM	125	*.70	90 MayoOn the Side 114^{hd}, Azeri $125^{7 1/4}$, Randaroo 121^{nk}	Gamely 4
03Apr04	9OP	fst	1 1/16	:46⅗	1:10	1:41	4 ↑ Ⓕ Apple Blossom H	500000	4	1	1	1	1	1	SmithM	123	2.00	92 Azeri $123^{1 1/2}$, Wild Spirit (Chi) $119^{1 3/4}$ (dq-p3), Star Parade (Arg) $114^{7 1/4}$	Steady handling 6

Previously trained by Laura de Seroux

28Sep03	6SA	fst	1 1/16	:47⅕	1:11⅕	1:42⅘	3 ↑ Ⓕ Lady's Secret BC H	300000	6	$5^{4 1/2}$	$5^{3 1/2}$	$5^{3 1/2}$	3^{2}	$3^{2 3/4}$	SmithM	128	*.20	88 Got Koko 118⅕, Elloluv $116^{1 3/4}$ (dq-p4), Azeri 128^{1}	No late bid 6
10Aug03	8Dmr	fst	1 1/16	:47	1:11	1:42	3 ↑ Ⓕ Clement L Hirsch H	300000	1	1^{1}	$1^{1 1/2}$	$1^{1 1/2}$	$1^{2 1/2}$	$1^{3 1/4}$	SmithM	127	*.30	89 Azeri $127^{3 1/4}$, Got Koko 118^{hd}, Tropical Blossom $108^{4 1/2}$	Handily 5
21Jun03	8Hol	fst	1⅛	:47⅕	1:10⅗	1:48⅗	3 ↑ Ⓕ Vanity H	250000	3	$2^{1/2}$	1^{hd}	2^{hd}	1^{1}	1^{2}	SmithM	127	*.30	91 Azeri 127^{2}, Sister Girl Blues 111½, Bare Necessities $118^{4 1/2}$	Driving 7
24May03	8Hol	fst	1 1/16	:46⅕	1:10	1:41⅗	3 ↑ Ⓕ Milady BC H	211800	2	2^{hd}	1^{1}	$1^{2 1/2}$	$1^{2 1/2}$	1^{3}	SmithM	125	*.20	92 Azeri 125^{3}, Enjoy 114^{3}, Tropical Blossom 111^{1}	Driving 6
05Apr03	8OP	fst	1 1/16	:48⅗	1:12⅕	1:43	3 ↑ Ⓕ Apple Blossom H	500000	4	3^{2}	$4^{2 1/4}$	$2^{1/2}$	$2^{1 1/2}$	1^{hd}	SmithM	123	*.40	92 Azeri 123^{hd}, Take Charge Lady $118^{3 1/4}$, Mandy's Gold 116^{2}	Classy 7

26Oct02	3AP	gd	1⅛	:46⅕	1:09⅗	1:48⅗	3 ↑ Ⓕ BC Distaff	2000000	4	1^{1}	1^{1}	1^{1}	1^{2}	1^{5}	SmithM	123	*1.80	98 Azeri 123^{5}, Farda Amiga 119^{hd}, Imperial Gesture $119^{3 1/4}$	Kicked clear 8
02Oct02	8SA	fst	1 1/16	:45	1:08	1:41	3 ↑ Ⓕ Lady's Secret BC H	217500	3	1^{hd}	$1^{1/2}$	1^{hd}	$1^{2 1/2}$	$1^{3 1/2}$	SmithM	127	*.30	89 Azeri $127^{3 1/2}$, Starrer 115^{hd}, Mystic Lady 116^{1}	Handily 7
11Aug02	8Dmr	fst	1 1/16	:47⅗	1:11	1:42⅗	3 ↑ Ⓕ Clement L Hirsch H	300000	3	1^{hd}	$1^{1/2}$	1^{1}	1^{3}	1^{2}	SmithM	126	*.10	87 Azeri 126^{2}, Angel Gift 114^{2}, Me Acabo (Chi) $114^{2 1/2}$	Drew clear 5
22Jun02	3Hol	fst	1⅛	:46⅗	1:10⅘	1:48⅗	3 ↑ Ⓕ Vanity H	250000	2	1^{1}	1^{1}	$1^{2 1/2}$	$1^{3 1/2}$	1^{3}	SmithM	125	*.30	90 Azeri 125^{3}, Affluent 119^{3}, Starrer 117^{1}	Handily 5
25May02	8Hol	fst	1 1/16	:46⅖	1:10⅕	1:42	3 ↑ Ⓕ Milady BC H	211400	4	1^{1}	1^{1}	1^{2}	$1^{3 1/2}$	$1^{3 1/2}$	SmithM	122	*.60	92 Azeri $122^{3 1/2}$, Affluent 119^{4}, Collect Call 115^{3}	Ridden out 6
06Apr02	11OP	fst	1 1/16	:47⅖	1:12	1:42⅗	4 ↑ Ⓕ Apple BlossomH	500000	5	4^{4}	4^{2}	$2^{1/2}$	$1^{1/2}$	$1^{1 3/4}$	SmithM	117	*1.00	92 Azeri $117^{1 3/4}$, Affluent 118¾, Miss Linda (Arg) 118^{2}	Best 5
10Mar02	8SA	fst	1⅛	:47⅕	1:11⅕	1:49	4 ↑ Ⓕ SantaMargarita H	300000	4	$3^{1 1/4}$	4^{2}	$3^{2 1/2}$	$2^{1/2}$	1^{3}	SmithM	115	2.20	97 Azeri 115^{3}, Spain 118^{1}, Printemps (Chi) 116^{4}	Clear late 7
09Feb02	8SA	fst	1⅛	:48⅕	1:12⅗	1:49⅕	4 Ⓕ LaCanada S	200000	6	5^{5}	$5^{4 1/2}$	5^{4}	$3^{1 1/2}$	2^{1}	SmithM	115	2.90	94 Summer Colony 119^{1}, Azeri 115^{1}, Ask Me No Secrets $115^{1 1/}$	Rallied 6
12Jan02	3SA	fst	1	:46⅘	1:10⅗	1:35⅘	4 ↑ Ⓕ AOC7	4100	4	$4^{2 1/4}$	$4^{2 1/4}$	$2^{1/2}$	$1^{1 1/2}$	1^{3}	SmithM	117	*.40	89 Azeri 117^{3}, Elaine's Angel 117^{nk}, Angel Gift 117^{5}	Handily 6

17Dec01	7Hol	fst	6½	:22	0:44⅗	1:15⅗	3 ↑ Ⓕ Alw	50700	5	$5^{3 1/4}$	1^{hd}	-	1^{1}	1^{3}	SmithM	118	*.50	96 Azeri 118^{3}, Burning Breeze $118^{4 1/2}$, Pine Lake Lady 118^{1}	Handily 7
01Nov01	4SA	fst	6f	:21⅗	0:43⅗	1:08⅗	3 ↑ Ⓕ Msw	49400	4	2^{hd}	1^{hd}	-	$1^{2 1/2}$	1^{6}	SmithM	120	17.30	93 Azeri 120^{6}, Southern Oasis $120^{3 1/2}$, Blushing Rahy $120^{2 1/2}$	Ridden out 9

Photo Credits

Miss Woodford:
Keeneland-Cook, 11, 13, 14,16-17, 23, 25

Imp:
Ross County Historical Society, 29, 31, 33, 34, 36-37; Keeneland-Cook, 41

Beldame:
Keeneland-Cook, 45, 48, 52, 54, 57, 59; *The Blood-Horse*, 51

Regret:
Keeneland-Cook, 61-63, 64-65, 70; National Museum of Racing, 66-67

Twilight Tear:
Bert Morgan, 77; World Wide Photos, 82; Acme, 85, 89; Joe Fleischer, 90-91; Imperial War Museum, 92; James Sames/ Livingston collection, 94, 95

Busher:
The Blood-Horse, 97, 100, 110; Turfpix, 101; Arlington-Washington Park, 103-105; Washington Park Jockey Club, 106, 109

Moccasin:
The Blood-Horse, 113, 123; Skeets Meadors, 116, 125; Turfotos, 119, 121; John Noye, 126

All Along:
P Bertrand et Fils, 129, 137; Barbara D. Livingston, 131; Milton Toby, 132; *The Blood-Horse*, 138; NYRA/Bob Coglianese, 141; Jerry Frutkoff, 143; John Noye, 144

Lady's Secret:
Four Footed Fotos, 149; Skip Dickstein, 152; NYRA/Bob Coglianese, 155; Jim Raftery, 160; Barbara D. Livingston, 162; Dan Johnson, 165; Anne M. Eberhardt, 167

Azeri:
Barbara D. Livingston, 169; Matt Goins/Equipix, 173; Coady Photography, 176-177, 179, 184; Skip Dickstein, 183

Cover Photos:
Azeri (Barbara D. Livingston); Regret (Keeneland-Cook); Lady's Secret (Skip Dickstein); Twilight Tear (Bert Morgan)

Back Cover Photos:
Beldame (Keeneland-Cook); All Along (Bob Coglianese); Miss Woodford (Keeneland-Cook); Imp (Ross County Historical Society); Moccasin (Skeets Meadors); Busher (Washington Park Jockey Club)

Book Design:
Sarabeth Brownrobie

Authors

Edward L. Bowen is the award-winning author of thirteen books, including biographies of Man o' War and War Admiral and a two-volume set on the great breeders entitled *Legacies of the Turf*. Bowen lives in Lexington, Kentucky.

Craig Harzmann is a freelance racing journalist and sixth-grade teacher. In addition to being the Southern California correspondent for *The Blood-Horse*, he has written for many industry publications including *California Thoroughbred* and *Paddock*. He and his wife Anna live in Lake View Terrace, California.

Avalyn Hunter is a mental health care professional and Thoroughbred pedigree researcher whose first book, *American Classic Pedigrees*, was published by Eclipse Press in 2003. Hunter lives in Lake City, Florida.

Steve Haskin is the award-winning national correspondent for *The Blood-Horse* magazine and author of several books, including biographies of John Henry and Dr. Fager. He lives in Hamilton Square, New Jersey.

Tom Hall is assistant editor for Eclipse Press, the book division of Blood-Horse Publications. He is the co-author of *The Calumet Collection*. Hall lives in Lexington, Kentucky.

Judy L. Marchman is managing editor of Eclipse Press, the book division of Blood-Horse Publications. She is the author of the *Kentucky Derby Glasses Price Guide* and co-author of *The Calumet Collection*. Marchman lives in Lexington, Kentucky.

John McEvoy is a well-known Turf writer and author of several books, including the award-winning *Great Horse Racing Mysteries*. McEvoy lives in Evanston, Illinois.

Eliza McGraw is a freelance writer living in Washington, D.C. Her work has appeared in *The Blood-Horse*, *EQUUS*, and *The Washington Post*. Her book, *Everyday Horsemanship*, came out in 2003.

Ray Paulick is editor-in-chief of *The Blood-Horse* magazine and the author of a biography of Sunday Silence. He lives in Lexington, Kentucky.

David Schmitz is a senior writer for *The Blood-Horse* magazine and writes the weekly column "Stud News." He lives in Lexington, Kentucky.